Routledge Revivals

Introduction to Philosophy

Introduction to Philosophy

A Handbook for Students of Psychology, Logic, Ethics, Aesthetics and General Philosophy

Oswald Külpe

Routledge
Taylor & Francis Group

First published in 1897 by George Allen & Unwin Ltd.

This edition first published in 2018 by Routledge
2 Park Square, Milton Park, Abingdon, Oxon, OX14 4RN
and by Routledge
711 Third Avenue, New York, NY 10017

Routledge is an imprint of the Taylor & Francis Group, an informa business

Publisher's Note
The publisher has gone to great lengths to ensure the quality of this reprint but points out that some imperfections in the original copies may be apparent.

Disclaimer
The publisher has made every effort to trace copyright holders and welcomes correspondence from those they have been unable to contact.

A Library of Congress record exists under ISBN: 82049641

ISBN 13: 978-1-138-60542-8 (hbk)
ISBN 13: 978-1-138-60543-5 (pbk)
ISBN 13: 978-0-429-46277-1 (ebk)

INTRODUCTION TO PHILOSOPHY

A Handbook for Students of

PSYCHOLOGY, LOGIC, ETHICS, ÆSTHETICS AND GENERAL PHILOSOPHY

BY

OSWALD KÜLPE

PROFESSOR OF PHILOSOPHY AND ÆSTHETICS IN THE UNIVERSITY OF WÜRZBURG

TRANSLATED FROM THE GERMAN (1895)

BY

W. B. PILLSBURY

INSTRUCTOR IN PSYCHOLOGY IN THE CORNELL UNIVERSITY

AND

E. B. TITCHENER

SAGE PROFESSOR OF PSYCHOLOGY IN THE CORNELL UNIVERSITY

LONDON: GEORGE ALLEN & UNWIN LTD.
RUSKIN HOUSE, MUSEUM STREET, W.C.
NEW YORK : : : : : : : : THE MACMILLAN CO.

FIRST PUBLISHED	*July*	1897
REPRINTED . .	*March*	1901
,, . .	*August*	1904
,, . .	*July*	1907
,, . .	*October*	1908
,, . .	*November*	1910
,, . .	*June*	1915
,, . .	*February*	1922
,, . .	*April*	1922
,, . .	*February*	1923

To

FRAU JOHANNA ROCHLITZ

AND THE MEMORY OF

GEORG ROSENBERGER

IN FRIENDSHIP AND VENERATION

TRANSLATORS' PREFACE

The text upon which this translation is based differs only in a few minor points from that of Professor Külpe's *Einleitung in die Philosophie*, as published in 1895. The author has modified passages in §§ 2, 6, 10, 23 and 30; has added to the list of literary references; and has made some forty verbal changes in the course of the work. The translators have added titles to the literature of several of the earlier sections, indicating the addition in every case by the use of square brackets, and have filled in a small number of cross-references which the author had left in general terms. They have been greatly tempted, in certain contexts, to write special paragraphs dealing with the English philosophers at more length than has been done by Professor Külpe. But the new matter would have considerably increased the expense of the book, besides breaking the thread of the original exposition. Moreover, the fact that the work was primarily intended as a text-book for German students of philosophy should not make it less interesting or valuable to their English-speaking contemporaries.

Cornell University,
March 20th, 1897.

AUTHOR'S PREFACE

THIS book has been written to supply a need which my experience as a teacher had brought home to me. At the same time, it is meant as a modest contribution to the philosophical work of the present day. On the one hand, I have striven to produce an elementary but complete guide to philosophy, past and present; and have thus been led to include in the work facts and arguments which have hitherto been confined to encyclopædias of philosophy. On the other, I have attempted, whether by way of criticism or by the adoption of a positive attitude to philosophical aims and problems, to further, or at least to stimulate, scientific work in the philosophical field. The reader will find, I hope, that the divergent schools of philosophic thought and the achievements of individual philosophers, ancient and modern, are treated with uniform interest and impartiality, and that the estimate of their value is based upon good reasons. Nevertheless, I am fully aware that a limited knowledge of the subject-matter, and a certain inevitable subjectivism in interpretation and selection, place such formidable obstacles in the path of my best endeavours that I am very far from realising the ideal which I had proposed to myself at the outset of my undertaking.

The law of brevity was imperative, but obedience exceedingly difficult. Many pages of exposition have been sacrificed to it; and whether I have always saved the most important part I cannot venture to decide. Grave difficulties were also encountered in the choice of works for citation under the various sections. I have mentioned those that seemed best adapted to the plan of the work. I shall be exceedingly grateful for any proposal or suggestion from the philosophical or the general reader — and I have tried to write for a wider public than is made up of students of philosophy — which may assist me in the preparation of a possible second edition.

WÜRZBURG,

June, 1895.

TABLE OF CONTENTS

INTRODUCTION.

B. Epistemological Schools.

C. Ethical Schools.

CHAPTER IV. THE PROBLEM OF PHILOSOPHY AND THE PHILOSOPHICAL SYSTEM.

INTRODUCTION TO PHILOSOPHY

INTRODUCTION

§ 1. *The Purpose of an Introduction to Philosophy.*

1. THAT the need of an Introduction to Philosophy was felt in the past is shown by the record of systematic lectures and the existence of books upon the subject. That the same need is felt to-day is proved by the advertisement of introductory lecture courses in philosophy at most universities. There is, however, at the present time a curious dearth of books, whether elementary outlines or advanced treatises, to be used as supplementary to oral teaching. Thus we have nothing that can compare for practical value with the *Einleitung in die Philosophie*, by Johann Georg Walch, 1727, which treated in three books of philosophy and philosophical knowledge in general, of the special philosophical disciplines, and of the philosophical mysteries, and gave its readers much historical information and numerous literary references. This work presents a comprehensive and detailed picture not only of the condition of philosophical thought at a particular time, but also (in spite of certain peculiar and erroneous historical statements) of the history of philosophy at large.

2. But not every Introduction to Philosophy has been written from this standpoint. We find that the problem, nominally the same but variously conceived, has been approached by two essentially different paths. (1) A first group of authors attempt to lead their readers to *philosophise*, by enumerating the principal

philosophical problems and indicating their solution. An exposition of this kind is contained in Suabediss' *Zur Einleitung in die Philosophie*, 1827, where it is expressly stated that an Introduction to Philosophy should point out the way in which one may oneself attain to philosophy. For this reason, the author goes on, it should be "neither a metaphysics nor an encyclopædia of philosophical knowledge, neither a *résumé* of the history of philosophy nor a critique of philosophical systems," but should tell us "what is the nature of philosophy, *i.e.*, what is the aim of philosophical thinking." A very similar standpoint is taken up by Simon Erhardt, in his excellent *Einleitung in das Studium der gesammtem Philosophie*, 1824. This clear and systematic little work, which deserves a place beside Herbart's much better known *Lehrbuch zur Einleitung in die Philosophie* (4th edition, 1837), falls into nine sections, which discuss the idea, object and final purpose of philosophy, its subdivisions, its sources and the aids to its study, its subjective condition (the philosophical temperament), the relation of philosophy to the empirical and positive sciences, the problems which it has to solve, and its history. The writer's general point of view is that of Schelling's 'identity' philosophy.

3. The above-mentioned work of Herbart also belongs to this class of Introductions. Its tone is dogmatic throughout, and its purpose simply to lead the reader to the understanding and acceptance of the special philosophy of its author, who, with this end in view, discusses the essential problems of logic, metaphysics and practical philosophy (æsthetics). It is only by an occasional piece of adverse criticism that one learns anything of divergent views, and only from a few historical notes that one gets a glimpse of the actual development of philosophical ideas and beliefs; so that while the book is valuable as a source of knowledge of Herbart's peculiar philosophical system, it is in no sense an Introduction to Philosophy, regarded as an already existing science.

Lastly, a very recent treatise on the subject, F. Paulsen's *Einleitung in die Philosophie* (3rd edition, 1895) may, upon the whole, be referred to this group. It is true that Paulsen pays much more attention than Herbart did to the history of philosophy, and is incomparably more reticent in the matter of formulating or advocating any personal theories; but the fact that he confines himself to the problems of metaphysics, epistemology and ethics, and even accords this last an entirely subordinate place, shows that he is not attempting a complete survey of the traditional field of philosophy; while he employs all the resources of a graceful and attractive literary style to plead the cause of a consistent modern theory of the universe.

4. (2) A second group of Introductions to Philosophy is characterised by the authors' desire to transcend the narrow limits of individual conviction, and give the reader a bird's-eye view of the whole extent of philosophy, past and present. This purpose can be served only by abundant historical citation and copious literary reference. The attempt made by J. Chr. Briegleb, in his *Einleitung in die philosophischen Wissenschaften*, 1789, is much less successful than that of Walch. Briegleb's historical references are often wrong, and at best very superficial; while the bibliography placed at the end of the volume, though more extensive than the text, is a mere list of titles without purpose or arrangement. Far more rationally conceived is Heydenreich's *Encyclopädische Einleitung in das Studium der Philosophie*, 1793. This author is a disciple of Kant, and draws freely upon the master's work, as well as upon C. L. Reinhold's 'elementary' philosophy. He gives a definition of philosophy, works out a philosophical system in detail, goes on to determine the ultimate purpose of philosophy in general, and concludes with the statement of certain "rules for the profitable study" of the subject. Useful references to modern philosophical literature are made in their proper places; but there is hardly any trace of historical orientation. On the other hand, we have in von Reichlin-Meldegg's *Einleitung in die Philosophie*, 1870, a critical history of philosophy, which tells the reader almost nothing of the range and status of philosophy at the time of its publication. Coming to quite

recent years, we find one work, and one only, which belongs to this second class of Introductions: Strümpell's *Einleitung in die Philosophie vom Standpunkte der Geschichte der Philosophie*, 1886. Although the author is a professed Herbartian, he discusses here, in a quite impartial spirit, the definition, problems, sub-divisions and tendencies of philosophy. The various schools are treated by a strictly historical method, and the criticism is always moderate. Unfortunately, references to modern literature are entirely lacking, and the writer's account of the separate philosophical disciplines leaves much to be desired on the score of completeness.

5. There can, in our opinion, be little doubt as to which of these two methods of writing an Introduction to Philosophy should have the preference. Works of the first type may, no doubt, stimulate an occasional student to philosophic thought, and so lead him to undertake a closer study of philosophy itself. But if one is trying to gain some real preparation for this study,—to find out what has been done in the past, to get a vocabulary of technical terms, to understand the reasons for the divergence of the schools, and the significance of the supreme efforts of our own time towards the advancement of philosophical science,—then recourse must be had to a work of the second class. In an age when philosophy was so highly prized by the whole educated public as it was in Germany in the eighteenth century or in Rome during the last days of the Republic, when the chief impulse to its study was not the desire of knowledge but the hope of personal happiness and private good fortune, the teacher might, perhaps, be content simply to lead men to philosophise. But to-day we hear, only too often, the voice that proclaims the approaching end of philosophy, or condemns it as a useless superfluity. Judgments of this kind cannot arise except from ignorance of what philosophy is and what it means, and cannot be corrected except by an accurate report of what the main business of philosophy has been in all times. And, all this apart, it is hard to see how a student of the systematic philosophy of our own day can better be sped upon his course than by an Introduction to Philosophy which pays equal regard to current doctrines and their historical conditions.

6. The great advantages possessed by works of the first type,—definiteness of fundamental principles, and the interest which is lent to all exposition by a warm personal conviction,—are not wholly denied to those of the other class. The survey of opposing tendencies and changing definitions cannot but impel anyone who thinks for himself to indicate what seems to him to be the probable solution or explication of the questions under discussion. But in thus passing the limits of objective statement the writer must never lose sight of his main purpose, and never suffer his opinion to become dogma.

While, then, works of the first category are, as a rule, entirely without the characteristics which we judge to be valuable in the others, it is quite possible to retain something of their stimulating quality while adopting the general plan of books of the second type. We shall, accordingly, ourselves endeavour in what follows—presupposing no special knowledge on the reader's part—to give a short account of the development and present status of philosophy. Chapter I. will be devoted to the definition and classification of philosophy; Chapter II. to a survey of the separate disciplines which are now included under the general name of philosophy; and Chapter III. to a characterisation of the more important schools of philosophic thought. Throughout, our chief aim will be to assist the student in the understanding of lectures and treatises upon special philosophical topics. The citation of the most important literature of the subjects discussed will also, we may hope, serve to call the attention of the beginner to the works which will aid him most in entering upon a more thorough course of study. In a brief final chapter (Chapter IV.) on the problem of philosophy and the philosophical system, we shall cast a glance over the whole range of philosophical investigation, from the new point of view which we have gained by our critical consideration of its nature and significance.

CHAPTER I.

DEFINITION AND CLASSIFICATION OF PHILOSOPHY

§ 2. *The Definition of Philosophy.*

1. A DEFINITION is a determinate relation between certain symbols (usually written or spoken words) and the objects which they indicate. It is, in other words, the meaning of a symbol, explicitly formulated. Hence any enquiry into the definition of philosophy must begin by answering the question what the word 'philosophy' means. We are met at once by a great divergence of opinion as to the significance of the term; so that our first task will be (*cf.* § 1. 5, 6) to collect and examine those proposed definitions which have proved most important, *i.e.*, have been most widely accepted. How far it may be possible to combine the various formulæ into a phrase which shall do equal justice to the present and the past, we cannot here decide; we shall recur to the point in Chapter IV. For the present we confine ourselves to definitions which have actually been offered, and say nothing of the ideal definition which we may ultimately find.

2. Little credence is now given to the statement of Heraclides Ponticus that the use of the word 'philosophy' to denote a science begins with Pythagoras. Herodotus was, in all probability, the first to employ the verb 'philosophise'; he makes Croesus tell Solon how he has heard that "from desire of knowledge Solon has traversed many lands, philosophising." The phrase "from desire of knowledge" (θεωρίης εἵνεκεν) sounds like a translation of the participle "philosophising" (φιλοσοφέων). Thucydides speaks in much the same sense of the Athenians in Pericles' incomparable funeral oration: "We are lovers of wisdom (we philosophise)

without effeminacy" (φιλοσοφοῦμεν ἄνευ μαλακίας). And Cicero says that knowledge of the best things, and the ability to use this knowledge, in whatever department they may be acquired, are termed 'philosophy.' All these uses of the word indicate that there is a peculiar province of knowledge which we are impelled to explore not by any practical need, but by the simple desire for knowledge itself. Now there can be no doubt that self-preservation or some other equally practical end lies behind the first beginnings of all knowledge. All the more remarkable, then, is this distinction of a special province of knowledge, which men investigate from the pure desire to know, without obtaining any direct profit for themselves or for the society in which they live. We employ to-day a single name for such knowledge in all its branches, and call it 'science.' Evidently, then, 'science' and 'philosophy' spring from a common root.

3. But philosophy came to mean a great deal more than this, even among the ancients. At first, before its results had been achieved, we find philosophical activity, philosophising, the centre of attraction. But as the stock of knowledge increased, and the thoughts of other generations could be regarded by the objective light of history, the name was gradually extended to a certain sum of acquired knowledge, products of this philosophical activity. When Socrates, pressing the etymological significance of the term, calls himself a philosopher (a striver after wisdom), as distinguished from the Sophists (teachers or possessors of wisdom), he is not really exalting with a sincere mind the endeavour after knowledge for knowledge' sake, but rather passing a sceptical judgment upon the certainty of knowledge or the possibility of knowing. His disciple Plato takes up a more positive and objective attitude on the question of what constitutes philosophy. Thus we read, *e.g.*, in the Theaetetus, of "geometry or any other philosophy"; while in the Euthydemus we find a general definition of philosophy regarded as acquisition of knowledge (κτῆσις ἐπιστήμης). More than this: there are passages which define the philosopher as one whose efforts aim at a knowledge of the eternal, of the essential nature of things, and thus give a quite definite objective meaning

to philosophy. We find a still closer definition in Aristotle's "first philosophy" (πρώτη φιλοσοφία) and "second philosophy" or physics. Aristotle means by 'first philosophy' philosophy proper, the highest or most general philosophy,—that which to-day is usually entitled metaphysics. But he also employs the word with technical precision, in its wider sense, as equivalent to 'science,' and as opposed to 'art' or the ability to make use of science (τέχνη).—*Cf.* Bonitz, *Index Aristotelicus*, 1870, *s.v.* φιλοσοφία.

4. The idea of philosophy undergoes yet another change at the hands of the Stoics and Epicureans. Alongside, or rather in place of, the strictly scientific meaning of the word, comes an emphasising of the value of the practical results of philosophic activity, and of the need for a comprehensive view of the purposes of human life and action. Thus Cicero exclaims: "Philosophy, thou director of our lives, thou friend of virtue and enemy to vice! What were we, what were the life of man at all, but for thee?" The individualistic thought of these schools found its chief interest in the endeavour after practical capacity or happiness. At the same time certain special fields of knowledge, such as mathematics and astronomy, begin to assume the rank of independent sciences.

It would be difficult to extract from the definitions of philosophy which we have mentioned hitherto any abstract formula which should be valid for all alike. Without attempting anything of the sort, we may, however, call the reader's attention to the fact that one and all lay special emphasis upon the natural desire for knowledge as an end in itself. This view also found representation in the middle ages, when the term philosophy was applied to knowledge attained by the natural light of reason, as contradistinguished from the supernatural knowledge owed to revelation. Philosophy thus comes to mean systematised natural knowledge.

5. The same distinction appears in the definition of philosophy as *scientia saecularis*, worldly wisdom or temporal science; for those who accepted it could not, of course, admit that any but temporal matters, the things of this world, were illuminable by the natural light of human reason. Even the rise of modern

philosophy produced no apparent change in this point of view: the only difference is that the value set upon temporal wisdom increases with marked rapidity, and that there is manifested a growing tendency to grant the claims of reason to be the sole and exclusive instrument for the attainment of real knowledge. In the writings of Descartes or Cartesius (1596–1650), the 'father of modern philosophy,' we find explicit acceptance of this standpoint; certain knowledge can be gained only through philosophy, and established only upon a philosophical basis. Here again, *i.e.*, philosophy stands simply for science, as it did in the ancient world. In England, the differentiation of temporal wisdom and theology was longer lived. The dominant note, both in Bacon's (1561–1626) classification of the sciences according to the faculties of knowledge,—in which philosophy is derived from reason,—and in Hobbes' (1588–1679) definition of philosophy as the knowledge of causal connections, would seem to be the same with that of mediæval thought. And the supposition is confirmed by the fact that the English universities have retained scholastic forms longer than any others, and that even to-day certain uses of 'philosophical' carry us back to the older and wider meaning of the word. Further to notice in this connection are the curiously hard and fast distinction between knowledge and belief, and the absence of a metaphysics, in the strict sense of the term, which are characteristic of English philosophy. Philosophy is made to do service in the investigations undertaken by the separate sciences; it remains specifically scientific, and is thus kept upon the safe ground of experience, and deals with facts of universal validity.

6. The chief end of continental philosophy, on the other hand, has been to accomplish a rational unification of knowledge and belief by help of a metaphysics erected by scientific methods upon a scientific basis. Descartes believed that the principal aim of philosophy was the complete knowledge of all things knowable, and that this involved the discovery of one supreme and final principle, from which every fact of knowledge might be rationally deduced. Later on Christian Wolff (1679–1754) defined philosophy as the "scientia possibilium, quatenus esse

possunt," *i.e.*, as the science of the possible, so far as it can become actual. For him too, that is, the task of philosophy consists in the establishment of most general principles, from which the data of knowledge can be derived. Nor is there any great difference of outlook in Kant's (1724–1804) definition of philosophical knowledge as "rational knowledge from concepts," in J. G. Fichte's (1762–1814) view of philosophy as a "science of knowledge" (*Wissenschaftslehre*), or in Hegel's (1770–1831) definition of it as a "science of the absolute." So we come by easy gradations to the definition of philosophy as the 'science of principles,' which is generally current at the present time. The definition proposed by Ueberweg (†1871) takes precisely this form; and the tendency of many modern philosophers to regard epistemology and logic as the sole or at least the central disciplines of a scientific philosophy is an indication of substantial agreement with his view.

7. But our survey would be incomplete if we failed to take account of some other attempts to formulate an unitary definition of philosophy. The rapid growth of the special sciences has led certain modern philosophers to assign philosophy a place among them, or to look upon it as supplementary to them. The original relation of the two departments of knowledge is thus reversed: philosophy has ceased to be the necessary presupposition of the work done by individual sciences, and this has come to be recognised as an adequate basis for philosophical labours. Herbart (1776–1841) approaches this point of view when he defines philosophy as the "working over of concepts," and explains that to 'work over' means, in the concrete case, to classify, correct and supplement by determination of relative value. Philosophy accordingly falls for him into three main divisions: logic, metaphysics and practical philosophy or æsthetics (*cf.* § 1. 3). Even here, then, we find that certain concepts are recognised as given, as data of experience. The same fundamental thought, expressed in greatly improved form, recurs in Wundt, who states that the problem of philosophy is the unification of all knowledge obtained by the special

sciences in a consistent whole; and in Paulsen, who defines philosophy as the sum total of all scientific knowledge. Such a view evidently regards philosophy as supplementary to the separate sciences, as something which they may, perhaps, be able to do without; and there can be no doubt that this idea of the business of philosophy is widely prevalent at the present time. Of less influence is the position held by Beneke (1798–1854) and Lipps, who assert that philosophy is psychology, or the science of the inner experience, and that it must therefore be looked upon as co-ordinate with natural science.

8. It is evident that none of these modern definitions seeks to appreciate or explain philosophy considered as a product of historic development; they are intended rather to give expression to the personal opinions of independent thinkers as to the best possible way of pursuing the study of philosophy at a particular time. Hence, while they may appeal to us as programmes for determinate systems, or as apt *résumés* of the views of individual philosophers, they cannot be regarded as attempts to summarise the permanent characteristics of philosophy in a formula of universal validity. As it is a matter of indifference for our immediate purpose which of the more general definitions of philosophy we adopt, we will take that proposed by Ueberweg (*cf.* above, § 2. 6), and try by its aid to illustrate the relation of philosophy to allied fields of thought. As a science of 'principles,' philosophy differs from the special sciences in that it is restricted to those most general concepts which they employ, but do not explain. Every science speaks of conditions, laws, forces, possibilities, realities, etc.; but no single discipline can undertake a comprehensive discussion of these and similar terms, if only for the reason that they are applied in the most diverse spheres, and by no means always endowed with the same attributes. As a 'science,' philosophy falls under the general heading of products of mental activity, while it is distinguished from other members of the same class, *e.g.*, from art and religion, by its endeavour to assure the universal validity of its statements.

9. The following criticisms may be passed upon this definition of philosophy:—

(*a*) The fact that philosophy has always had an *individual* significance, *i.e.*, that it has been the work of particular philosophers, may well make us hesitate to predicate the term 'science' of the sum total of philosophic achievement. We do not speak of Helmholtz' or Maxwell's physics, of Berzelius' or Liebig's chemistry, of Ranke's or Taine's history, of Savigny's or Wächter's jurisprudence. If the name of an individual occurs in the exposition of any of these sciences, it is only that some definite discovery may be accredited to its author, or some definite hypothesis, which has not met with general acceptance, be associated with those investigators upon whose authority it rests. Philosophy is to a much greater degree the work of particular men; and it is as yet only in certain of the philosophical disciplines that we can see personal opinions beginning to consolidate about a nucleus of generally accepted laws.

(*b*) But neither does philosophy deal with 'principles,' in all the departments of knowledge which pass under its name. Ethics, *e.g.*, purports to be a direct scientific investigation of the facts and laws of the moral life, and to state the conditions which must be fulfilled by every action which is to be made the matter of a moral judgment. Æsthetics, in the same way, is the science of the facts and laws of æsthetic pleasure. Neither of these two disciplines, which are universally ascribed to philosophy, can be regarded by the impartial critic as anything else than a special science (*cf.* §§ 9 and 10),—unless, indeed, he is prepared to accept a definition of philosophy as bizarre as that proposed by Lotze, who declared that it is the investigation of the thoughts which constitute our principles of judgment in daily life and in the separate sciences. And even then it would not be hard to show that the definition, generous as it looks, cannot cover a very considerable portion of the field of philosophic work.

We must conclude, then, that one of the commonest of current definitions of philosophy is inadequate in its statement, both of the 'genus proximum' and of the 'differentia specifica.' The conclusion serves to justify the attempt, which we propose to make later on, to find a better definition of the essential purpose of philosophy.

NOTE.—We sometimes read of 'sources' of philosophical activity, philosophy being regarded as the product of a definite impulse or emotion. Plato, *e.g.*, makes *wonder* (θαυμάζειν), and Herbart *doubt*, the origin of philosophy. But curiosity as to the existence or nature of something, and doubt as to the correctness or validity of some statement, are emotions which underlie advance in all departments of science, and can be brought into special relation to philosophy only by the instancing of some peculiarity in philosophic subject-matter, by which they are there aroused. In saying this, however, we do not wish to deny that a special capacity or specific talent is the presupposition of a successful handling of philosophical questions.

LITERATURE.

R. Haym, 'Philosophie,' in the *Allgemeine Encyclopädie* of Ersch and Gruber. Sect. 3, Part 24, pp. 1-11. 1848.

F. Ueberweg and M. Heinze, *Grundriss der Geschichte der Philosophie*. 8th ed., I., pp. 1-5. 1894. Trs. of 4th ed., by G. S. Morris. 1891.

W. Windelband, *Geschichte der Philosophie*, pp. 1-6. 1892. Trs. by J. H. Tufts. 1893.

§ 3. *The Classification of Philosophy.*

1. Classification in philosophy must always be classification along the lines laid down by a definition of philosophy. Hence the differences of definition which we have discussed in preceding paragraphs mean corresponding differences of classification. As a matter of fact, however, not every philosopher who has given us a more or less clear definition of philosophy has also attempted a definite classification of his subject-matter. The earliest of which we have record is that of Plato. Plato distinguishes, in treatment though not in name, between three disciplines: dialectics, physics and ethics. Dialectics embraces epistemology and metaphysics; it is a science of ideas or concepts, of the essential nature of things. Physics includes natural science, natural philosophy and psychology, and can therefore, perhaps, be best rendered by the phrase 'natural knowledge.' Lastly, ethics covers for Plato the same

field that it does for us, *i.e.*, is the science which deals with moral conduct. It is plain that this specification of parts of philosophy does not constitute a system, in any true sense of the word, but is intended simply to bring out some of the more prominent characteristics of the science. But its adoption by the Stoics and Epicureans made it of great influence upon subsequent philosophic thought, and it dominated philosophy as late as, and even later than, the middle ages.

2. The influence of the Platonic classification is also due, in part, to the fact that no systematic arrangement of the philosophical disciplines had come down from Aristotle. It is true that Aristotle is customarily accredited with the division of philosophy into theoretic, practical and poetic, on the strength of the sentence: πᾶσα διάνοια ἢ πρακτικὴ ἢ ποιητικὴ ἢ θεωρητική. But we have seen (*cf.* § 2. 3) that Aristotle knew and employed a much narrower definition of philosophy; and as the divisions of his system show no traces of any such triple distinction, it seems probable that the word διάνοια should not be translated 'philosophy.' On the other hand, we find a little further on the phrase φιλοσοφίαι θεωρητικαὶ used to cover the sciences of mathematics, physics and theology; so that we are bound to assume, at least, that Aristotle recognised a complementary 'practical' philosophy. However this may be, it is readily intelligible that the Aristotelian definitions could have but little influence upon later thought.

At the beginning of modern philosophy we are met by a comprehensive classification of philosophy upon an entirely new principle. It occurs in Bacon's work (1623) *De dignitate et augmentis scientiarum* (*cf.* § 2. 5). Bacon begins by classifying the faculties of knowledge, and thus enunciates for the first time a principle that has never since wanted for advocates,—the principle that psychological enquiry must form the basis of all philosophy, indeed of all science. The faculties of knowledge are memory, imagination and understanding or reason. From the first arises the science of history; from the second, poetry; while reason gives us philosophy. Philosophy itself is subdivided according to its subject-matter. It may be concerned with God, nature or man, and falls accordingly into three parts, entitled theology, natural philosophy and anthropology. Within each of these departments Bacon draws a further distinction between practical and theoretical investigation, and in this way, and by the more exact specification of subject-matter, splits up the three primary disciplines into various other sciences. The far-reaching influence of this comprehensive classification of the sciences is attested by the fact that d'Alembert kept it practically unchanged in his *Discours préliminaire* to the famous *Encyclopédie* (1751 *ff.*).

3. The fruitfulness of the new principle is further evidenced by the classification of philosophy proposed by C. Wolff (*cf.* § 2. 6), which also has its root in psychology. Wolff distinguishes a *facultas cognoscitiva* and a *facultas appetitiva*, a faculty of knowledge and a faculty of desire, and so obtains two main divisions of philosophy, the theoretical (*metaphysica*) and the practical. The classification proceeds on the basis of subject-matter. Theoretical philosophy, which has to do with God, the mind and the world, falls into theology, psychology and cosmology (physics). Behind these special theoretical disciplines lies the fundamental science of ontology, whose business is the discussion of the most general concepts of the understanding (categories). Practical philosophy, in its turn, is divided into ethics, economics and politics, which treat of man respectively as an individual, as member of a family, and as citizen of a state.[1] These, too, have their fundamental science, 'general practical philosophy.' A general introduction to both the practical and theoretical philosophies is afforded by logic, which Wolff considered to be a purely formal discipline. Lastly, this whole arrangement is crossed, and to a certain extent interfered with, by a classification in terms of the method employed in the separate philosophical sciences. The mathematical method of deduction, which derives facts from most general principles, is pronounced to be intrinsically preferable; but an induction, which starts out from individual facts, is also recommended

[1] Similar divisions of the 'practical philosophy' of their master had already been made by the Aristotelians.

and expounded. Wolff accordingly opposes the rational to the empirical disciplines. Alongside of rational theology stands experimental theology or teleology; and we have similarly a rational and empirical cosmology or physics, and a rational and empirical psychology. The opposition is primarily no more than a difference in manner of exposition; the contents of the science remains the same, but the methods followed are divergent. None the less it contains within it the suggestion of a separation of philosophy from the special sciences, of which before Wolff's time we find but little trace. Originally, cosmology or physics covered the whole field of natural knowledge. Later on, philosophers availed themselves of the two different terms, in order to give convenient expression to the difference between the investigations of natural philosophy and natural science.

4. The most important classification of philosophy in modern times is that given by Hegel. He distinguishes a science of the origin of absolute knowledge from a specific exposition of its contents. The former he calls the 'phenomenology' of mind. This sets forth six stages in the gradual development of knowledge, until it reaches its culmination in 'absolute knowing.' The method by which these stages are developed is logical, not psychological: it is the method of 'dialectic,' which Hegel employed with such rigorous consistency. The keynote of the dialectic is that the higher stages of knowledge do not simply replace the lower, but take up all that is good in these into themselves; so that the highest stage, of absolute knowledge, contains in it the truth of all the lower stages. Hegel defines 'logic' as the science that treats of the contents of absolute knowledge, which he developes, by the same dialectic method, from the universal contentless concept of being to the absolute idea, the richest in contents of all concepts. Logic gives rise to two special philosophical disciplines,—the 'philosophy of nature' and the 'philosophy of mind.'

We find a similar set of divisions, despite a wide difference of general standpoint, in Wundt's classification of philosophy. We may first of all, Wundt says, enquire into the origin of the whole contents of knowledge: this enquiry is the task of epistemology. But, secondly, we may investigate this same contents with reference to the systematic connection of the principles of knowledge: this enquiry is the task of a 'theory of principles.' This falls again into a general theory of principles, or metaphysics, and a special theory of principles, which may in its turn be subdivided into the philosophy of nature and the philosophy of mind. It is clear that this classification is at bottom very similar to that of Hegel; though the divergence in method and the restricted meaning of the phrase 'theory of principles' are more than sufficient to differentiate the two.

Herbart's classification has already been mentioned (§2. 7). We cannot here discuss certain quite recent attempts to furnish a new classification of philosophy.

5. Remembering our definition of philosophy as a science of principles (§ 2. 8), we must now raise the question in what sense such a science is capable of division into separate disciplines. It is plain that, if subdivision is to be possible, the term 'principles' must be so defined as to admit of it; and a definition of the kind, recognising the distinction of classes under the general rubric 'principles,' seems to be implicit in Wundt's assumption of a general and special theory of principles. But no attempt at a systematic classification of the disciplines which rank as 'philosophical' can be successful, so long as no single and universally acceptable definition of philosophy can be found. Indeed, it is not difficult to show that all the classifications quoted above fail to accomplish their purpose. In the first place, we must take exception to the idea of a 'philosophy of mind.' If the phrase means a philosophical consideration of the mental sciences, philology, jurisprudence, history, etc., there is no place made for ethics and æsthetics: while the statement that psychology is the fundamental discipline of these mental sciences does but scant justice to the peculiar position which it occupies in general philosophy. This apart, however, we can see that there is absolutely no hope of success for any attempt at a systematic classification on the basis of a single and universally acceptable

definition of philosophy. We have only to look at history, to remember that disciplines once accounted philosophical have now lost that title; in a word, to recall the changes of meaning that the term philosophy has undergone (§ 2). Wolff, *e.g.*, did not hesitate to include empirical psychology and physics under philosophy; while Wundt regards the former as a special science, and accordingly excludes it from the circle of philosophical disciplines, and experimental physics has long been treated independently of philosophy, as a special natural science. Descartes still regarded medicine and mechanics as parts of philosophy, and Newton called his famous masterpiece, *Naturalis philosophiae principia mathematica*, without having the least intention of writing a 'natural philosophy' in the present sense of the words. A. Comte (1798-1857) and Herbert Spencer have made sociology a part of philosophy, thus filling a gap left by Bacon in his classification of the sciences; but the time seems not far distant when it, too, will cut loose from philosophy, and take rank as a separate science. If philosophy were a single science, with a permanent and definite subject-matter, all this change of opinion with regard to its divisions and subdivisions would be quite incomprehensible.

6. A critical examination of current classifications, then, has led us to the same result as our investigation of the customary definition of philosophy. The original problem still confronts us; and we find fresh reason for the endeavour to lay down a new definition of philosophy, which shall be adequate to all that is of universal validity in its nature and contents.

We must, however, adopt some sort of classification for the survey of the admittedly philosophical disciplines which we shall essay in the following Chapter. For this preliminary purpose we may divide up our subject-matter into *general* and *special* philosophical disciplines, the former having reference to the whole contents of our knowledge, whether as its presupposition, completion or exposition, the latter only to certain departments of scientific achievement. We say nothing at all here upon the question whether or not the sciences mentioned under the head of special philosophical disciplines deserve the general name of philosophy in the light of any definition hitherto proposed. Our sole purpose in making the classification is to obtain a thread upon which to hang our discussion of the different sciences which are to-day generally regarded as philosophical,—to satisfy the demands of logic without committing ourselves to any definite conception of philosophy as a whole. Among the general philosophical disciplines we include metaphysics, logic and epistemology; among the special, natural philosophy, psychology, ethics and the philosophy of law, æsthetics, the philosophy of religion and the philosophy of history. Sociology is here embraced under the title 'philosophy of history.'

Literature.

W. Wundt, "Ueber die Eintheilung der Wissenschaften." In *Phil. Studien*, vol. v., pp. 1 ff. 1889.

[H. Spencer, "A Classification of the Sciences." In *Essays*, vol. ii., p. 74.]

CHAPTER II

THE PHILOSOPHICAL DISCIPLINES

A. THE GENERAL PHILOSOPHICAL DISCIPLINES

§ 4. *Metaphysics.*

1. The name 'metaphysics' is of purely accidental origin. The editors of Aristotle's writings placed his most general investigations after the works on natural science and natural philosophy, and since the latter were called τὰ φυσικά, the former were naturally known as τὰ μετὰ τὰ φυσικά. This arrangement, originally chronological only, was later looked upon as logically correct; and it is no unusual thing to find philosophers, even as late as the eighteenth century, judicially discussing the double meaning of the μετά. The Aristotelian metaphysics treated of the most general determinations of being, and attempted to elaborate a theory of the universe. Hence it is by no means true to say that Aristotle created the science to which his writings have furnished a name: metaphysics had already been studied by the philosophers of both the earlier and later Ionian schools,—among others, by Plato. The term 'dialectics,' which occurs in Plato (*cf.* § 3. 1), covers the discussion of topics similar to those examined by the Aristotelian metaphysics. At a later time, however, the word fell into disrepute, through its scholastic associations. Dialectics was one of the regular subjects in the curriculum of the schools of the middle ages, but came to be regarded as nothing more than an apprenticeship in hairsplitting and barren disputation. Nevertheless, Schleiermacher (1768–1834) revived the term, to cover metaphysical and epistemological disquisitions; and Hegel brought it

into temporary favour by his use of the dialectical method (*cf.* § 3. 4). More recently still, E. Dühring has called his acute essay on space, time, causality and infinity 'natural dialectics' (1865).

2. Keeping to our definition of philosophy as a science of principles (§ 2. 8), we must regard metaphysics as the science of the *most general* principles. It will, therefore, be concerned with such concepts as those of being, becoming, possibility, actuality, necessity, etc. Many philosophers, however, following Wolff, have regarded these matters as the subject of a special branch of metaphysics, ontology. Lotze, *e.g.*, divides his metaphysics (2nd ed., 1884; Eng. trs., 1887) into ontology, cosmology and psychology, and assigns to the first-named the duty of deciding the most general determinations of being. From another point of view, metaphysics has been conceived of as a theory of the real, in contradiction to the theory of the phenomenal, which is furnished by the special sciences. Its problem would then be the cognition of the self-existent, of that which must be regarded as existing, absolutely, behind the world of appearances. We find this idea of metaphysics in Descartes and Spinoza (1632–1677), Leibniz (1646–1716) and Herbart, Schopenhauer (1788–1860) and E. von Hartmann; though the reasons that each of these philosophers gives for regarding such a science as possible differ pretty widely from those given by the others. Metaphysics, then, takes shape as a theory of the universe; something which rounds off and in a certain measure corrects the knowledge attained by the separate sciences. And it is in this meaning of metaphysics that we have the root of that individuality which characterises not it alone but all philosophy. For a theory of the universe, to use popular language, is not only the work of the 'understanding,' not only an intellectual analysis and recomposition of scientific data, but also the creation of 'feeling' and 'will,' of a mind which approaches those data with definite needs and requirements. It must satisfy the demands not only of the intellect, but also of the will,—in more general phrase, of human life. Hence it is this sense of the word metaphysics that philosophers have in

view when they distinguish a whole number of divergent 'schools'; the terms monism and dualism, materialism and spiritualism, etc., stand for metaphysical opposites. Even Kant, who set out to rob metaphysics of its title to existence as a part of scientific knowledge, admitted that he was dealing with an irrepressible requirement of human reason, and did not for a moment believe that his criticism had made all attempts at metaphysics impossible.

3. The chief result of Kant's 'critique of all metaphysics' is the proof that every metaphysics must be preceded by an investigation into the limits of our faculty of knowledge. It is on this account that Kant is known as the representative of a 'critical' philosophy. His demonstration of the unscientific character of current metaphysical essays in all the three departments of theoretical philosophy distinguished by Wolff—rational psychology, cosmology and theology—is irrefragable. It runs somewhat as follows.

(1) The conclusion of rational psychology, the assumption of an imperishable and substantial mind, rests upon a paralogism or erroneous inference: it involves argument from the 'I' familiar to everyone as logical subject to an 'I' as substantial existence.

(2) Cosmology makes certain statements with regard to the spatial, temporal and causal attributes of the universe, and declares that they possess universal validity. The claim is unfounded: for precisely opposite assertions can be demonstrated to be equally worthy of credence. Thus arise what are known as the 'cosmological antinomies.' The finitude and infinitude of space, time and causality are proven with equal cogency.

(3) Finally, Kant subjects the customary proofs of the existence of God offered by rational theology—the ontological, cosmological and physico-theological—to a destructive criticism, and again succeeds in showing that the methods of proof employed are scientifically inadequate. We cannot argue from the idea of a supreme or most perfect being to his existence; we cannot infer a final cause from the fact of an order of nature in the universe; and we cannot conclude from the purposive course of natural phenomena that it is the work of a supreme regulating intelligence (*cf.* §22).

To the metaphysical ideas which find treatment in these different connections, Kant opposes the extremely happy and fruitful conception of a 'regulative principle.' He understands by this an hypothesis which is intended to regulate scientific investigation, without putting forward any claims of its own to independent significance, *i.e.*, a highest principle which owes its place simply to considerations of expediency. Since in the scientific investigation of nature, *e.g.*, it is convenient to set out from the assumption of the infinity of the universe, this, and not the contrary assumption of its finitude, is raised to the rank of a regulative principle; but its adoption does not pledge the investigator to include the metaphysical doctrine of infinity in his general theory of the universe. When, however, Kant comes to discuss the question of the freedom or determination of the will, he is led to the conclusion that we may at least assert the possibility of an uncaused beginning of any series of events, provided that they lie outside the sphere of phenomena—the only objects of scientific knowledge—or of possible experience. It was on this basis that Kant, later on, worked out his metaphysics of ethics, in which he demanded the acceptance of freedom of the will.

4. The post-Kantian philosophy is perhaps more rife in metaphysical speculation than that of any other period. We shall look for metaphysics, however, less in the works of the 'idealists,' Fichte, Schelling and Hegel, than in Kant's 'realistic' followers, Herbart and Schopenhauer. For the realists made an express attempt to obtain knowledge of the essential nature of things, to get an idea of the character of the 'thing in itself,' which Kant believed to lie behind the world of phenomena, but which he declared, in his critical discussion of the limits of human knowledge, to be wholly inaccessible to scientific determination. Fichte, Schelling and Hegel, on the other hand, desired primarily merely to systematise the Kantian philosophy. C. L. Reinhold (1758–1823) began in the same way, with the search for a general principle valid for the whole faculty of knowledge. The result of his efforts was a supreme principle of ideation, by means of which unity was brought into the critique of pure reason,

Kant's theoretical philosophy. Fichte went a step farther, endeavouring to trace back both the critique of pure reason and the critique of practical reason (the ethics) to ultimate principles. The concept of the self proved to be best adapted to his purpose: Kant makes it a final logical presupposition of knowledge, *i.e.*, of the theoretical philosophy; and 'will' is defined in the practical philosophy as the thing in itself which lies behind the complex of phenomena constituting the nature of man. The idea of the ego can thus be regarded as the culmination of Kant's theoretical and practical philosophy alike. Schelling (1775–1854) and Hegel, with the same end in view, rose to a yet higher abstraction. Schelling introduced the idea of absolute identity as the supreme principle of all philosophical knowledge; Hegel made use of the corresponding idea of absolute existence, or, simply, of the 'absolute.'

It is evident from the above historical sketch that for these three philosophers metaphysics was a secondary result, not a chief end of philosophical enquiry. Indeed, Hegel's recognition of thought and being, reason and reality, as two completely distinct fields, is a sufficiently clear indication of his rejection of a special metaphysics as science of the existential nature of things. The modern tendency to make Hegel's 'speculative' metaphysics responsible for the general discredit into which philosophy subsequently fell is, therefore, historically unjustifiable. Hegel's undertaking was, as a matter of fact, conceived entirely in the spirit of latter-day science; he planned to give a comprehensive logical deduction and exposition of things as they were. Objection cannot be taken to his intention, but only to his manner of carrying it out.

5. In England metaphysics has never succeeded in obtaining a permanent foothold. English philosophy is an expressly empirical philosophy; and it seems never to have occurred to the great English thinkers, even as a possible problem, to combine natural philosophy and psychology with ethics, and so to approach the questions which form the peculiar subject-matter of continental metaphysics They will have philosophy

studied just as if it were a special science, or at least employed for the furtherance of the special (more particularly the natural) sciences. The few exceptions—Berkeley (1685–1753) and some of the Scottish philosophers—simply serve to prove the rule. This position with regard to metaphysics has recently been defended in detail by Herbert Spencer, and has become known as *agnosticism*. Spencer admits the existence of an absolute, corresponding to Kant's thing in itself, and lying behind the world of phenomena, but makes all knowledge consist in relations, and thus leaves the absolute indefinable,—not even to be characterised by any negative statement that might serve to determine its nature. The thinkers of this school are also frequently called *positivists*. Positivism originally meant the conception of philosophy expounded by A. Comte in his *Cours de philosophie positive* (6 vols., 1830–42); the idea of philosophy as nothing more than a systematisation of the special sciences. Recently, however, the name has been used with a wider signification, and there are not a few philosophers at the present day who might properly be classed as positivists. Characteristic of the positivist attitude are the rejection of all metaphysics, and the recognition of philosophy as a universal science and of experience as the sole source and sole object of knowledge. In this sense of the term, David Hume (1711–1776) was a positivist. E. Laas, whose book on 'Idealism and Positivism' (3 vols., 1879–1884) is a critical and historical account of the differences between these two great branches of philosophical thought, puts the dawn of positivism as far back as the sophist Protagoras. And the Neo-Kantians of our own time, whose chief representatives are F. A. Lange († 1875), H. Cohen, P. Natorp, K. Lasswitz, etc., have by their insistence upon the critical side of Kant's teaching taken up an attitude to metaphysics which shows the closest resemblance to that of positivism.

6. We cannot decide between these conflicting opinions until we have definitely marked out the field of metaphysics. If we understand by metaphysics what is still sometimes understood by it, the theory of the most general concepts employed for the

determination of empirical data (*cf.* § 4. 2), no objection can be urged against its claim to scientific recognition. Its pursuit would be entirely confined within the limits of possible experience, and could not of itself lead to any general view of the universe. We believe, however, that a metaphysics of this kind is best called 'epistemology,' since (as we shall have occasion to show later in detail: *cf.* § 5) it is precisely the investigation of the most general determinations of empirical data which constitutes the peculiar problem of that science. We accordingly exclude it from metaphysics.

There now remains for metaphysics nothing but the elaboration of a theory of the universe. That such a theory must transcend the limits of possible experience needs no special proof, the gaps in our knowledge are obvious enough. It is only against this second conception of metaphysics, therefore, that criticism, agnosticism and positivism can bring any valid arguments. But even here we cannot admit that their attack is wholly justified, or even that it is in keeping with the spirit of the Kantian philosophy. For metaphysics is, surely, to be combated and driven back within its borders only when it puts forth a claim to universal scientific validity. As an irrepressible requirement of the human reason it will still maintain its ground wherever a theory of the universe is found indispensable, and religion—the only other ministrant to similar needs—proves unable to supply a comprehensive view of life and the world. The motives from which religion took its origin are wholly practical. Its office is to assure an encouraging outlook, to provide a firm foundation, for the life of moral action and moral endeavour. But the ideas in which its purpose is realised are subject to the natural influences of scientific progress. Hence the desire must soon arise for a reconciliation or compromise between scientific laws on the one hand and the imperishable elements in religious conviction on the other. The details of such a compromise will differ at different times, since the postulates advanced upon the scientific side are constantly changing. But the reconciliation itself has always been entrusted to metaphysics.—In our opinion, then, metaphysics is a theory of the universe, based partly upon practical motives, partly upon the demand for a consistent rounding-off of scientific knowledge. With the stones supplied by the special sciences, at some given stage of their development, for its building material, it erects a complete and comprehensive structure, wherein each separate scientific fact finds its modest but definite and recognised place. And in the second instance it takes account of those practical requirements which have necessarily determined the first beginnings of every theory of the universe. Metaphysics thus appears as a science, in the sense that scientific knowledge constitutes the only real basis of metaphysical enquiry. At the same time, it can never attain to the scientific ideal, and become a system of universally valid propositions, for the simple reason that the continual progress of scientific knowledge prevents the final co-ordination of underlying facts, and compels us to supplement what is known by more or less probable hypotheses.[1]

7. If we ask under what conditions the need of a theory of the universe, however differently satisfied, is universally felt, we are met primarily by the four following: (1) some measure of uncertainty in political and legal relations; (2) insecurity and discomfort in the affairs of social life; (3) lack of exact knowledge of natural processes, and of the means whereby they can be adapted to human ends; and (4) insufficient experience of one's own inner life, and of the prerequisites of self-control. Whenever, that is to say, the external and internal worlds in which the individual is obliged to pass his life leave him dissatisfied because things are of this complexion or are not of that, there arises a desire for a more ideal existence, such as can best be pictured by help of a new theory of the universe. And these are also the influences which lead to the adoption of a metaphysics. Now and again the metaphysical spirit seizes on a population already stirred by other and similar impulses,

[1] The reader should compare with this paragraph Wundt's original attempt (*System der Philosophie*, 1889) to derive the right of metaphysics to transcend experience from similar procedure within the limits of the special sciences

and is confirmed and reinforced by their presence. Thus Wolff's systematisation of Leibniz' theory of the universe came before the German public at a time when the intellectual and emotional life of the nation, in the most widely different departments of activity, was eminently favourable to its reception. Wolff's idea of reality as something accidental and confused, something calculated rather to hinder the advancement of knowledge than to furnish its necessary basis, and the correspondingly high value which he set upon clear and distinct rational knowledge, upon thought and understanding, coincided with a rationalistic art, a pedantic etiquette in the intercourse of daily life, and an universal preference for the subtle and artificial. Hence it is not surprising that his doctrines displaced scholasticism and Cartesianism in the universities, that they were heard from the pulpit, and that they furnished the principles upon which children's books were written. Nor were the sciences—theology, jurisprudence, medicine—behindhand: they investigated and expounded upon Wolffian lines. Special societies were established for the propagation of the truth according to Wolff, and even *belles lettres* became, under his influence, a refinement of mental gymnastic that could be taught and learned. Contrast with this universal participation in a philosophical theory of the universe the spirit of our own time, with its delight in the real, its rich store of scientific knowledge, its vast material improvements and its high standard of social well-being!

8. This general change of view has, of course, left its imprint upon the metaphysics of our day. Slowly but surely the relation between reason and reality has been altering. Kant still inclined upon the whole to place the rational above the real, though he recognised that reality was at least the necessary starting-point for any extension of human knowledge. But it was Hegel who taught us to see that the real and the rational must be coincident, *i.e.*, must be given equal weight in a theory of the universe. Lotze went further, declaring that reality is much richer than our thought; and, lastly, Wundt makes the directly experienced reality of the 'object of idea' not only the foundation of his

epistemology, but the end and aim of metaphysical enquiry into the ultimate nature of things. Indeed, Wundt does not hesitate to assert that the rational determination of certain aspects or constituents of this direct reality, as it is undertaken by the special sciences, and more particularly by natural science and psychology, depends upon a wholly artificial distinction, and leads to results which are merely conceptual, not real. Here we have the relation between reason and reality completely reversed; and the change is strictly paralleled by a reversal of the values attached to them in popular estimation.

A survey of the *literature* of metaphysics would mean a survey of the philosophical systems of all ages. We will, therefore, only mention here two short treatises written from different points of view, and on that account well calculated to bring home to the reader the lack of universal validity in metaphysical expositions. They are the *Grundzüge der Metaphysik*, by K. Dieterich (1885), and the *Elemente der Metaphysik*, by P. Deussen (2nd edition, 1890; trs. 1894). The first-mentioned author is a follower of Lotze, the latter of Schopenhauer.

§ 5. *Epistemology.*

1. In the wider sense of the term, epistemology or theory of knowledge means the science of the material and formal principles of knowledge; in its narrower sense, it is the discipline which is exclusively concerned with the material principles of knowledge. The word 'logic' is also often used in a broad sense to cover the whole field, while a more restricted usage confines it to the science of the formal principles of knowledge. We shall employ both terms only in their more limited meanings, regarding logic and epistemology as two complementary sciences, the one of which treats of the most general contents, the other of the most general forms of knowledge. Both together may be said to constitute the 'science of knowledge' (in Fichte's terminology, *Wissenschaftslehre: cf.* § 2. 6).

For the ancients epistemology did not exist as a separate discipline. Plato included epistemological investigations under what he calls dialectics (*cf.* § 3. 1), and we find them also in

Aristotle's metaphysics (*cf.* § 4. 1); but there is no sharp line of division between epistemology on the one hand, and the properly metaphysical or specifically logical discussions on the other. The principal epistemological questions in ancient philosophy are those which centre round the truth and universal validity of knowledge. There is hardly any trace of the problems which have loomed so large in modern thought,—the relation between the subjective and objective factors in knowledge, the parts played by object and by knowing subject in the process of perception or knowledge, and the determination of the limits of knowledge and of the nature of pure experience.

2. The English philosopher, John Locke, must be regarded as the real founder of epistemology as an independent discipline. His great work, ***An Essay concerning Human Understanding***, which appeared in 1690, contains the first systematic enquiry into the origin, certainty, nature and limits of knowledge. Locke was led to undertake an investigation of the kind by the experience that in matters of metaphysics, moral philosophy and religion agreement of opinions was hardly to be obtained. The universal source of knowledge lies for him in external and internal perception, 'sensation' and 'reflection'; and a comprehensive classification of the 'ideas' which are derived from these two sources leads him to assume a certain limited number of elementary constituents, which in manifold connection and combination make up our developed knowledge. The distinction between primary and secondary qualities of physical bodies (already clearly drawn by Galilei, who in his turn may have followed Democritus), whereby certain attributes of things are looked upon as permanent and necessary, others as transitory and contingent, due to our own special organisation,—in other words, the doctrine of the *subjectivity of the qualities of sense*, of colours, tones, tastes, etc.,—is raised by Locke to the epistemological antithesis of outer and inner, subject and object.

3. It is readily intelligible that this first attempt at an epistemology—the first, despite the preparatory work already done by Hobbes—was not wholly successful. Locke, like all the episte-

mologists of that period, made the curious mistake of regarding the psychological point of view as natural and original, and basing the recognition of any objective factor in knowledge upon a mere argument from probability. But his penetrating analysis of the materials of human knowledge, his introduction of logical categories (substance, mode, relation, etc.) which allow of a simpler, more useful and more systematic arrangement of the objects of knowledge than Aristotle's tenfold grouping by where, how, to what end, etc., and finally his careful discussion of the various stages and certainty of knowledge, have all been of lasting service to the science. How great an impression his work made upon philosophy is shown by the fact that Leibniz wrote his *Nouveaux essais sur l'entendement humain* (the publication of which was postponed on account of Locke's death, and which consequently appeared posthumously in 1765) in direct criticism of Locke's theories. Leibniz is principally concerned with the attack upon the doctrine of innate ideas to which Locke had devoted his first book. Locke formulates his position in the words of an old aphorism: *Nihil est in intellectu quod non prius fuerit in sensu;* Leibniz adds: *nisi intellectus ipse.* We must remember that in the continental philosophy of the time the universal validity of knowledge is always referred to an innate endowment of the mind, of whose existence we are assured by intuition, and in contrast with which the teachings of experience possess only a contingent, or at most a probable value (*cf.* § 4. 7).

4. This idea pervades the thought of Kant, who, after Locke, has done most toward the establishment of epistemology upon a scientific basis. Stimulated by the critical discussions of David Hume, the first to rouse him from his 'dogmatic slumber,' Kant essayed to explain what to him was an indisputable fact: the existence of universally valid scientific knowledge in the form of mathematics and mathematical natural science. He was led by his enquiry to the assumption of *a priori* elements both in sensuous knowledge and in knowledge of the understanding. Space and time are the forms of all perception, which lie ready in the mind, and render an universally valid science of number and space

possible. In the same way, the twelve categories which constitute the original possession of our understanding enable us to express the fundamental propositions of natural science with regard to matter, change and the uniform connection of phenomena, in necessary formulæ. This *a priori*, then,—which in Kant himself still has many of the attributes of an innate mental character, though by the modern representatives of his epistemology, the Neo-Kantians, it is used more correctly to designate a presupposition of scientific knowledge that is independent of experience,—this *a priori* is the root of all necessity and universality. At the same time, the *a priori* elements cannot of themselves, in Kant's opinion, furnish us with knowledge. They become fruitful only when applied to the material of experience. Hence their employment beyond the limits of possible experience, in what is called the 'transcendent' sphere, is merely pseudo-scientific, and can lead to no result (*cf.* § 4. 3). The works in which Kant expounds his epistemological views are the *Kritik der reinen Vernunft* (1781) and the *Prolegomena zu einer jeden künftigen Metaphysik* (1783).

5. In the writings of Kant's immediate successors epistemology appears under different names. We have already mentioned Fichte's term *Wissenschaftslehre*, science of knowledge (*cf.* §5. 1). In his elaboration of this discipline Fichte comes to definite metaphysical conclusions as to the principle which underlies the order of the universe, and passes far beyond the limits of epistemology proper. The same thing is true of Schelling's 'philosophy of identity,' of Hegel's 'logic,' of Herbart's 'metaphysics' and of Schopenhauer's system. No one of these authors makes any attempt to define the boundaries of strictly epistemological enquiry. Since the sixth decade of the present century the conviction has grown among German philosophers that a sound epistemology can alone furnish an adequate basis for philosophy in general, and a reliable criterion of the inferences drawn from the investigators of the special sciences. Materialism, the metaphysical assumption that matter is the principle of all things (*cf.* §16), was the direct occasion of the return to Kant which this conviction brought with it. Hegel's speculative philosophy crumbled beneath

the attacks of the empirical disciplines and of this cautious new philosophy, and philosophical science began by slow degrees to recover its lost ground. To-day, the first thing demanded of a philosopher is a complete familiarity with epistemology, which there is a great tendency to regard as actually equivalent to 'philosophy,'—so far, at least, as philosophy can lay claim to any scientific import; and the high value set upon epistemology has extended beyond philosophy. Men of eminence in the special sciences, like Helmholtz, Fick, Mach, etc., have attempted to answer the epistemological questions which lie behind their sciences. So in Protestant theology: Ritschl's school, in particular, are convinced that the scientific exposition of the contents of the Christian religion presupposes not a metaphysics, but Kant's or Lotze's epistemology.

6. There can be no doubt that epistemology deserves the high position thus accorded to it. But in face of the multiplicity of opinions concerning its special problem, we are called upon to delimit its sphere of application as precisely and definitely as we can. If one understands by 'knowledge' the obtaining of knowledge or knowing, *i.e.*, the acts or processes which lead to knowledge, epistemology evidently becomes a part of psychology. For these activities cannot imply anything but psychical functions; indeed, we often hear of a 'psychology of knowledge,' whose subject-matter consists of all the conscious processes involved in the acquisition of knowledge,—sensation, perception, memory and imagination, attention and thought, etc. The old psychology spoke in the same sense of a *facultas cognoscitiva*, within which it distinguished between lower and higher faculties of knowledge. The point of view from which all these processes are considered is that of the purpose which they are conceived to fulfil or to be capable of fulfilling: what must be the nature of those psychical functions—so the question runs—which lead, have led and can lead to knowledge? This teleological standpoint, which is thoroughly characteristic of the older psychology, makes the psychology of knowledge an applied science. Epistemology as thus defined, would, therefore, be a department of applied psychology. We trace the same tendency in certain modern names

for psychical processes. The phrases 'sensation of weight,' 'sensation of resistance,' 'sensation of movement,' denote those simple sensation qualities which give rise to the idea of a heavy, fixed or moving object.

7. If epistemology were nothing more than a part of applied psychology, it could not (1) form the presupposition of all the disciplines engaged with a certain subject-matter, but would itself presuppose the quite definite science of psychology. (2) Moreover, on such a definition it must be looked upon as one of the special sciences, since empirical psychology, which constitutes its foundation, has already become a special science (*cf.* §8. 9). (3) Further, it would bear no relation to the weighty questions of the validity and limits of human knowledge; for no amount of applied psychology could help us to determine the value or extent of possible knowledge. (4) Finally, it would be wholly unable, under these circumstances, to undertake any objective investigation of the general problems of the distinction between subject and object, of causality, of development, etc. All that it could do would be to show the course which the processes of scientific enquiry or acquisition most usefully take in the mind of some particular individual; but then it would entirely lose the character of a scientific philosophy and general philosophical discipline. It seems evident, therefore, that epistemology cannot be regarded as a theory of knowing.

The other meaning which we can give the term is that of the science of the results of obtaining knowledge or knowing, the science of knowledge as acquired. But again, in this very general sense, epistemology would run the risk of confusion with logic and the special sciences. Now we can distinguish logic from epistemology (as we shall see later: § 6) by entrusting to it the exclusive treatment of the formal principles of knowledge; and if we hand over the special contents of knowledge to the special sciences, we are obviously left with an epistemology whose peculiar province is that of the *general contents* of knowledge. The discipline would, on this view, be occupied with those concepts whose comprehensive application in different special sciences made them the logical presuppositions of these sciences, and prevented their adequate discussion within the limits of any individual science.

8. Epistemology treats, then, not of any special facts which can be separated from other special facts, nor yet of those more general contents of knowledge which can still be disposed of within a restricted field of scientific enquiry, but of matter so general that it is common and essential to all, or at least to great groups of the special sciences. The reader will better understand what is meant if we give a list of the objects which come under this category.

(1) The first business of epistemology will be the definition of the phrase 'contents of knowledge' in its most general sense,—an examination of the question of the possibility of knowledge. Such an examination is of special importance in connection with the 'limits' of knowledge, which are generally admitted and often enough make their appearance in the course of a scientific discussion. Closely related to this last question are (*a*) the distinction between 'transcendence' and 'immanence,' between what lies beyond all experience and what is contained in experience; (*b*) the antithesis of the *a priori* and the *a posteriori*, of what in human knowledge is independent of experience and what is dependent upon experience; (*c*) the enquiry into the conditions of the 'necessity' and 'universal validity' of statements, *i.e.*, into the nature of the contents which make these statements possible, etc., etc. (2) In the second place, epistemology will have to test the fundamental division of the contents of knowledge into 'subjective' and 'objective.' This division is so far-reaching that it differentiates the two great departments of natural science and psychology; all that can be regarded subjectively is handed over to psychology, all that can be objectified, to natural science. It is clear that the examination could not be carried out by a psychological epistemology; and it follows that the school of subjective idealism, which adopts the psychological point of view and looks upon every datum of knowledge as an idea of the knowing subject (*cf.* § 26. 1 ff.),

has barred the way to any solution of the problem involved. (3) In the third place, epistemology must consider the not less fundamental division of knowledge into 'formal' and 'material' constituents. (4) As a fourth problem we might set down the investigation of being and becoming, or change, and of one of the more special forms of change, development. Besides these enquiries, which constitute the logical presupposition of all the special sciences, epistemology will be occupied with certain less general concepts, common only to definite groups of sciences. (5) Under this head fall the concepts of matter, force, energy, life, mind, the relation between psychical and physical processes, etc. As a rule, however, these special questions are discussed in particular philosophical disciplines, such as natural philosophy or psychology.

9. We need use no argument to prove that our definition gives epistemology the significance of a fundamental philosophical science. On the other hand, we may pause for a moment to notice that it completely nullifies a difficulty which has often been urged from the dialectic standpoint against the recognition of epistemology as a separate discipline. The question has been raised, how the value and validity of knowledge can be determined when we are always obliged to use the knowing mind in coming to our determination. If we posit the validity of knowledge in the latter case, it is plain that no further investigation of the validity of knowledge is necessary. If we do not, then we have no criterion by which to judge of validity or invalidity at all. Now this line of argument will, evidently, hold only as against the conception of epistemology as a theory of *knowing*. It has no force whatsoever when brought against our definition of the discipline as a science of the most general contents of knowledge.

There can be no doubt that epistemological investigations are among the most difficult in the whole realm of philosophy. Not only does their conceptual character require a very peculiar capacity for abstract thought; their dependence upon the progress of the special sciences—which cannot but exert great influence upon our knowledge of the most general contents of science—demands, at the same time, a familiarity with the status of all the special branches of scientific work. Moreover, through the action of a psychological law of universal validity, which cannot be further discussed at present, we find that the most general concepts are those first formed by popular and philosophical reflection; so that epistemology runs a risk of suffering from the confusion of popular linguistic usage and from association with all sorts of metaphysical theories and beliefs. Although the science is, in principle, as capable of attaining to necessity and universal validity as any other discipline, still the difficulties which it has to meet are fully sufficient to explain the fact that epistemological antitheses still play a part in philosophy, and that the conception of the study as a whole cannot as yet be said to have become wholly clear and definite. We may note that in the special sciences, too, it is the most general theories which are least capable of a formulation which shall exempt them from discussion and disagreement.

10. The varying use of the term 'logic' has led to the frequent inclusion of epistemological expositions in works which bear that title, and which also deal with the problems peculiar to logic in its narrower sense. We shall here, then, merely mention the names of those modern writers who have given epistemology a place in their logics: Schuppe, Lotze and Wundt. The works themselves will be cited under § 6. We append a list of strictly epistemological treatises.

H. Cohen, *Kant's Theorie der Erfahrung*, 2nd ed., 1885. (The chief epistemological work of the Neo-Kantians.)

A. Riehl, *Der philosophische Kritizismus*, 2 vols., 3 parts, 1876–87. (The first volume contains an historical exposition, beginning with Locke.)

R. von Schubert-Soldern, *Grundlagen einer Erkenntnisstheorie.* 1884.

J. Volkelt, *Erfahrung und Denken.* 1885.

R. Avenarius, *Kritik der reinen Erfahrung.* 2 vols. 1888–90.

G. Heymans, *Die Gesetze und Elemente des wissenschaftlichen Denkens.* 2 vols. 1890–94. (Contains also a short sketch of logic.)

F. Erhardt, *Metaphysik. I. Erkenntnisstheorie.* 1894. (Takes up a position nearly allied to that of Kant with regard to the apriority of space and time.)

L. Busse, *Philosophie und Erkenntnisstheorie.* I. 1894. (Contains a critical discussion of different epistemological tendencies, in connection with the question of the possibility of a metaphysics, together with an outline of a system of philosophy.)

[L. T. Hobhouse, *The Theory of Knowledge.* 1896.]

A history of epistemology is much needed, but still remains to be written.

§ 6. *Logic.*

1. Logic, defined as the science of the formal principles of knowledge, was founded by Aristotle. True, we find in earlier thinkers anticipations of and contributions to the science: many of the Platonic dialogues, in particular, contain discussions of the formation of concepts, of definition, and of the deductive procedure. But it was not till the time of Aristotle that logic was raised to the rank of an independent discipline and its divisions systematically classified. The theory of inference and proof Aristotle calls 'analytics' (τὰ ἀναλυτικά); in the prior analytics he treats of inference, in the posterior of proof, of definitions, of classifications and of the inductive procedure. The theory of dialectical inference or reasoning from probabilities he calls 'topics' (τὰ τοπικά). The book περὶ ἑρμηνείας deals with the proposition and the judgment; the book περὶ κατηγοριῶν (of doubtful authenticity) discusses fundamental concepts. The editors and commentators of the Aristotelian writings named all these logical treatises, taken as a whole, the ὄργανον, and the science which they expounded, logic: Aristotle himself had used only the term analytics. The Stoics, of whom Zeno and Chrysippus deserve special mention, supplemented the Aristotelian logic by epistemological disquisitions and the theory of hypothetical and disjunctive inference. After the sixth century A.D., the most important propositions of the organon were included in the text-books of the 'seven liberal arts,' and thus took a prominent place in the curriculum of the Christian schools of the middle ages. The name of the discipline was now changed to dialectics, to accord with the Stoic subdivision of logic into dialectics and rhetoric (*cf.* §§ 3. 1; 4. 1). Logic came to be a favourite field of philosophic activity among the scholastics, and the Aristotelian 'syllogistic,' the theory of inference, was developed with great subtlety. Elaborate deductions of permissible and impermissible inferences were made, the criteria being the general or special form and the positive or negative

quality of the judgments contained in them. At the same time an important part was played by the controversy between nominalism and realism. The nominalists maintained that general concepts are merely names (*universalia sunt nomina*); the realists asserted that they are real determinations, the real nature of the objects which they designate (*universalia sunt realia*).

2. In the modern period the Aristotelian logic held its own for some length of time. Melancthon's text-books retained it even in the Protestant schools. But the general revolt against Aristotle and the scholastics which characterises the beginnings of modern philosophy led to various changes, more or less violent and radical, in the complexion of the science. Petrus Ramus (†1572), it is true, diverges much less seriously from the Aristotelian conception than his zealous polemics would lead us to infer. His service consists in a systematisation of logic, which has persisted with but slight alteration to our own day; logic is divided into four parts, the theories of the concept, of the judgment, of inference and of method. Bacon's attack is more energetic. He discards the syllogism and the deductive procedure altogether, on the ground that they do not further knowledge and cannot lead to any advance in science, and eulogises induction in their stead as the one true and normal path to scientific knowledge. His opposition to Aristotle is expressed even in the title of his work upon logic, the *Novum Organon*. We must admit that the method which Bacon describes as induction could not pass muster under that name at the present day. But nevertheless the impulse which he gave, perhaps a little too vigorously, to the development of the methods employed in the past and to be employed in the future by the empirical science whose awakening he saw, has had a very considerable influence upon the history of logic. The enquiries undertaken by his successors, Hobbes, Locke, Berkeley and Hume, into the concept and its relation to the word are not only acute but of permanent value.

The methodical rules prescribed by Descartes have had far less effect. Apart from his adoption of clearness and distinctness of knowledge as the test of truth, he demanded no more than the analysis of difficulties, the orderly arrangement of thoughts, and complete synopses or enumerations. Mathematics supplied him with an ideal of scientific exposition. Spinoza held mathematics in still higher esteem; while Leibniz and Wolff try to found the procedure of all the sciences, so far as possible, upon mathematical models. Wolff wrote a systematic logic, which he regarded as the foundation of philosophy in general (*cf.* § 3. 3). He divides logic, in his usual way, into a theoretical and practical discipline. The former deals with concept, judgment and inference, in Aristotelian fashion; the latter seeks not only to formulate technical scientific methods, but also to lay down similar rules for the conduct of life.

3. We owe to Kant the separation of logic from epistemology, and a new and fruitful classification of its subject-matter. He defines it as the science of the right use of reason and understanding according to the *a priori* principles of 'how the understanding should think,' *i.e.*, subsumes it on the one hand to the idea of end, making it to some degree a technical or normative discipline, and on the other assigns to it a purely formal function. His division of logic is best shown by the following table:

- Logic.
  - General.
    - Pure.
      - Doctrine of Elements.
      - Methodology.
    - Applied.
  - Special.

The feature of this scheme which has found most general acceptance is the distinction of methodology, the theory of method, from the theory of the elements (concept, judgment and inference). In modern times there has appeared a whole series of excellent and formative treatises on logic. The palm of highest merit among them all must be awarded to the work of John Stuart Mill († 1872), the first logical reformer. Mill's *System of Logic, Ratiocinative and Inductive*, was published in 1843, and had run into eight editions before the death of its author. Following the traditions of English logic, Mill makes induction the centre of his whole enquiry, and attaches very little importance to deduction and the syllogism. F. Ueberweg's *System der Logik* (5th ed., revised by Jürgen Bona Meyer, 1882) is especially valuable for its numerous historical excursus. M. W. Drobisch has attempted in his *Neue Darstellung der Logik* (5th ed., 1887) to work out a purely formal logic, upon Herbartian principles (*cf.* § 2. 7). The most recent German works, on the other hand, have endeavoured to steer a middle course between Hegel's metaphysical conception of the science (*cf.* § 3. 4) and Herbart's purely formal standpoint. At the same time many important changes have been introduced in the treatment of certain parts of logic. Thus C. Sigwart (*Logik*, 2nd ed., 2 vols., 1889–93; tr. by Helen Dendy, 1894) gives judgment the most prominent place in his discussions, while B. Erdmann (*Logik*, vol. I., 1892) has, in name at least, completely eliminated the theory of the concept. H. Lotze (*System der Philosophie. I. Logik*, 2nd ed., 1880; Eng. tr., 2nd ed., 1888), W. Schuppe (*Erkenntnisstheoretische Logik*, 1878) and W. Wundt (*Logik*, 2nd ed., 2 vols., 1893 ff.) combine epistemological disquisitions with the development of properly logical theories. Th. Lipps' *Grundzüge der Logik*, 1893, is a brief but very clear and suggestive exposition of logic from the psychological point of view. Lastly, among historical treatises we may mention the monumental work of K. von Prantl, *Geschichte der Logik im Abendlande*, whose four volumes (1855-70) bring the reader, unfortunately, no farther than the first thirty years of the sixteenth century, and F. Harms' *Geschichte der Logik* (1881).

4. Logic is, without doubt, the most advanced of all the philosophical disciplines, both as regards the mode of formulation and the certainty and finality of its statements. Nevertheless, we find here as elsewhere differences in method of treatment and in individual theory. Hegel's assumption of the identity of thought and existence, and the metaphysical logic which grew out of it, may, it is true, be considered to have been definitely abandoned at the present day, thanks more especially to the adverse criticism of Trendelenburg's *Logische Untersuchungen* (3rd ed., 1870). But alongside of this an epistemological, a purely formal and a psycho

logical logic have grown up and flourished, while the last few decades have added a mathematical logic to the list. *Epistemological* logic treats of the general contents of knowledge in connection with the properly logical questions. The purely *formal* logic takes no account at all of contents or of the significance of the forms of thought for scientific knowledge. The *psychological* view makes logic a department of psychology; thought, and, in particular, correct thought, are considered as psychical processes. Finally, *mathematical* logic has earned its special title by the invention of a new system of symbols, a logical algorithm or calculus. Again, we may draw a distinction between logical treatises according as they emphasise the *normative* character of the science, the laying down of rules and precepts for the operations of thought, or merely look upon scientific thought itself as the object of a *descriptive* or *explanatory* investigation. In face of these divergences of opinion, we cannot attempt to give any detailed criticism of separate theories, but must confine ourselves to the presentation, in a consistent way, of what we take to be the prevailing view of the problems of logic.

5. We defined logic above (§ 5. 1) as the science of the formal principles of knowledge. By 'formal principles' we mean the general relations, presupposed in every instance of the acquisition of knowledge, between the objects of knowledge and the symbols (words, letters, figures, etc.) which designate or represent them. The dictionary may be said to give us these relations, in so far as it gives the meanings of particular words; and conversation or communication of any kind presupposes a knowledge of the relations obtaining between the expressions employed and the objects to which they refer. With logic, however, it is different. Logic does not try to find out all the possible meanings of particular symbols; it is content to furnish a scientific exposition of the general facts and laws of these relations, *i.e.*, to state the conditions under which every special system of nomenclature or terminology must be worked out and applied. But, further, it concerns itself only with that sort of knowledge which leads to scientifically valid results, and accordingly claims the title of propædeutic to

all scientific knowledge. Since, however, limitation of the aim of a science necessarily means a sharp definition of the purpose which it subserves, logic turns aside from the consideration of the various possible paths to knowledge, and even of those which have actually been trodden in the past, and becomes a *normative* discipline, *i.e.*, a science whose object is not a datum, something given, but must be termed ideal, realisable only under certain conditions. The ideal aim of all science is a universally valid formula or a system of universally valid formulæ. Logic, therefore, shows us the conditions under which this ideal can be attained, *i.e.*, lays down definite rules for scientific investigation in general. In this sense we can accept the current definition of it as the 'art of thinking,' including under the word 'thinking' all the operations which constitute the objective conditions of the attainment of the purpose described above. Such conditions would be the formation of useful concepts, a system of classification, an inductive or deductive procedure, etc. And since, again, a complete scientific account of all these rules presupposes a knowledge of the elements which go to determine them, logic is not only a methodology, but also a theory of the elementary processes. Thus the concept, the meaning of a symbol, is a logical element in every scientific formula; and judgment, the scientific formula itself, is an element in more complicated thought-connections; and inference, the logical colligation of scientific formulæ, is the next higher element in a comprehensive scientific argument. In this way the theory of concept, judgment and inference becomes a necessary propædeutic to the higher normative function of logic, which it must attempt to discharge in the form of a methodology.

6. A few critical remarks upon the psychological and mathematical methods of treating logic may help to explain and justify our view of its nature and purpose. No one can deny that scientific formulæ, with all that appertains to them, are spoken or written by subjects, and may therefore be regarded as the voluntary actions or thought-activities of individuals. But this is no reason for subsuming logic to psychology. For (1) logic and epistemology, as forming part of a general science of know-

ledge, have to determine the presuppositions of all the sciences, inclusive of psychology. Logic, then, obviously, cannot be a department of psychology; if it were, it could not do its duty, at any rate so far as psychology was concerned. (2) We may say that where the subject-matter of logic and of psychology is the same, it is treated from an entirely different point of view. Psychology, in dealing with concepts, tries to show how they take shape in the course of the individual life, and what psychical states are implied in their use. It has to answer questions as to the general or special nature of the ideas, as to the reproduction of symbols by various perceptions, as to the peculiar conditions under which the hearing, reading and writing subject is placed. The logical discussion of concepts is completely foreign to these enquiries. For logic, concepts are simply the relations between name and object; and it deals only with the general forms of such relations and the objective conditions of their employment. (3) The fact that judgments must be termed voluntary actions or operations of thought tells us absolutely nothing of their validity, their truth or falsehood. On the contrary, the dependence of scientific formulæ on the subject who may happen to use them is for logic entirely irrelevant. It is a matter of complete indifference whether the judgment is read, heard or written; whether it arouses this association or that; how far the attention is involved in it, etc. (4) It is only when we separate logic and psychology in this way that we can understand how logic could attain as early as it did to the form of an exact science, and could remain as little affected as it has, even down to the present time, by the changes and advances in psychological knowledge.

7. The new science of mathematical logic seeks to represent all the relations existing among concepts, analytically, by means of appropriate symbols, and to derive conclusions or deduce new facts from these data by mathematical conversions and transformations. The foundation of the logical algorithm, in its strict form, was laid by G. Boole in his work, *An Investigation of the Laws of Thought* (1854). After him W. S. Jevons, J. Venn,

C. S. Pierce and E. Schroeder (*Vorlesungen über die Algebra der Logik*, I., 1890) have done most to develope the science. We may illustrate its procedure by one simple example. The fundamental form of all categorical judgments is expressed in the relation $a \nless b$, when the sign = indicates equality of extension, and the sign (the subordination of a to b. If, now, $a \nless b$ and $b \nless c$, it is inferred that $a \nless c$. A grave objection to the view that this logic can ever be the whole of logic is that it confines all relations among concepts to the extension of the concepts. Recently, however, an attempt has been made, with some success, to transcend this exclusive logic of extension, and subject the contents of concepts to a similarly mathematical mode of exposition (logic of contents). We would, nevertheless, call attention to the following arguments:

(1) With a few entirely trivial exceptions, mathematical logic is a superfluity. Nothing is gained by it which cannot be gained, and gained more easily, by means of verbal logic. It presupposes not only familiarity with the expressions current in ordinary logic, but the further knowledge of the symbolic language peculiar to itself.

(2) The method of treatment often does violence to logical terms, never exhibiting them except as dressed out quantitively and deductively in mathematical garb. Indeed, there is a great deal (the theory of the concept or of induction, *e.g.*) which cannot be adequately represented at all in mathematical form.

(3) The experiment was frequently tried, in earlier times, of representing certain logical proportions or relations in a simple and pictorial way by aid of geometrical figures or brief analytical proofs. But this procedure is simply a procedure sometimes followed by mathematics itself—a concrete realisation of the logical connection—and not in any sense a mathematical logic.

(4) It is clear that logic gains nothing in force or accuracy by mathematical formulation; for it is the logical element, of course, that gives mathematics its force and accuracy. It is only because mathematics is freer than any other science of all the confusing properties natural to a knowledge whose contents is

sharply defined, or whose subject-matter has penetrated to the popular consciousness, that it gives us most directly and plainly the impression of logical precision and necessity.

(5) Mathematical logic—though its representatives usually fail to see this—consists simply of a peculiar technique, a special method of colligating concepts and judgments with one another; it is not a theory of thought or of the purposive employment of the functions of knowledge. But then it cannot be logic itself, whose business it is to supply us with just this theory.

LITERATURE.

La logique ou l'art de penser. 1662 and later. (This is the 'Port Royal' logic; one of the most famous works of the Cartesian school: *cf.* p. 41).

F. H. Bradley, *Principles of Logic*, 1883 (*cf.* p. 42).

[B. Bosanquet, *Logic or the Morphology of Knowledge*, 1888.]

B. THE SPECIAL PHILOSOPHICAL DISCIPLINES.

§ 7. *Natural Philosophy.*

1. The philosophical thought of ancient Greece begins with natural philosophy. The two principal schools of pre-Socratic philosophers are usually termed the 'earlier' and 'later' natural philosophy; and all the various attempts of the time to determine the nature of things were directed predominantly upon nature, upon the external objects of perception. Indeed, this purpose played so large a part in the scientific enquiry of the age that, even when attention was given to man himself and the things of mind, the activities which attracted greatest notice were those that seemed to contribute most to a knowledge of external nature. It is not difficult to find a reason for the prominence accorded to nature at a period when interest in general philosophical investigation was just awaking.

(1) Even to-day, popular thinking looks upon 'things'—solid, heavy, coloured, resonant things—as having absolute existence, and entirely disregards the share which the perceiving subject undoubtedly has in the perception of such objects. Objectification, that is, is the most natural attitude for us to take up towards

experience, and only a mature reflection can teach us that what seems so objective is in part a product of internal and external factors, in part something given—primarily, at any rate—solely in our idea. Philology bears out this judgment by showing that names for the objects of sense perception are earlier developed than names for the subjective functions of seeing, hearing, sensing, perceiving, etc.

(2) The exclusive interest which a primitive civilisation takes in the external in nature is determined by the supreme importance of a knowledge of natural processes, in order that they may be subjugated, calculated, foreseen. Indeed, it is true to say in general that the impulse to knowledge, when we first meet with it, is rooted in the impulse to self-preservation; and that even when (as here in philosophy: *cf.* §2. 2) it begins to develope a force of its own, its course is for some time determined by considerations of the value and advantage of the knowledge obtained for the purposes of practical life.

2. The most important theory of natural philosophy in old Greek thought, if not in that of the whole of antiquity, is the theory propounded by the Atomists. They were the first to draw any sort of clear distinction between the external world, as determinable only in a quantitative way, and the internal, as determinable only in terms of quality. It can be proved that this purely mechanical view of nature, which reappeared at the beginning of modern philosophy, was to some extent a necessary corollary of Anaximenes' theory that air was the essence of all things. In later Greek and mediæval thought, however, the atomistic theory, important as it might have been for scientific investigation, was displaced by the doctrine of Plato and Aristotle, who taught that natural things have no real existence at all, but are rather the negation of real existence,—or at most contain the possibility or potentiality of existence,—while true reality is to be found in form, in ideas or concepts. Alongside of this subordination of matter went the substitution of a teleological or purposive theory for the purely mechanical, causal view of the colligation of natural processes. Plato discusses the questions of natural philo-

sophy in the *Timæus;* Aristotle principally in the τὰ φυσικά or φυσικὴ ἀκρόασις—the treatise ordinarily cited as the *Physics.* Neither in the Atomists nor in Plato and Aristotle do we find any distinction made between a special natural science and a more general natural philosophy.

The interest in natural philosophy shows a great falling off in the succeeding schools. Epicurus, however, deserves especial gratitude for having accepted Democritus' doctrine of the atoms, practically unchanged. The contempt for nature which is so marked a feature of Christian philosophy is to be explained, in part, by the influence of Platonic ideas; the sensible and material is not simply appearance, mere phenomenal existence, but also evil, the bad principle (*cf.* § 9. 3). It is only occasionally in the middle ages that we come across any less negative attitude toward natural objects and occurrences. Roger Bacon († 1294) is marked out by his greater knowledge of their import and personal share in their investigation.

3. With the beginning of modern natural science—with the coming of men like Copernicus, Galilei and Kepler—all this is altered. It is not by chance that just where we find the first trace of the new philosophy, in Nicolaus Cusanus (1401–64), Bernardinus Telesius (1508–88) and the rest, we find also the greatest emphasis laid upon natural philosophy. But how close the connection still was between philosophy and special science is seen in the fact that Galilei and Kepler both regarded themselves, primarily, as philosophers, and arrived at their great discoveries by way of very general considerations. The results of all these enquiries have exerted a vast influence upon the philosophical view of the universe. We may conveniently arrange them under the five following heads.

(1) The first important result of modern natural science to be mentioned here, was the disproof of the 'heaven of fixed stars' of the ancients, and the consequent hypothesis of the infinity of space. Out of this grew that antithesis of the sensible and the supersensible or insensible, of which every religiously coloured metaphysics had thenceforth to take account.

The solid vault of the sky was turned to an infinite mass of vapour, and those who still clung to the religious ideas of a world beyond this world could not now think of it as realised in sensible form, but only in insensible. The antithesis soon came to be identical with that between bodily and mental, physical and psychical.

(2) A second great result was the discovery of a strict uniformity in the relations of all bodies, and of the possibility of a thorough-going application of mathematics to natural phenomena. This banishes all arbitrariness and indeterminism from the realm of perception, and drives them to take refuge in the only region left,—that of mind or morals. The antithesis of sensible and supersensible or insensible thus takes over a new meaning from that of nature and mind or morals, mechanism and freedom.

4. (3) In the third place, the basal assumptions of modern natural science have led to an exact definition of matter as objective, and to the important doctrine of the subjectivity of the qualities of sense (*cf.* § 5. 1). Galilei distinguishes between the essential and the accidental properties of bodies. In the former class he puts form, relative magnitude, position, time, movement or rest, number, and isolation or contiguity with other bodies. All these attributes are inseparable from the idea of body. On the other hand, it is not necessary to the existence of a body that it should be white or red, bitter or sweet, resonant or mute, pleasantly or unpleasantly odorous; these are all expressions for the effects of bodies upon our sense organs. Here again it is evident that the antithesis of physical and psychical assumes a new and more exact form.

(4) A fourth principal result is the change in our estimation of the importance of the earth, and of ourselves who live upon the earth and are devoted to the acquisition of knowledge concerning it. The earth has ceased to be the centre of the universe, and is now merely one of the numerous planets which circle round the sun, an infinitesimal point in the infinity of space. The proud claim of man to be the final purpose of the world's

development gives place to a more modest conception of his destiny; and the dogmatic theories of earlier centuries are transformed to a sceptical valuation of the capacity of our faculty of knowledge. We are brought to a consciousness of the subjectivity, the inevitable limitation of human knowledge and human appreciations.

(5) Fifthly and lastly: the impression produced by these pioneer researches in natural science meant a better understanding of the value which all observation and all experience have for all knowledge, if only they are controlled by a rational purpose and combined with the deductive activity of the understanding. Galilei declares that a thousand reasons are not able to prove a real experience untrue. At the same time, however, the new antithesis of outer and inner experience is brought upon the stage of philosophic thought.

5. There is no trace of any theoretical separation of natural science from natural philosophy until towards the end of the eighteenth century. Descartes' *Principia philosophiae* combines the two. Wolff's terms 'experimental physics' and 'rational cosmology' are indicative rather of different methods of exposition (*cf.* § 3. 3) than of a difference in subject-matter. Nor did Newton, to whom we owe the establishment of the fundamental concepts of modern physics, draw a distinction between physics and philosophy. Natural philosophy may be said to have assumed an independent place with the appearance of three works, at the end of the eighteenth century: the *Système de la nature* of 1770, Kant's *Metaphysische Anfangsgründe der Naturwissenschaft* (1786), and Schelling's *Entwurf eines Systems der Naturphilosophie* (1799). The aim of the first of these was rather propagandist than scientific. The name Mirabaud appeared upon the title-page; but the actual author was, in all probability, Baron Holbach († 1789). The book proceeded, however, from the group of 'Encyclopædists,' and evidently contains contributions from other hands,—from Diderot in particular. Its first volume is devoted to the exposition of a purely materialistic metaphysics (§ 16). The whole of the second volume is a polemic against religion, and especially the Christian

faith. The results attained by the natural science of the time are worked up with great skill into a single system of natural phenomena; but no account is taken of any definite investigation. Kant's *Metaphysische Anfangsgründe* is simply an attempt to establish the *a priori* principles of all natural science, and consequently deals exclusively with the most general concepts,—those of matter, motion, force, etc. Kant arrives at what is called a *dynamic* conception of nature, and finds the essential character of the phenomena of external nature in forces which are distributed in space, and act and react upon one another. At this point Schelling takes up the question. He developes the Kantian theory of nature, more especially upon the organic side, applying the teleological arguments (*cf.* § 20) which Kant had set forth in his *Kritik der Urtheilskraft* (1790). The whole of nature, he thinks, is a graduated system of purposes, beginning with its lowest, most insignificant and crudest forms, and rising to its highest, richest and most delicate manifestation in the mental life of man. Here, then, the question of the development of natural phenomena is set in the forefront of philosophical enquiry.

6. Schelling's theory of development was largely and boldly conceived, and despite the fantastic form which it assumed in the hands of its author and his more immediate school—of whom Steffens was most prominent in geology and Oken in biology—found general acceptance among workers in natural science at the beginning of the nineteenth century. Not a few of the men who later did good work in the field of exact research were originally adherents of Schelling's natural philosophy. The widespread disrepute into which it fell when its scientific inadequacy was realised, taken together with the overthrow of the Hegelian philosophy, led to a general distrust in any contributions to natural science, in the wider sense of the term, offered by philosophers proper. We can see now that limited material was chiefly to blame for the insufficiency of the natural philosophy in matters of detail, and that its great value lay not in the special knowledge which it embodied, but in its ability to satisfy the craving for a consistent explanation of things, an explanation that should include the whole of nature,

organic as well as inorganic, psychical as well as physical. Recently it has grown to be the custom for scientific workers to try and satisfy their own philosophic needs, and for philosophers to approach the special problems of natural philosophy only under the more general formulation of metaphysics or of epistemology and logic. This state of affairs is not one for us to congratulate ourselves upon. The philosophical ideas propounded by the representatives of natural science are invalidated, almost without exception, by ignorance of the history of philosophy and by a prejudiced estimate of conclusions drawn from experiences and results within one special field. On the other hand, we hope to show in what follows, by an enumeration of the objects with which a natural philosophy would have to do, that the task of instituting a general investigation into the principles of natural science confronts philosophy to-day just as it did a century ago.

7. It is plainly characteristic of natural philosophy to overlap metaphysics on the one side and epistemology and logic on the other. The collection and working-over of scientific results are exceedingly important for a general theory of the universe, while natural science specialises, by particular application, the most general contents and forms of knowledge. We abstract here from the possible import of natural philosophy for a theory of the universe. Its remaining problems fall into three groups.

(1) The first group consists of certain definite epistemological questions. Chief of these are the questions of the reality of the external world, of the meaning of 'law,' and of the concepts of causation, substance and development. That their discussion is a purely logical prerequisite of work in natural science is clear enough; all of the concepts named, as well as the hypothesis of the existence of an external world, play a part in the expositions of the special sciences,—but none of them receive that careful and comprehensive treatment which their very general significance would lead us to expect. They can obtain it only at the hands of a natural philosophy.

(2) In the second place, natural philosophy must critically examine the methods and fundamental concepts of the natural

sciences. The problems mentioned under (1) are not confined to the domain of natural science, though they are there given a special application; the problems of this second group are couched in terms of concepts and methods which have been shaped by the natural sciences, and find scientific use only within their limits. Here belong matter, force, energy, motion, and the spatial and temporal factors of natural occurrence. These concepts, like the others, although they constitute quite special preconditions of scientific knowledge, are not subjected to the critical examination they deserve by natural science itself. And those refined procedures, by which the natural sciences are ever attaining to greater knowledge, must also furnish weighty matter for logical consideration.

8. (3) Finally, we must entrust to natural philosophy the task of thorough analysis and appreciation of scientific theories, or at least of those which possess any wide significance: the atomic theory, the biological theory of evolution, the mechanical and vitalistic theories of life, etc. Under this heading we shall look for an epistemological determination of the meaning of the term 'theory,' as employed by natural science, and a decision between the many opposing hypotheses, made on the basis of an intimate knowledge of the facts upon which they rest, and with an eye to their metaphysical value. It need hardly be said that familiarity with the methods and results of scientific investigation is indispensable for the solution of all these questions.

It follows from what was said above (*cf.* § 7. 6) that the modern literature of natural philosophy is exceedingly scanty. Special contributions have come from workers in natural science, and there are chapters dealing with natural philosophy in various epistemological and metaphysical treatises. Apart from these, we may call attention, in the first place, to the *Philosophie der Naturwissenschaft*, by F. Schultze (2 vols., 1881–82). The first part contains a history of natural philosophy down to Kant; the second gives a systematic exposition of 'critical empiricism.' The author has, however, confined himself to a discussion, from the Kantian standpoint, of the most general problems of natural philosophy. We may recommend, secondly, K. Kroman's valuable work, *Unsere Naturerkenntniss* (1883; from the Danish). The book is devoted to an exclusively epistemological treatment of mathematics and natural science. K. Lasswitz' *Geschichte der Atomistik* (2 vols., 1890) is also a noteworthy contribution to the history of natural philosophy. [*Cf.* W. Whewell, *History of the Inductive Sciences* and *Philosophy of the Inductive Sciences*, 1837 and 1840.]

§ 8. *Psychology.*

1. While the distinction between exact work within the natural sciences and a philosophical consideration of the general principles underlying them was fully recognised in the eighteenth century, the analogous separation of psychology as a special science from psychology as a department of philosophical enquiry is only now in course of making. Our survey of the development of psychology must, therefore, touch upon questions which really belong to a definite and specialised discipline.

The first thing necessary to the working-out of a psychology is a more or less clear and precise idea of the relation between physical and psychical, or a delimitation of the two fields of natural science and psychology. The contents and method of any 'psychology,' therefore, depend upon its author's personal conception of the nature of the psychical. We may conveniently distinguish three periods in the history of the science.

(1) In the first, mind, the substrate of all psychical phenomena, is identified with the vital principle. This view carries with it a very broad interpretation of psychology.

(2) In the second, the province of mind is limited by the definition of 'mental' as that which can be known by internal perception. At this stage, *i.e.*, the division of physical and psychical depends upon a sharp opposition of external and internal perception.

(3) The third and, probably, final period, which has found its explicit formulation in quite recent times, makes the psychical co-extensive with the subjective, *i.e.*, with what is dependent upon the experiencing individual. That element in direct, unmediated, unreflecting experience which is dependent upon the

experiencing subject, and gives evidence of this dependence, is the psychical element in the experience. On the other hand, that element in it which is independent of the subject, and whose existence and mode of operation depend upon laws of their own, is termed objective or physical.

2. The view of the first period as to the nature of mind prevailed in antiquity and throughout the middle ages. It meets us unmistakably in the earliest systematic treatise upon psychology that has come down to us, Aristotle's περὶ ψυχῆς. In the first book Aristotle gives a critical survey of previous psychological theories. In the second, he defines mind as the entelechy of the body, *i.e.*, as its actualisation or formative principle. At the same time he describes its faculties or divisions in detail. The lowest mental faculty is the nutritive function; this belongs only to plants, the lowest organisms. Next above it stands the sensitive mind, which together with the nutritive is present in animals. The highest level of mental development is reached with the rational mind. Aristotle makes this the distinguishing characteristic of man, who possesses it along with the other two. Now an author who attributes the nutritive function to mind is evidently of the opinion that mind and vital principle are one and the same, *i.e.*, that mind is the source of all those peculiar phenomena which we group together under the name of 'life,' and oppose to the lifeless, to inorganic matter. The second book concludes with remarks upon the senses. In the third, Aristotle discusses perception and idea (memory, imagination), the understanding, feeling, desire, and movement Christian philosophy took over from Aristotle the idea of a separation, conceptual if not actual, of the rational mind from the lower mental faculties. The division was not only useful as pointing the difference between man and the animals,—it distinguished a perishable and an imperishable element in the final work of creation, and provided a simple psychological basis for the sharp contrast of sense and reason, of the faculty for the things of time and of this world and the sense for things eternal and the world beyond.

3. The same view obtained at the beginning of modern philosophy. The Italian natural philosophers generally divided mind into mortal and immortal, reasoning and merely perceiving parts. They laid, perhaps, an even greater stress upon the advantages possessed by the immortal part of mind in the acquisition of true knowledge. Its procedure is intuitive; it knows the truth by an immediate perception; whereas the mortal part is dependent upon the senses and upon demonstration or deduction. The mortal part, that is to say, is the substrate even of those activities which are ordinarily ascribed to the understanding,—inference from given assumptions, the logical colligation of concepts.[1]

At this point the road lies open to a more consistent idea of psychology. When once it is realised that the 'intuitive' knowledge of the human mind has not dwelt in it from all eternity, *i.e.*, is not a connate possession of the mind, but little is needed to do away with the unnatural separation into mortal and immortal parts, and set up a new and better definition of 'mental.' The honour of effecting this reform in psychology belongs to John Locke, the founder of modern epistemology (*cf.* § 5. 2). With him the second period of psychology begins—the period characterised by the definition of mind as the substrate of the internal sense. It is clear that this theory must look upon all purely organic processes as physical and not psychical; for the processes of organic life are known through external perception in precisely the same way as inorganic phenomena. The wide acceptance of the two forms of sense or perception is seen in Leibniz' use of the terms 'perception' and 'apperception,' the counterparts of Locke's 'sensation' and 'reflection.' The German psychology of the eighteenth century employed the words simply to mean the activities of the external and internal senses.

[1] The Cartesian differentiation of mind and body, by thought and extension, is simply a special expression of the same fundamental idea. It has been more important for metaphysics than for psychology. What had previously been called the 'mortal' part of mind, was by Descartes referred to the physical realm. It followed as a matter of course that animals were mindless and automatic.

4. Even to-day the difference between psychical and physical is often referred to Locke's difference between internal and external perception, though a very little reflection shows that no clear idea of their relation can be gained from it.

(1) In the first place, there is no 'internal sense,' in the strict meaning of the phrase, but only external senses, *i.e.*, definite organs for the reception of stimuli. The expression can, therefore, never be used otherwise than figuratively, and even so is dangerous unless a clear idea of the nature of the function which it indicates has been previously acquired in some other way.

(2) The antithesis of external and internal perception cannot be allowed to pass as an adequate expression for differences in the world of given facts. Modern epistemology has proved that our original experience does not fall apart into two different worlds, but is entirely unitary. The relations expressed by the phrases 'internal' and 'external perception' are of later growth, and depend upon all sorts of observations; there are not two radically and intrinsically different functions. In other words, the terms are not necessary and unequivocal names for separate, co-existent acts, but merely figurative expressions—not too happily chosen—of a deeper-lying distinction.

(3) Finally, if the hypothesis of an external and internal perception were correct, we should be entirely at a loss in regard to the qualities of sense, *i.e.*, to what is now called 'sensation.' For modern natural science, while it uses them as aids to the knowledge of objective processes, refers them as facts to the knowing subject (*cf.* § 7. 4). On the other hand, there can be no doubt that (as Locke himself definitely stated) they originate in external and not in internal perception; so that psychology would be precluded from discussing what is obviously a part of mental life.

5. Psychologists have thus been led, in recent years, to attempt another definition of the 'psychical.' The third period begins with a reference to the epistemological idea of the subject or the 'subjective.' The unitariness of all the original data of experience is admitted, but a distinction drawn between a

subjective and an objective factor, from whose co-operation they result. 'Sensation,' 'idea,' 'perception,' are names for the subjective factor; 'objects,' and the 'properties,' 'states' and 'relations of objects' are expressions for the objective factor. But there are also phenomena in the original experiences which are of a purely subjective nature—the 'images' of memory, feelings, desires, volitions—and which accordingly admit only of psychological examination. It is evident that those who look to the difference of subject and object for the distinction between psychical and physical take a great deal of work upon them; they have to determine in each particular case what proportion of an experience is referable to subjective factors. But this is precisely what the workers in natural science do. Everyone who has had occasion to make scientific investigations knows that the first thing aimed at is a knowledge of the object,—of the objective, that is, with all its subjective accretions stripped off. The very idea of an 'error of observation,' above and beyond inaccuracies of circumstance or technique, is an indication that subjective states have something to say in the investigation of natural phenomena; and the popular notion that we see or hear 'something that isn't there,' or that what seems to be seen is 'only in our eye,' takes us straight to the selfsame difficulty. For the developed consciousness, as for the naïve, every experience is an unitary whole; and it is only the habit of abstract reflection upon experience that makes the objective and subjective worlds seem to fall apart as originally different forms of existence. Just as a plane curve can be represented in analytical geometry as the function of two variables, the abscissæ and the ordinates, without prejudice to the unitary course of the curve itself, so the world of human experience may be reduced to a subjective and an objective factor without prejudice to its real coherence (*cf.* § 26. 12 f.). E. Mach (*Beiträge zur Analyse der Empfindungen*, 1886) and R. Avenarius (*cf.* § 5. 10) were the first to work out this view with full theoretical consistency. The author believes that he has given the first exposition of psychology, from the same standpoint, in his *Grundriss der Psychologie* (1893, tr. 1895).

6. From the earliest times attempts had been made, more or less independently of the prevailing opinion as to the nature of mind, to determine the interrelations of psychical and purely bodily processes. The theory of 'animal spirits' (*spiritus animales*), propounded in the second century A.D. by Claudius Galenus, found wide acceptance as an explanation of the vital processes of the human body and their connection with certain psychical functions. It remained the current view, with but little modification, down to the end of the eighteenth century. The nerves were conceived of as very fine tubes, fitted directly to the most delicate branches of the blood vessels. Only the most fiery, mobile and subtle particles of the blood could force a way into them; and these particles formed the 'animal spirits.' The heart thus becomes the real central organ of all vital phenomena. Its heat, the vital warmth, causes the movement of the blood, which it propels to the remotest branches of the vascular system. As late as 1772, E. Platner, in his *Anthropologie*, gave a physiological theory of attention based upon the hypothesis of animal spirits. But in the sixteenth and seventeenth centuries it was more especially the affective processes that were singled out for physiological explanation. Descartes (*Les passions de l'âme*, 1650) regarded the emotions as the peculiar effects of an interaction between mind and body, and sought to reduce them to perceptible changes in the action of the heart. So had Melancthon—in the main a good Aristotelian —done before him, in the *De anima* of 1530. One of the most important adherents of this school was the Spanish philosopher Ludovicus Vives (*De anima et vita*, 1539). There can be no doubt that the physiological interpretation was greatly supported by the separation of the mind into mortal and immortal parts (§8. 2 f.); the idea that the mortal psychical functions depended upon certain bodily processes had nothing either dangerous or repugnant about it.

The first logical systematisation of all the efforts of this age to formulate an exact theory of emotion is given by Spinoza, in the fourth book of his *Ethics*. We have in it an impartial examination of the interrelations between psychical and physical processes, but one which must of necessity undergo essential change with the entrance of psychology upon its second period. As a matter of fact, Locke's work was followed, especially in Germany, by the development of a pure psychology of internal perception, which, with more or less of consciousness, completely disregarded the physical conditions of mental phenomena. This is the *Erfahrungsseelenlehre*, or 'empirical theory of mind,' which took its title from Chr. Wolff's *psychologia empirica* or *experimentalis*.

7. Pre-eminent among these psychologists of pure internal experience is J. N. Tetens. Certain chapters of his *Philosophische Versuche über die menschlische Natur und ihre Entwicklung* (2 vols., 1777) still possess considerably more than a mere historical interest; their summary of the facts, as then known, is thorough and impartial, and their logical connection carefully worked out. Similar attempts to erect a consistent theory of psychical phenomena upon the basis of internal perception alone have been made down to our own day. Herbart's *Lehrbuch zur Psychologie* (1816 and later) and *Psychologie als Wissenschaft* (2 vols., 1824–25) are among the most important. Herbart tried further, by aid of certain metaphysical assumptions concerning the nature and powers of the mind, and of mathematical formulæ, to write an exact psychology, a mental 'statics and mechanics.' Among modern psychologists, F. Brentano (*Psychologie vom empirischen Standpunkt*, I., 1874) and Th. Lipps (*Die Grundthatsachen des Seelenlebens*, 1883) may be mentioned as representative of the same school. Besides Herbart, F. E. Beneke (*Lehrbuch der Psychologie als Naturwissenschaft*, 4th ed., 1877) made a creditable attempt to build up a psychology without physiological assistance. There can be no doubt at all that such a treatment of the science is possible in itself; indeed, that it is the only available method of dealing with some of the more complex mental states. When we are asked to describe the psychological mechanism of some æsthetical, ethical, logical or religious idea, emotion or voluntary action, we shall get no help towards a solution of our problem by referring the process in question to any sort of brain function. For the real problem here is simply the analysis of a complex mental experience, not

the determination of its bodily conditions. If we can describe the elementary processes and their mode of co-operation in the complex whole with scientific accuracy, we have done everything in the way of an 'explanation' of the phenomena that can reasonably be demanded of us. A psychology of the internal experience only becomes exceptionable when it is obliged to have recourse to all kinds of auxiliary concepts or secondary hypotheses, which are themselves not deducible from internal experience. But our mental life, so far as we know anything about it, is by no means self-complete; so that, as a matter of fact, most of the psychologists of this school are compelled to make a more or less free use of the 'unconscious' in order to fill the gaps that they cannot but find in internal experience, and to base their theory of the elementary psychical processes on the hypothesis of a substantial mind, which stands behind the facts of consciousness, and controls and arranges them. Neither assumption can be said to satisfy the requirements of science.

8. So it has come about that physiological psychology, the beginnings of which we mentioned just now, has gradually risen to greater and greater importance. And since the new definition (that of the third period) of the subject-matter of psychology has also led to the connection of the subjectively conditioned, the psychical, with its condition, the corporeal individual, modern psychology has become a science of those elements in pure, primitive experience which depend upon corporeal experiencing subjects. We have been brought to this result not only by the work of psychologists proper, but also by that of the physiologists. It was the general custom, some years ago, to include mental phenomena in physiology, as specific functions of living beings. To be mentioned among the psychologists of the last century are D. Hartley (*Observation on Man*, 1749), J. Priestley († 1804) and C. Bonnet (*Essay de Psychologie*, 1755 and later). H. Lotze's *Medicinische Psychologie* (1852) marked a great advance in the scientific direction.

Lastly, the new psychology received systematic formulation in W. Wundt's *Grundzüge der physiologischen Psychologie* (1874;

2 vols., 4th ed., 1893). This work is dominated by the idea of a thorough-going psychophysical parallelism, *i.e.*, by the hypothesis that some physical or physiological process can be correlated with every psychical process discoverable by internal perception. Everything that other theories would ascribe to the unconscious or to a substantial mind falls, on this view, within the purely physiological domain. The principle thus assures to physiological psychology the advantage of having none but observed, or at least observable, processes to describe and explain in the course of its exposition of mental phenomena. Psychophysical parallelism is not a metaphysical principle, and therefore has nothing to do with materialism (*cf.* § 16), which makes material movements the cause of psychical phenomena: the bodily is the 'condition' of the mental in the sense that one magnitude is dependent upon another in a mathematical function, *i.e.*, that uniform relations of change obtain between the two. In other words, it is only a 'regulative' principle (*cf.* § 4. 3).

9. It is only on the assumption of an uniform connection of bodily and mental processes that we can make use of a new and valuable aid to psychological investigation,—experiment. The beginnings of psychological experimentation are to be found in certain of the older contributions to the physiology of the senses. The dependence of colour sensation upon definite properties of the physical stimulus, light, and the analogous relation of auditory sensation to acoustic phenomena, led to results, far back in the history of physical discovery, which a psychology of sensation can turn to good account. But experiment for explicitly psychological ends is a comparatively late feature of the science. Tetens (*cf.* § 8. 7) and Bonnet now and then give brief descriptions of experiments. It was not till 1849, however, when E. H. Weber published his famous work on the sense of touch and common feeling (*Ueber den Tastsinn und das Gemeingefühl*, in R. Wagner's *Handwörterbuch der Physiologie*), that any real impetus was given to a systematic employment of the experimental method; and not till 1860 that experimental psychology took shape from the fruitful investigations of G. T. Fechner

(*Elemente der Psychophysik*, 1860; 2nd ed., unchanged, 1889). Fechner meant by psychophysics an exact theory of the interrelations of physical and psychical, and based the applicability of experiment upon the assumption that the dependence of sensation on stimulus can be mathematically expressed. Following him, Wundt has introduced experimental methods and results into his physiological psychology.

We may take it, then, that the field of psychology as a special science has now been definitely marked out. In includes: (*a*) the reduction of more complex facts of consciousness to more simple; (*b*) the determination of the relations of dependency which hold between psychical processes and the physical (neural) processes which run parallel to them; (*c*) the application of experiment, to obtain an objective measure of mental processes and an exact knowledge of their nature. The history of the development of the psychical life may, perhaps, be made the subject of independent scientific investigation. Herbert Spencer (*The Principles of Psychology*, 1855 and later) has written consistently from the developmental standpoint—onesidedly, however, since the whole of animal psychology and the psychology of childhood fall under the general rubric. Lastly, we may note that M. Lazarus and H. Steinthal have distinguished a 'psychology of peoples' from the ordinary individual psychology. Its purpose is the study of all those mental phenomena which cannot be explained from the individual organisation, but originate in and are peculiar to entire groups of individuals, 'peoples.' Language and custom are examples of such phenomena.

10. It is evident that all the objects of enquiry which we have grouped together in the preceding paragraph belong to psychology in the sense of a special science, and not to a philosophical psychology; for all alike are as truly ultimate data, sheer facts, as are any 'natural' phenomena. If we define philosophy as the science of principles, we cannot call these psychological investigations philosophical. Indeed, there is general agreement on the point among experimental or physiological psychologists. But it thus becomes all the more necessary to ask whether there

may not be a philosophical psychology alongside of the scientific, and, if so, in what relation it stands to the philosophy of mind or of the mental sciences which, since Hegel's day, we have been accustomed to oppose to the philosophy of nature. We can best begin our answer to the question

(1) By giving a list of the special problems which would fall within the sphere of a philosophical psychology (*cf.* §7. 7). In the first place (*a*) philosophical psychology has to discuss the epistemological and logical presuppositions of scientific or empirical psychology. These include the concepts of subject and individual, of psychical causality and psychical measurement, of the analytic, synthetic and genetic methods, etc. (*b*) It must further undertake a critical examination of the fundamental concepts employed by empirical psychology: consciousness and the unconscious, mind and its relation to body, the mental element, etc. (*c*) It must bring together the general theories of empirical psychology, and scrutinise them in the interests of philosophy: the theories of spatial and temporal ideas, of sensation, of association, etc.

(2) We come very close to metaphysics in the theories of substantiality and actuality. The former assumes a mind-substance, the latter asserts that the acts of consciousness, as directly given, constitute mental reality.

(3) The discipline would be concerned with the antithesis of intellectualism and voluntarism. Intellectualism finds the ultimate elements of mental experience in the intellectual processes, thought or idea; voluntarism looks upon the phenomena of will as typical of the mental life at large.

(4) The terms 'monism' and 'dualism,' 'materialism' and 'spiritualism' (which we shall discuss in detail in Chapter III.) are indicative of different solutions that have been offered of the problem of the relation of psychical to physical.

We find numerous essays of this philosophical-psychological tenor between the covers of epistemological and metaphysical works, or included in what is, for the most part, a scientific treatment of psychology. The first attempt in modern times to make philosophical psychology an independent discipline, is to be found in J. Rehmke's *Lehrbuch der allgemeinen Psychologie* (1894). Rehmke's example has been followed by G. T. Ladd, in *The Philosophy of Mind*, 1895.

11. A philosophical psychology in this meaning of the phrase is not a philosophy of mind or of the mental sciences: it has to do simply with the special presuppositions, basal concepts or theories of empirical psychology, and not by any means with those of all the 'mental' sciences. If these include empirical psychology itself, then, in the author's opinion, philosophical psychology can never be more than a part of a general philosophy of mind: the other departments would be those of the philosophy of law, the philosophy of religion, the philosophy of history, and, perhaps, ethics and æsthetics. With such a variety of disciplines to be covered by the single title, it would seem well to dispense with the idea of a general philosophy of mind, or of the mental sciences, altogether—all the more, as it does not offer any real contrast to the philosophy of nature. Æsthetics, *e.g.*, is obliged, in some respects, to take account of 'natural' processes; and it would not be fair to the objective significance of law, art, religion and history, if we considered them merely as mental products.

In conclusion, we may mention certain works upon psychology, which have not been expressly named in the text.

W. Volkmann, *Lehrbuch der Psychologie*, 4th ed., 2 vols., 1894 f. (The standpoint is essentially that of Herbart. The work is characterised by detailed historical excursus and numerous references to the literature. The text is, in places, entirely out of date.)

A. Bain, *The Senses and the Intellect*, 1855 and later; *The Emotions and the Will*, 1859 and later. (The author is a representative of the 'associationist' psychology, which regards association as the fundamental phenomenon in every psychological uniformity.)

H. Höffding, *Psychologie in Umrissen*, 2nd ed., 1893. (From the Danish. English translation from the 1st ed. of the German, by M. G. Lowndes, 1891.)

W. James, *The Principles of Psychology*, 2 vols., 1890.

W. Wundt, *Vorlesungen über Menschen- und Thierseele*, 2nd ed., 1892. (English translation, 1894.) *Grundriss der Psychologie* (also in English trs.), 1897

E. B. Titchener, *An Outline of Psychology*, 2nd ed., 1897.
G. F. Stout, *Analytic Psychology*, 2 vols., 1896.
F. Jodl, *Lehrbuch der Psychologie*, 1896.
F. A. Carus (*Geschichte der Psychologie*, 1808) and F. Harms (*Geschichte der Psychologie*, 1878) have written general histories of psychology; but both are very incomplete. The two volumes so far published (1880, 1884) of H. Siebeck's admirable *Geschichte der Psychologie* extend only as far as Thomas Aquinas.

§ 9. *Ethics and the Philosophy of Law.*

1. With ethics and æsthetics we enter upon an entirely new field. The philosophical disciplines which we have discussed hitherto rest upon one, if not upon a whole number of special sciences; but these two have no such basis. They themselves possess the character of special sciences, dealing with definite and ultimate facts. Ethics or moral philosophy is ordinarily regarded as a normative science (*cf.* § 6. 4, 5), and its problem defined as the exact determination of the conditions which must be fulfilled if human volition and action are to be made 'moral.' In this sense it may be termed the art of conduct, just as logic is the art of thought. Since, however, the definition of the attribute 'moral' cannot be purely arbitrary, ethics has at the same time to take account of the historical development of moral judgments, and by analysing the principles or ideals which it finds in actual life, to try and make its precepts rational and consistent. Whether it performs this task well or ill, ethics, at any rate, always draws a distinction between conduct as it is, and conduct which is enjoined, prescribed, or (at least) desired. Indeed, if the distinction is not made, there is no room for any special application of the predicate 'moral,' over and above the other attributes, to human sentiment, impulse, etc. True, it is sometimes said to-day, as it has been in the past, that there is no real difference between 'moral' and natural volition and action. But we may agree to this, and yet not admit any exception to our rule. For if a 'natural' action is opposed to the action that, as a matter of fact, we find occurring, with the sanction of social usage and

other ethical influences, we have, though in different words, the very distinction which our statement emphasised.

2. The first question that meets the moralist, therefore, is that of the origination of this antithesis between unregulated, impulsive conduct and conduct regulated by some kind of law, precept or maxim. He will find it definitely answered by the results of investigation in the sphere of ethnic psychology. The first beginnings of a normative judgment of human conduct take the form of religious ideas and practices, and of those customary usages and rules of social intercourse which seem to be as old as society itself. At a very early stage of civilisation these two influences put a constraint upon the individual; his actions are largely subjected to outside control, and his life follows a definitely prescribed course. It is not till comparatively late that the various regulative factors are split up into well-marked groups. When this happens, we find religion, custom, law and morality to have been the chief elements in the originally undifferentiated total sanction. Still later is the demand for the separate scientific investigation of the different classes of phenomena. Though poetry and the language of daily life gradually come to distinguish between religious and worldly wisdom, the consciousness of their connection is very slow to die. Hence it should not be surprising that Socrates, who is generally looked upon as the founder of ethics proper, expressly mentions two sources of moral order—the written laws of the state, and the unwritten laws of the gods. At the same time, the moral decay that he saw around him led him to attempt for his age what all later moralists have attempted for theirs, the discovery of universally valid moral principles. So he came to regard virtuous or moral conduct as the result of knowledge, something that could be communicated and taught.

3. Plato, like Socrates, tried to determine the conditions of the universal validity of moral standards. In the *Phædrus*, *Phædo* and *Republic*, ethics is brought into close connection with metaphysics. The antithesis of the sensible material, matter, and the form or idea or essence of things, becomes a contrast of

values: matter is the principle of what is base and evil, the 'idea' the precondition of everything good. For Plato there can be but one virtue. And this is, in a sense, the condition of its universal validity; for we are apt to say of truth, too, that it must be one. All that is good comes, in the last resort, from God; and true happiness is found only in the immaterial world of pure ideas. Beauty alone can give sensible knowledge the imprint of the good, of moral value, and so enable us to catch a glimpse in it of the higher beyond it. The full realisation of virtuous endeavour presupposes a certain form of society, the state. In his ideal republic Plato describes the special conditions under which mankind might live a life that should satisfy all the requirements of human nature.

Happiness (*εὐδαιμονία*) had been regarded by the pre-Socratic moralists as the contents of the ideal good, the one thing worth striving for. But we find no systematic formulation of a happiness-ethics before Aristotle. In the Nicomachean Ethics happiness is declared to be a state which may exist at many different degrees or stages, and the conditions for its attainment are said to vary correspondingly. Whereas the school of Aristippus of Cyrene (the 'Hedonist' or 'Cyrenaic,' as he is called), in the fourth century B.C., made simple sense-pleasure (*ἡδονή*) the end of action, Aristotle is of the opinion that only a permanent happiness—an equable cheerfulness of temper, not to be ruffled by the accidents of life—can lay claim to the highest value, and therefore rank as the final goal of all human effort. We achieve this happiness by the help of reason; reason alone can assure a wise moderation of passion and desire, and protect us from the too much or the too little. Virtue is the golden mean between the two extremes. Aristotle, like Plato, emphasises the ethical importance of the state; but places the contemplative life of the sage and the philosopher higher than any form of political activity.

4. In the post-Aristotelian schools ethics shows a still more definite tendency to become an art of conduct. The Stoics did most for the continuance of ethical interest. They limited the field of the science by their very noteworthy idea of the *ἀδιάφορα*—

indifferent neutral actions, which obtain ethical value only as means for the attainment of good ends. They further drew a sharp line of division between virtuous, dutiful, rational conduct (κατόρθωμα), and vicious, passionate action, emphasising it by the personal contrast of the wise (good) man and the fool. We see, then, that ancient ethics had drawn a whole series of valuable distinctions. The purpose and regulation of human volition and action, of goods, duties and virtues—all these had received close consideration.

Christianity, however, introduced an entirely new point of view, characterised by three principal ideas: the idea of inevitable guilt, the command to love all men, and the belief that future blessedness or condemnation is necessarily determined by the moral quality of the life lived upon earth.

(1) Ancient ethics is always convinced of the possibility of a realisation of its ethical ideals; Christianity teaches that no man, however much he try, can attain to a guiltless life. Hence there is need of a liberating, saving power to remove the weight that must otherwise crush humanity down, and to hold out hope, at least, of a pure and happy existence.

(2) We find traces, in ancient literature, of the idea of a love for humanity in general; but it does not appear as a duty, still less as an obvious duty, till Christianity has come to declare that all men are the children of God, and therefore brothers.

(3) And though the ancient world was familiar enough with the idea of happiness or misery after death, Christianity, here too, introduces a new factor, by setting the doctrine of future reward and punishment in close connection with the moral struggles and progress of the individual. That we reap what we sow in the moral as in other fields—that our whole hope must centre in the grace of God, who will pardon even the sinner if he repent—these are the essential elements in the Christian doctrine, and not any special notions about heaven and hell.

5. Among the ethical problems which were brought into prominence for the first time by the rise of Christianity was the very important question of the freedom of the will. The ideas of merit and guilt, now so strongly emphasised, have no meaning

unless man can be considered free to choose between various possible courses of action. In the Christian ethics of the middle ages the freedom of the will came up, for the most part, only as connected with the further problem of the relation of man and human freedom to God and omnipotence. Nevertheless we find a clear recognition of the antithesis of determinism and indeterminism,—distinct affirmations and denials of the freedom of the will (*cf.* § 21).

Yet another revival of ethical interest, prompted by religious motives, occurred at the Reformation. The asceticism and shrinking from the world that characterised the middle ages, and, to a certain extent, the primitive Christians also, now gave way to the belief that a vocation in the world is the one thing which satisfies all the requirements of the moral life, that our works here upon earth have a positive value, and that pleasure in earthly matters is permissible, since the world and all that is in it come from the hand of God. Along with this conviction went a deepening of the religious sentiment. Not by any outward works can we acquire a claim to happiness, to the grace of God, but only by a steadfast inward faith that triumphs over the world; and if we lack this faith, no outward ceremony may give us freedom or redemption from guilt. He who will be moral is thus taught to look to himself: his regeneration must take place within himself; his fight with the evil power of sinful passions is an inward conflict; and only faith in God and His mediator, Christ, can assure him courage, joy and peace.

6. Modern ethics endeavours, as Socrates endeavoured, to obtain an universally valid basis for moral standards. Very different paths have been followed in this attempt. One way, the most superficial, in which the problem has been attacked, is to model ethics upon mathematics. Thus Spinoza gives us an *Ethica ordine geometrico demonstrata*; and both Hobbes and Locke believe—though they give what are at least very ingenious reasons for their belief—that ethics can be deductively presented, and its conclusions made as strict and universally valid as those of mathematics. Apart from this superficial and analogical

method, we can distinguish four different types of scientific ethics in modern philosophy.

(1) Ethics is marked off from religion and metaphysics, and the empirical scientific treatment of moral questions advocated.

(2) Ethics is based upon some already existing empirical science, such as psychology, political economy, biology, etc., and in this way itself acquires the character of a special science.

(3) The 'moral' is identified with what is 'useful,' either to the individual or the community. This reduction of the idea of morality to other terms makes it possible to give a comprehensive and fairly precise formulation of moral rules.

(4) Lastly, ethics is built up on aprioristic foundations; moral laws or judgments of conscience are an original function or connate possession of the human mind, and morality is, therefore, independent of all the varying theories of experience.

These four views can be separated only in abstract reflection; in the concrete they are as a rule found together, and serve to supplement one another. Thus the independence of ethics as regards religion and metaphysics is confirmed by the relation in which it is brought to certain positive sciences, or by an aprioristic mode of treatment, etc. But as there seems to be no theoretical need of any particular grouping of the different standpoints, while, as a matter of fact, the history of ethics supplies instances of very various forms of colligation among them, we may be allowed to distinguish them for our present purpose as representative of the principal ideas underlying all the ethical activity of modern times.

7. At first, we find the ethical interest strongest in the English philosophy. Bacon gives occasional suggestions towards an independent treatment of moral philosophy; Hobbes attempts to work out a definite ethical system. He sets out from the hypothesis of isolated and purely selfish individuals, and so comes to the conclusion that social life and peace are made possible only by a reasoned and calculating compliance of each with the demands of all: morality originates in reasoned reflection upon the useful and harmful. Locke, in a similar way, makes the

relation of human volition and action to some kind of law the principal topic of ethical discussion. Agreement with the law means moral conduct, disagreement with it, immoral. But there were, for Locke, three different kinds of law: the law of God, the law of the state, and the law of public opinion. Hence there must be three different forms of moral conduct. Under the divine law, action is dutiful or sinful; under the law of the state, guilty or innocent; under the law of public opinion, virtuous or vicious. Shaftesbury's definition of morality ("An Inquiry concerning Virtue and Merit," in the *Characteristics of Men*, etc., 1711 and later) is somewhat different. Ancient ethics had tended to connect the ethical with the æsthetical; and Shaftesbury, too, finds the essence of morality in the harmonious relation of the selfish and social emotions, in the beauty of proportion or symmetry, and in the absence of any unnatural or aimless inclinations. At the same time, he combines happiness with harmony, and declares that the form in which morality is first presented to us is that of a judgment of value. The English ethics of the seventeenth and eighteenth centuries, however, is not wholly free from aprioristic elements. R. Cudworth, S. Clarke and J. Butler believed that all moral judgments and modes of conduct take their source from an original disposition or function. Hume (*An Enquiry concerning the Principles of Morals*, 1751) and Adam Smith (*Theory of Moral Sentiments*, 1759) give a very careful psychological analysis of the moral sentiment and judgment; and Smith, in particular, completely establishes the independent existence of, and true moral justification for, benevolence or sympathy.

8. Continental philosophy shows us a close connection of ethical discussion and metaphysics. It is only here and there, at least in the earlier period, that we find any advocacy of a treatment of morals apart from religion and from a preconceived metaphysics. Bayle (†1706) and Helvetius (†1771) were the principal champions of an independent ethics. For the most part the essence of morality was found in clear cognition and in the regulation of the emotions by the rational will. Upon this point Descartes,

Spinoza and Leibniz are at one, despite their many differences on special questions. Perfection, defined in a purely theoretical, intellectualistic way (*cf.* § 30. 5), appears alongside of happiness, as the ethical ideal. We have already seen (§ 5. 3f.) that apriorism was generally recognised at this time as the condition of universal validity and necessity; so that we can understand Kant's endeavour to give ethics scientific rank by basing it upon *a priori* principles. Kant declares, in direct contradiction of Rousseau, the representative of the 'natural' element in moral philosophy, that a 'categorical imperative,' which is in opposition to all our natural tendencies, determines the will towards morality. He further argues, however, against any attempt to define the contents of the moral law by reference, *e.g.*, to the happiness of all or the perfection of the individual; for if an empirical element regulates moral conduct it is useless to pursue an enquiry into the conditions of the universal validity of ethics. The works in which Kant put forth his views upon moral philosophy are the *Kritik der praktischen Vernunft* (1788), the *Grundlegung zur Metaphysik der Sitten* (1785), and the *Metaphysik der Sitten* (1797). Ethics is here made the basis of a new metaphysics. The fact of a moral law which demands unconditioned realisation seems intelligible only on the assumption of a will freed from all constraint of natural causation; and the incongruity that exists, as a matter of fact, between virtue and happiness requires, Kant thinks, the immortality of the soul, and a divine being whose compensative justice can remove the contradiction. The post-Kantians have made ethics in most cases one of the most important aids to a metaphysics. J. G. Fichte extends its range of influence still further. Knowledge is, to a certain extent, conditioned by the moral will. And the reality of other beings besides ourselves is the necessary precondition of our own moral efforts, of an ego struggling towards morality (*System der Sittenlehre*, 1798).

9. Ethics is not now accredited with this wide-reaching significance. Even Schelling and Hegel look upon it only as a transition science, a stage on the road to higher things, not itself furnishing the ultimate and supreme ideal. Herbart (*Allgemeine*

praktische Philosophie, 1808) effected its complete separation from theoretical philosophy. On his view the attribute 'moral' cannot be regarded as determining the essential nature of any object or objects; but is simply the predicate in a judgment of taste, a determination of value. This kind of judgment contributes nothing to our knowledge of things; it is merely the expression of our subjective attitude to them. Now the passing of a judgment of value presupposes a standard of comparison; and this is given by the ideas of inner freedom, perfection, benevolence, justice and recompense. All five ideas furnish original and independent judgments of taste. Schopenhauer (*Die beiden Grundprobleme der Ethik*, 2nd ed., 1860) follows Kant in the postulation of freedom, but restricts it to the first steps in the formation of character, the peculiar feature of an individual will. On the other hand, he refuses to accept the Kantian view of the purely formal significance of the moral law, and declares—in accordance with his pessimistic metaphysics—that sympathy is the ethical impulse *par excellence*. Schleiermacher's contribution to ethics (*Grundlinien einer Kritik der bisherigen Sittenlehre*, 1803) is the distinction between theory of goods, theory of virtues, and theory of duties: each in its own way containing an exposition of the whole of moral science. In quite recent years, since the epistemological zeal of the sixties has somewhat cooled, there has been very great activity in the ethical field. A large number of good and suggestive works have been published, of which only a few can be mentioned here. Much labour has been devoted in particular to the strengthening of the foundations of ethics, and the discovery of new facts of ethical import by investigation in certain of the special sciences—political economy, sociology, psychology, etc.

We may mention the following works:—

E. von Hartmann, *Phänomenologie des sittlichen Bewusstseins*. 1879. Second Edition under the title *Das sittliche Bewusstsein*. 1886.

H. Spencer, *The Principles of Ethics*. 1879-93.

W. Wundt, *Ethik*. 2nd ed., 1892. Trs. in preparation.

F. Paulsen, *System der Ethik*. 2 vols., 3rd ed., 1893.

G. Simmel, *Einleitung in die Moralwissenschaft*. 2 vols., 1892-93.

H. Sidgwick, *The Methods of Ethics*. 3rd ed., 1884.

We may also mention three admirable histories of ethics:—

T. Ziegler, *Geschichte der Ethik.* I., *Die Ethik der Griechen und Römer*, 1881. II., *Die christliche Ethik.* 2nd ed., revised, 1892.

F. Jodl, *Geschichte der Ethik in der neueren Philosophie.* 2 vols., 1882–89.

[H. Sidgwick, *Outlines of the History of Ethics.* 2nd ed., 1888.]

10. This hasty glance at the historical course of ethical thinking is enough to show that there has been a great diversity of opinion among moral philosophers. Indeed, there is no philosophical discipline, except metaphysics, which has given rise to so many schools and standpoints as has ethics. Terms like Intellectualism, Intuitionism, Eudæmonism, Evolutionism, etc., all stand for divergences of ethical theory, whether as regards the origin of moral precepts, or the real end of moral conduct, or the motives of moral action. This lack of agreement in first principles, as manifested in the history of the discipline, may be referred to the constant change to which moral ideals and judgments are subject. What we to-day look upon as moral, good or meritorious, may, in earlier times, have been called by other names, or have lain altogether beyond the sphere of human volition. But the divergence of opinion obtains not only between period and period; we find it at every moment of every period. We have only to look round us now to discover it; very little examination of different individuals, or, better still, of different social classes, will bring to light fundamental differences of moral judgment. This uncertainty as to the essential nature of morality extends, however, only to its contents; no one disputes that requirements, laws, norms of some kind, have their place in the consideration of human conduct. Not a particular contents, but the form of the law or regulation, that is, has universal validity in the ethical realm. What direction the law takes, with what contents its form is filled, depends upon the needs, customs and opinions of a particular time. Under such circumstances an ethics which attempts to do more than bring out these general factors, and determine, with so much of probability as it may, the character of the morality conditioned by them, must possess a merely temporary significance.

The same thing is true of the philosophy of law and political economy, whose contents are similarly determined by the stage of development to which the consciousness of justice and the code of law have attained, and by the economic conditions of the time. If, therefore, ethics is to become an empirical science, like these two, the first aim of the moralist must be the collection of facts over a wide range of conduct. Speculations as to the possible or necessary nature of moral volition and action expose him to the obvious risk of travelling out of the main current of the moral development of his age, and thus condemning himself to fruitless labour and universal disregard. It is by mere chance, so to say, that an ethics of this sort can arouse any general interest.

11. The principal task, then, which we must assign to a scientific ethics, regarded as a separate discipline, is the collection and analysis of the ethical opinions current in its day. We are here in full accord with Herbart when he says that the form in which morality is first presented to us is that of certain judgments of value passed upon human volition and action. These judgments take two main forms, corresponding to the two headings of the quality and the intensity of the will judged. The terms 'good' and 'bad' belong to judgments of quality; the terms 'merit' and 'guilt' to judgments of intensity. Since, however, every determination of intensity presupposes some volitional quality, whose intensity it is, every appreciation of the strength or force of the will must carry with it an estimate of will-quality. Hence only acts of the good will can be meritorious, and only acts of the bad will guilty:—a proposition whose truth must not cause us to lose sight of the relativity of the concepts 'good' and 'bad.' Armed with some such simple scheme as this, the moralist would have to collect the moral judgments of various individuals, professions, social classes, etc., and discover, by careful sifting of his material, whether any unitary laws or consistent theories were to be obtained from them. That done, proposals could be made, with real hope of successful result, for the improvement or perfection of the moral consciousness. Only in this way does it seem possible to bring ethics into living contact with the moral

development of a national life. It is not by leaning upon psychology, or political economy, or sociology, or any other special science, that ethics can attain to the rank of a universally valid discipline, but rather by taking its stand upon the facts which are peculiarly its own, accessible solely to its methods. The analysis of the moral consciousness as it is, and then the freeing of it from contradictions and inconsistencies,—those are the tasks set to a purely empirical ethics. Its character as a normative science is assured by the nature of the second problem. We need not decide, for the present, whether there can be a philosophical ethics side by side with the empirical. The question has never been raised, and may accordingly remain a *cura posterior*.

12. The philosophy of law may be dealt with much more briefly. It was originally an integral part of ethics, and is still generally treated as an appendix to moral philosophy. As 'justice' and 'morality' diverge, however—the former finding its expression in definite laws, promulgated and enforced by the state—the sciences that have to do with them become more and more distinct. A further ground of difference is seen in the division of the science of 'justice' into a philosophy of law and a special science of contemporary law; there is no such special science of 'morality.' The separation of the science of law from its philosophy is due to H. Grotius († 1645). The science has to do with *jus civile*, positive law; the philosophy with *jus naturale*, the law of reason or nature. Since Grotius' time, attempts have constantly been made to determine by *a priori* deduction the natural basis or real ground of law, regarded as independent of the will of a law-giver. Kant drew a sharp line between legality and morality, defining legality as outward compliance with legal prescription. The philosophy of law has, further, been somewhat influenced by the work of K. Chr. F. Krause († 1832), whose pupil, H. Ahrens, gained a wide reputation by his elaborate *Naturrecht oder Philosophie des Rechts und des Staates* (6th ed., 2 vols, 1870-71).

We may also mention :—

A. Trendelenburg, *naturrecht auf dem Grunde der Ethik*. 2nd ed., 1868

W. Schuppe, *Grundzüge der Ethik und Rechtsphilosophie.* 1881.
A. Lasson, *System der Rechtsphilosophie.* 1882.
R. von Ihering, *Der Zweck im Recht.* 2nd ed., 2 vols., 1884-86.
R. Wallaschek, *Studien zur Rechtsphilosophie.* 1889.
K. Bergbohm, *Jurisprudenz und Rechtsphilosophie.* I. 1891.
In the last-mentioned work the doctrine of natural law is vigorously attacked, and the philosophy of law defined as a philosophy of positive, *i.e.*, actual, current law.
[J. Lorimer, *Institutes of Law.* 1880.
Sir H. Maine, *Ancient Law.* 11th ed., 1888.
J. H. Stirling, *Lectures on the Philosophy of Law.* 1873.]

13. The true problem of the philosophy of law is usually obscured by a bad use of terms. It is customary to contrast the philosophy of law with the science of law, a mode of expression which would lead us to suppose that the philosophy can say something more or something better than the science upon the facts of law, as they lie before us for treatment, or that the philosophy has a special kind of law for its subject-matter, different from the law of jurisprudence, the positive law established by human enactments and based upon human convention. Really, of course, the problem of a philosophy of law must be similar to the problem of a philosophy of nature (*cf.* §7. 7); it does not deal directly with the facts of law, but simply discusses the fundamental principles presupposed and the general theories developed by the corresponding special science. 'Law' for the philosophy is precisely the same as 'law' for the science: this latter including, we may note, not only the systematisation of existing laws, but also the 'general theory of law,' as it is called, and comparative jurisprudence. We can therefore state the problems which confront a philosophy of law, on lines similar to those which are followed in the cases of natural philosophy and philosophical psychology (*cf.* §§7, 8). They are three in number.

(1) The philosophy of law must examine the epistemological and logical presuppositions of the science of law. Here belong all concepts of general significance which are applicable outside the special limits of jurisprudence, and therefore cannot be adequately defined by a particular science: those, *e.g.*, of action, intention,

will, attempt, accident, causality, law, freedom, etc. All these are general terms employed by other sciences than jurisprudence. Here belongs, further, the logical examination of the procedure, the peculiar method, of the science of law.

14. (2) The philosophy of law must undertake a critical investigation of the fundamental ideas which find expression in the science, *i.e.*, of the concepts employed exclusively by jurisprudence. Here belongs, in the first instance, the idea of justice. The very various definitions of the term given by jurists, in the present as in the past, necessitate a critical examination of the facts from which the idea has taken shape. Further to mention are the ideas of punishment, responsibility, the juristic 'person,' property, possession, etc. Here, too, we find divergent opinions, leading to more or less radical differences of school or standpoint.

(3) Lastly, a philosophy of law must examine the general theories of jurisprudence. It is hardly possible to draw an exact line of division between these last two problems, since a number of the fundamental ideas given under (2) have been made the basis for general theories. Thus there is a very great diversity of opinion as regards the meaning and purpose of 'punishment,' so that we have the 'deterrent' theory, the 'reformation' theory, the 'retribution' theory, etc. In the same way there is dispute as to the origin of justice, and different schools of law have given very different answers to the question, in the form of particular theories. Two have persisted to the present day: the theory that justice is referable to an original capacity or need of the acting individual, and may, perhaps, be deduced from the idea of a free personality; and the contrary theory, that always and everywhere justice means a sum of precepts or rules of human conduct, supported by some kind of sanction, and that to understand or define it we must look to history and experience, not to *a priori* likelihood or arguments of pure reason.

NOTE.—We may here say a few words about pedagogy. It is usual at the present day, to exclude pedagogy from the circle of philosophical disciplines proper, despite the close connection of its topics, both in history and in fact, with those of philosophy. Herbart (*Allgemeine*

Pädagogik, 1806), whose pedagogical doctrines are still dominant at least in Germany, sought to make pedagogy an applied ethics and psychology. Ethics shows the goal of education, determines its end and aim; psychology furnishes the method by which the end may be achieved. Such a view, however, can be correct only if ethical ends are made absolutely pre-eminent, and æsthetic and intellectual needs subordinated to them. And even so, it would hardly be right to call a pedagogy which aimed to be not merely a theory of education but also a theory of instruction, an 'applied ethics.' The aim or goal of instruction can be brought only by a very roundabout way into the sphere of ethical problems and definitions. On the other hand, the connection of pedagogy with psychology cannot be disputed. The process of learning and the process of instruction—the development of character and the work of education—are alike unintelligible unless considered from the psychological point of view. And it were much to be desired that the intimate relation between the two disciplines should be explicitly recognised, so that pedagogy might adapt itself without more delay to the living progress of psychology. The continued veneration for Herbart's pedagogy does not encourage us, however, to hope for any such result in the near future.

§ 10. *Æsthetics.*

1. Æsthetics, like ethics, is concerned with the investigation of particular facts; it is not a critical appendix to some special science, whether the history of art, as Vischer believed, or any other. The aim of modern æsthetics, then, must be the same with that of modern ethics: to become a positive science. The two groups of facts with which it has primarily and most directly to do are the æsthetic judgments of pleasure and displeasure, and art and artistic production. They are clearly distinguished in ancient philosophy. Plato, Plotinus and Longinus gave most attention to the ideas of beauty and sublimity, *i.e.*, to the contents of the æsthetic judgment; Aristotle was principally desirous of contributing something towards a theory of art, and accordingly propounds a theory of poetry, especially tragedy. Plato's views upon æsthetics are set forth for the most part in the *Phaedrus*, *Symposium* and *Philebus*; Plotinus treats æsthetic questions in the first and fifth Enneads, and Aristotle chiefly in the *Poetics*. It is doubtful whether Longinus is the author of the work περὶ ὕψους. In all

these books, however, the philosophy of beauty is still mixed with ethics and metaphysics, and is very far from being a simple empirical investigation of given æsthetic judgments. And it is much the same with the æsthetics of the middle ages and the æsthetic theories of modern times. Philosophic interest has centred in the establishment of certain ideals of artistic creation, and in general hypotheses as to the significance of beauty in the universe. At the same time, some writers, especially in England, —Shaftesbury, Burke and Home, for example,—have done much to further the psychological investigation of æsthetic feeling and appreciation. Home's *Elements of Criticism* (1762 and later) forms with Kant's work upon æsthetics the most valuable contribution to the science made by the eighteenth century.

2. The philosophy of art, as is readily intelligible, became a kind of empirical science at a comparatively early period. The name might with some reason be applied to Aristotle's *Poetics* itself, as well as to Leonardo da Vinci's treatise on painting, the *Art poétique* of N. D. Boileau (†1711), the *Réflexions critiques sur la poésie, la peinture et la musique* (1719 and later) by J. B. Dubos, etc., etc. But æsthetics does not appear as a comprehensive discipline until the years 1750–58, when Alexander Gottlieb Baumgarten (1714–1762) published his *Aesthetica* (2 vols.). The book was intended to fill a gap in Chr. Wolff's philosophical system. Wolff had contrasted the higher and the lower faculties of knowledge, and defined logic as the science of the higher. There seemed to be no corresponding science of the lower faculty, of sensible knowledge; and the new æsthetics was written to supply the deficiency. The ideal of all higher knowledge is truth, complete clearness of ideas. Lower knowledge is always confused, obscure. Baumgarten finds the ideal of this latter sort of knowledge in beauty (a position, by the way, which had already been indicated by Leibniz). Beauty is the perfection of sensible knowledge, just as truth is the perfection of the knowledge of the understanding. The problems assigned to theoretical æsthetics, which Baumgarten, in the spirit of the Wolffian classification of philosophy, marks off from practical (*utens, specialis*) æsthetics, are three in number.

(1) It has to show what parts of sensible knowledge are beautiful, and so aid in the discovery of beauty. This portion of æsthetics is termed Heuristics.

(2) It has to show what arrangements of these beautiful elements are beautiful, and therefore to be observed. This is the Methodology.

(3) It has to ask how the beautiful and beautifully arranged elements may be beautifully expressed. This enquiry is termed Semeiotics.

Baumgarten himself treats only of the first portion of this system of theoretical æsthetics. His pupil, G. F. Meier (*Anfangsgründe aller schönen Künste und Wissenschaften*, 2nd ed., 1754), is an even more zealous advocate of the independence of æsthetics. With him began a period of energetic work upon the new science: and very soon, as the psychology of the time developed, there came to be a feeling that the subject-matter of æsthetics was not what Baumgarten had declared it to be; that, in particular, beauty could not be termed off-hand the perfection of sensible knowledge, or, indeed, knowledge at all. The assertion, from the side of psychology, of an independent faculty of feeling led to the view that the true source of æsthetics must be sought on that side of mind, in feeling.—Alongside of these attempts to determine the essential contents or object of the æsthetic judgment, we find a large number of essays in the philosophy of art. Thus J. J. Winckelmann endeavoured to set up general rules for the plastic arts, and G. E. Lessing and J. G. Herder to formulate a new theory of poetry.

3. Kant is the true founder of scientific æsthetics; his *Kritik der Urtheilskraft* (1790) is an attempt to reconcile the conflicting views of his predecessors. Æsthetics is there divided into two distinct parts: the theory of beauty and sublimity, and an investigation of the nature of art and methods of æsthetic classification. In the first part, Kant is mainly concerned to separate æsthetics as clearly as possible from ethics, logic and sense pleasure. It rests upon an *a priori* principle, viz., the assumption of the communicableness of æsthetic impressions, and of a teleological harmony between the faculties of knowledge,—imagination

and understanding or reason. Beauty is direct disinterested pleasure in forms and relations; sublimity is direct pleasure in something that baffles the interest of the senses, *i.e.*, whose magnitude or power puts it beyond the grasp of sensibility. The philosophy of art shows that a work of art must awaken an idea of the beauty in things, and that genius is the subjective condition of exemplary work in art. Kant classifies the arts, according to the means employed for the expression of beauty, as those of words or articulation (the arts of speech), of gesticulation or deportment (the formative arts), and of modulation or tone (the arts of the play of sensations). The beautiful and sublime derive their greatest value, however, from their character as perfect symbols of the moral or the good. Kant's æsthetic theories had a marked influence upon Schiller's work in the same field (*Briefe über die æsthetische Erziehung*, 1795). In substantial agreement with Kant as regards first principles, Schiller gives a less formal interpretation of the various phenomena of artistic activity, lays greater emphasis upon the value of æsthetics, and attaches greater importance to the beautiful as opposed to the moral (*cf.* the admirable presentation of the relations of the two systems in E. Kühnemann's *Kant's und Schiller's Begründung der Aesthetik*, 1895).

4. The speculative tendency of the post-Kantian philosophy is clearly manifested in its æsthetics. A deductive procedure, of derivation from universal principles, is everywhere followed. Especially important is the discrimination of an 'æsthetics of contents' and an 'æsthetics of form.' Hegel is the representative of the former; Herbart the founder of a purely formal æsthetics. Hegel (*Vorlesungen über die Æsthetik*, 1836–38: vol. x. of the collected *Werke*) defines æsthetics as the philosophy of art; and art is, for him, the lowest form of reality of the absolute mind, which realises itself in the three stages of art, religion and philosophy. It follows, of course, that natural beauty is merely a first step towards beauty properly so called, the beauty of art. The essence of artistic beauty resides for Hegel in the revelation of idea by matter, or in the manifestation of the eternal and unconditioned in the temporal and finite.

Such a conception of beauty lays most emphasis upon the *idea* which forms the real value of the æsthetic impression. At the same time, the various arts, and the history of art in general, show a serial development: we have first the predominance of matter over idea, then a counterbalancing of one by the other, and finally a predominance of idea over matter. In this way Hegel obtains three different forms of art, the symbolic, classical and romantic, realised historically in Oriental, Greek and Christian art, and systematically in architecture, the plastic arts, and the trinity of painting, music and poetry. The Hegelian æsthetics, or æsthetics of contents, has found many disciples. We may mention the works of Ch. H. Weisse, *System der Aesthetik*, 1830; Fr. Th. Vischer, *Aesthetik*, 3 parts, 1846–58; A. Zeising, *Aesthetische Forschungen*, 1855; M. Carrière, *Aesthetik*, 2 vols., 3rd ed., 1885; and K. Koestlin, *Aesthetik*, 1869.

5. Among these the great work of Vischer takes first rank. True, it is—as the author himself came to see—sadly lacking as regards system and method; but its wealth of historical notes and of detailed references to the various special arts makes it a mine of valuable information even for the modern student of æsthetics. Vischer defines his subject as the theory of the beautiful, and gives æsthetics second place, next after religion, in Hegel's trinity of art, religion and philosophy. The work is divided into three parts: a metaphysics of beauty, which deals with the general idea of the beautiful; a theory of beauty 'in one-sided existence,' *i.e.*, as existing objectively in nature and subjectively in imagination; and a theory of the 'subjective-objective reality of the beautiful,' *i.e.*, of art. Vischer classifies the arts according to the three forms of imagination, the constructive, receptive or sensitive and poetic. Architecture, sculpture and painting correspond to constructive imagination, music to the receptive, and poetry to the poetic.

In Herbart the term æsthetics has an entirely different significance, including not only what is ordinarily called æsthetics, but ethics as well (*cf.* § 2. 7). It is the science of the supplementing of what is by determinations of value. The faculty which enables us to make such determinations is named by Herbart, quite generally, 'taste.' Hence not only æsthetical but ethical judgments are 'judgments of taste.' Æsthetics in the narrower sense has to do with our pleasure in forms; and its problem is to discover the simple relations which run through all the more complicated works that evoke the æsthetic impression, and to define the ideas or ideals which govern æsthetic judgments of beauty and ugliness. These simple forms and relations Herbart finds, *e.g.*, in the harmony and disharmony of tones and colours, in rhythm, as a pleasing or displeasing relation of time periods, and in symmetry, as a similar relation of spatial extents. He thinks it necessary, in æsthetics, to abstract entirely from the matter or contents of the pleasing or displeasing relations and forms, although the total effect of any work of art is largely determined by it. The Herbartian standpoint has been systematically worked out by R. Zimmermann (*Aesthetik.* I., *Geschichte der Aesthetik als philosophischer Wissenchaft*, 1858; II., *Allgemeine Aesthetik als Formwissenschaft*, 1865). Zimmermann pays special attention to the ideals of perfection, unity, etc., which Herbart had not defined at all exactly.

6. Romanticism brought with it an exaggeration of the æsthetical point of view. Schelling, Fr. Schlegel and Schopenhauer, the principal philosophers of the romantic school, all lay stress, though each in his own way, upon the supreme importance of beauty and art. In Schelling, everything appears in the form of a work of art: nature is a work of art, and the organism, and indeed the whole universe; and beauty takes its place in the developmental series of subjective creations as the higher synthesis of science and morality. Schlegel, too, at a certain period of his philosophical development, fell into a sort of hero-worship, a cult of genius. The autocracy of genius, its full magnificence, finds expression in free criticism (irony) and free creation, unspoiled by any law. Lastly, Schopenhauer looks upon the state of æsthetic enjoyment as the highest form of earthly existence, the one condition in which we can conquer the cause of all suffering—

will. It makes an end of unrest and struggle; for him who is sunk in pure contemplation of the beautiful, intellect and idea have obtained the wished-for mastery over will; he is brought well-nigh to that saving last state of human existence, which is will-less nothing. On the other hand, Schopenhauer regards music as the highest of all the arts, because it is not, like the others, a form of idea, but a direct image of will itself, the essence of all things.

7. In quite recent times this metaphysical and logical standpoint has been largely given up, and a radically different conception of the object and methods of æsthetics has begun to take its place. To put it briefly, æsthetics is on the road to become empirical, instead of speculative or constructive; and the empirical method is being applied not merely to judgments of pleasing impressions, but also to the arts themselves and the creative activity of the artist. Thus H. Taine (*Philosophie de l'art*, trs. 1865) discourses of art mainly from the point of view of an historian of civilisation, emphasising the factors which seem to have determined the course of artistic production in time. It was he who introduced the words 'milieu' and 'moral temperature,' which have since become so popular, to designate the total condition, mental and moral, of a given period. On the other hand, Grant Allen (*Physiological Aesthetics*, 1881) and Georg Hirth (*Aufgabe der Kunstphysiologie*, 2 parts, 1891) have attempted to discover the psychophysical conditions of the vogue of works of art, especially of plastic art. Finally, G. T. Fechner (*Vorschule der Aesthetik*, 2 parts, 1876) examined the empirical conditions of æsthetic pleasure and displeasure, and was able to demonstrate the validity of a very promising method, that of æsthetic experiment. Fechner distinguished three principal modes of experimental procedure: the methods of choice, of production and of application. The method of choice consists in the picking out of the most pleasing term of a whole series of different simple forms, geometrical figures, etc. That of production consists, *e.g.*, in the drawing of some given figure or form in the proportions most satisfactory to the subjective feeling of the

draughtsman. The method of application consists in the investigation of fashionable art-objects, or any objects of daily use, tc determine the simple form-relations that arouse æsthetic pleasure. Zeising (4, above) had already made a large number of measurements by this last method, all of which seemed to indicate that the most pleasing relation of two lines is that known as the 'golden section,' the proportion 8:13. Fechner confirmed Zeising's result for simple figures by the method of choice. There can be no doubt that experimental æsthetics may be extended to cover all pleasing relations in the sphere of sense impressions; and that it will bring to light a large number of new uniformities, and do away with the obscurity and arbitrariness of the older constructive æsthetics.—Another very important point in Fechner's work is the distinction of a direct and an associative factor in the æsthetic judgment. By the former he means the immediate conditions of pleasure lying in the object under consideration, quite apart from any secondary ideas aroused by it; by the latter, reproduced ideas of the meaning of the object, previous experiences, etc. The distinction is evidently of crucial importance for the experimental investigation of æsthetic judgments.

8. There can be no question that these recent enquiries inaugurate a new period in æsthetics, characterised by the purely empirical treatment of its subject-matter. The objects investigated by the science are on the one hand judgments of æsthetic pleasure and displeasure, and on the other works of art. The separation of the two groups shows that there was truth in the old distinction between a philosophy of beauty and a philosophy of art. The æsthetic judgment extends beyond works of art, since there is a beauty of nature as well as of art; and works of art give us more than the æsthetic judgment, since when we have decided as to the pleasingness or displeasingness of their impression we can go on to discuss the conditions of their origination, the relation between portrayal and portrayed, between form and contents, copy and model, etc., etc.

(1) The first part of æsthetics, the theory of the æsthetic judgment, may be regarded as a portion of psychology, and, of

course, of applied psychology. Its problem is to furnish an exact definition of the æsthetic judgment and its conditions in terms of psychology. When viewed in relation to its objects, however, and especially in relation to the beauty of art, it takes on the character of a normative discipline, stating the external conditions which any given object must fulfil in order to be æsthetically pleasing. The dominant method of this part of æsthetics can and must be the method of experiment.

(2) The province of the second half of empirical æsthetics, the theory of art, is negatively defined by the limits of a number of already existing purely technical disciplines: harmony and theory of composition in music, the rules of designing, colouring, engraving, etching, etc., in the plastic arts, and prosody in the art of poetry. That is to say, the technique of art, the statement of the objective conditions of the production of a work of art, may be ruled out of æsthetics. The problem that remains for the theory of art is (*a*) an investigation of the general relation of portrayal and portrayed within the work of art. The names idealism, realism and naturalism stand for different conceptions of this relation. (*b*) It has also to raise the question of the subjective conditions of the work of art, the temperament, imagination, memory, etc., of the creative artist. This part of æsthetics, like the first, is evidently psychological in nature, but can also take on the normative character,—rising above the mere determination of the mental attitude and furniture of the artist to the ideal construction of those features of his mental constitution which are most favourable for the production of a work of art that shall satisfy the canons of a severe (or, perhaps, of the severest) criticism.

9. In æsthetics, as in ethics, we are met by the problem of the existence of a philosophical discipline, over and above the special science of the same name; and there are not a few philosophers at the present day who emphasise the value of a philosophy, or even a metaphysics, of the beautiful. But there is no occasion here to discuss the possibility of a philosophical æsthetics in any detail. The development of the science in the near future must be pre-eminently an advance along empirical lines; and the philosophy of

beauty or of art cannot take permanent shape until a certain measure of strictly scientific knowledge has been acquired. The objection so often urged against a scientific æsthetics, that judgments of taste are purely individual in their nature, and that therefore anything in the way of an universally valid proposition in æsthetics is an impossibility, is met by the fact that, so far, in all cases where it has been possible to examine the æsthetic judgment under unexceptionable conditions, *i.e.*, experimentally, no trace has been found of 'purely individual' taste, or even of irregularity in the formulation of taste-judgments. On the contrary, there has been manifested a most surprising agreement in æsthetic judgment, an agreement which obliges us most emphatically to continue along the same path of enquiry. The belief in individual differences, expressed in the current phrase, *De gustibus non est disputandum*, is easily intelligible when we remember the complexity of the impressions which form the objects of æsthetic appreciation in ordinary life. Diversity of interests, differences in the associative factor, in attention, and even in the actual object of observation, are conditions which readily account for divergence of 'taste' in every-day matters.

The following works may be added to the literature quoted in the foregoing paragraphs:

E. von Hartmann, *Aesthetik.* I., *Die deutsche Aesthetik seit Kant.* 1886; II., *System der Aesthetik.* 1887.
H. Cohen, *Kant's Begründung der Aesthetik.* 1889.
K. Groos, *Einleitung in die Aesthetik.* 1892.
K. Grosse, *Die Anfänge der Kunst.* 1893.
J. Walter, *Die Geschichte der Aesthetik im Alterthum.* 1893.
H. von Stein, *Die Entstehung der neueren Aesthetik.* 1886.
M. Schasler, *Kritische Geschichte der Aesthetik*, two parts. 1872.
[B. Bosanquet, *History of Aesthetics.* 1892.]

§ 11. *The Philosophy of Religion.*

1. We are helped towards a preliminary definition of the philosophy of religion by the distinction drawn above (§ 9. 13) between a philosophy of law and a science of law. On that

analogy, we should have to oppose theology, as science, to the philosophy of religion, as a part of philosophy in general: the one dealing with some determinate positive religion, the other examining and testing the general concepts employed or assumptions made by a special theology. As a matter of fact, however, we find that in the philosophy of religion, as in that of law, this simple conception has been ousted by another, quite different view. Just as the law of reason or nature is contrasted with the positive law of the state, so, within a given form of religion, the natural or rational elements have been separated off from the revealed. They consist of the religious ideas or feelings which can be deduced *a priori* from the nature of man himself, and more especially from his highest faculty, reason. It is even probable that this division in religion served as model for the similar distinction in the sphere of law, where its application is evidently quite different and much more correct. In law, external enactments and outward conduct have the principal part to play; but the essence of religion has always been placed in a purely inward, subjective attitude, which manifests itself in all kinds of conduct, but constitutes a reality entirely apart. And, indeed, when we consider how frequently the religious life of the individual departs from the articles of belief and ceremonial duties prescribed by his creed, we cannot doubt the existence of an inward religion, a religion which has grown up from personal experience and by conflict with all manner of scientific objections, altogether aside from the objective, historical form assumed by a particular revealed religion. Hence it is intelligible that the philosophy of religion has always asserted its right to investigate the facts of religion in relative independence of theology, and has only occasionally approached the problem which we assigned to it just now—the discussion of the value and philosophical significance of the fundamental theological concepts.

2. It was not till a comparatively recent period that the philosophy of religion received independent treatment. In ancient philosophy it formed an integral part of metaphysics; and in

modern times, even down to our own day, the feeling has generally been that judgments of religion must be made from the metaphysical standpoint. Hence the attitude of a philosopher to religion or the idea of God has come to be looked upon as a criterion of his metaphysics; witness the terms theism, deism, pantheism and atheism (*cf.* § 22), which give clear expression to the relation of the two disciplines. Moreover, it was metaphysics that offered the first opposition to Christian dogmatics. Then again, in the English philosophy, the epistemological examination of the idea of revelation has led to a criticism of positive religion in general. The earliest independent treatment of the philosophy of religion is, perhaps, to be found in the writings of the English 'free thinkers' of the seventeenth and eighteenth centuries, Toland, Tindal, etc. These men set out to lay a new foundation for the contents of religion in a criticism of Christianity and the doctrines of the church. The result of their efforts was a deism, a purely mechanical conception of the universe, accepted under stress of the discoveries of modern natural science, and leaving no room for a God who should interfere with the destiny of the world. Deism cut away the ground from under the feet of natural religion in the original, metaphysical or epistemological and psychological meaning of the word; so that it had to be given an entirely new foundation, if a religious life apart from positive theology were once more to seem philosophically possible. This work was done by Kant. He characterised the chief objects of religious belief as postulates of the moral consciousness, and thus endeavoured to assure them against all protest from the side of theoretical ratiocination. The universal rule of mechanical laws stops short at phenomena; things in themselves constitute a realm of freedom, which receives its necessary complement in the assumption of personal immortality and of an all-powerful and all-good God (*cf.* § 9. 8). Kant defines religion, however, as the recognition of our duties as divine commands, and his own philosophy of religion (*Die Religion innerhalb der Grenzen der blossen Vernunft*, 1793) consists in a rationalistic interpretation of the dogmas of the Christian religion, which does not differ in any essential point from the older attempts of the period of the Illumination towards a religion in accordance with reason.

3. Kant was chiefly concerned to make religion a normative science and defend its right to a place within a philosophical system. Schleiermacher (*Reden über die Religion*, 1799) discusses it as a factor in history and a datum of psychology, and comes to the conclusion that all religion consists in the feeling of an absolute dependence. Hegel, on the other hand, brings religion into relation with philosophy once more, describing it as the obscure and confused anticipation of philosophy. In recent times, the development of the philosophy of religion has followed three principal lines: the historical, psychological, and epistemological and metaphysical. Historically, it has as an object of investigation the origin and progressive evolution of religion; psychologically, it attempts to describe the psychical processes constituting the religious life of the individual; epistemologically and metaphysically, it asks for the justification of religious ideas and examines their connection with a general theory of the universe. Enquiries of this latter kind not infrequently result in the establishment of a new religious ideal, whose compatibility with the scientific and metaphysical theories of the age renders it acceptable where positive religious ideas have proved unsatisfactory.

The philosophy of religion has been treated from this standpoint by:

E. von Hartmann, *Das religiöse Bewusstsein der Menschheit im Stufengange seiner Entwicklung*, 1881; and *Die Religion des Geistes*. 1882. 2nd ed., 1888.

O. Pfleiderer, *Religionsphilosophie*. I., *Geschichte der Religionsphilosophie von Spinoza bis auf die Gegenwart*. 3rd ed., 1893. II., *Genetisch-speculative Religionsphilosophie*. 2nd ed., 1884.

L. W. E. Rauwenhoff, *Religionsphilosophie* (trs. from the Dutch by von Hanne. 1889. New titular edition. 1894.)

H. Siebeck, *Lehrbuch der Religionsphilosophie*. 1893.

R. Seydel, *Religionsphilosophie im Umriss mit historisch-kritischer Einleitung über die Religionsphilosophie seit Kant*. 1893.

[E. Caird, *The Evolution of Religion*. 1893.]

[J. Martineau, *A Study in Religions*. 1888.]

4. It is clear from the preceding paragraphs that the position of the philosophy of religion within the circle of the sciences in general, and of the philosophical disciplines in particular, cannot be very simply or definitely described. At one time it is occupied with the depiction and explanation of a given set of facts (historical and psychological standpoints), at another with a critical examination of the possibility of these facts, or the establishment of a new religious ideal in connection with a determinate metaphysics (and ethics). In the former case, it is simply a special science. Many students of the philosophy of religion draw a distinction at this point between the speculative and empirical modes of treatment, and entirely exclude the latter from their consideration. The division seems to be wrong in theory, and impossible in practice. It is only because the general history of religion and general psychology leave untouched a number of problems which can be discussed by a philosophy of religion, that historical and psychological investigation can be regarded as its special province. Reasoning from analogy in other fields, we may expect that the philosophy of religion will some day shake off its present hybrid character. And the reform will probably begin on the side of the history of religion, since the student of the philosophy of religion generally lacks the wide range of previous knowledge that mastery of the historical material requires. In its psychological aspect, on the other hand, the philosophy of religion will probably continue to form a department of applied psychology; the independence and comprehensiveness of the religious life make it impossible to do full justice to the subject within the limits of a general psychology. The properly philosophical part of the science, however, is to be found only in its treatment of the second of the two problems mentioned above. As a philosophy of theology it has an extremely important function to discharge: it must carefully analyse the basal theological concepts, the ideas of God, revelation, sin, justification, worship, etc., and at the same time bring them into connection with related ideas in other fields, metaphysics, ethics, etc. It is noteworthy that this, the true vocation of a philosophy of religion, has (so far

as the author's knowledge extends) never yet found explicit recognition.

§ 12. *The Philosophy of History.*

1. The extraordinary complexity of the range of facts which we include under the name of history makes it probable that the science of history, not less than its philosophy, is among the latest products of human thought. And indeed it is only in our own century that we find any real distinction between a scientific treatment of historical facts and amateurish and dilettante writing upon past events. No previous age recognised that a special method and special preparation and training are required to obtain scientifically valid results from historical sources. And even at the present day, and among the representatives of historical science, we meet with the statement that the artistic factor is of as much importance in historical work as the purely scientific: a sure indication that a science of history, in the strict sense of the word, does not yet appear to students in the historical field the obvious and only thing to work for. We need not be surprised, then, to discover that the philosophy of history shows the same imperfections and obscurities as its corresponding science. Three different views of its aim and province can be distinguished.

(1) On the first of these, it has to do with the same subject-matter as the science of history, but must adopt, in contradistinction to the science, a speculative or pragmatic or explanatory mode of treatment. While the science of history, that is to say, merely narrates what took place in the past, the philosophy of history must furnish an explanation, a reasonable basis, for the succession of events, and so introduce a rational connection into the sequence of things. In attempting such an explanation it takes into account various classes of facts which would otherwise be neglected: climate, the geographical position of a country, the racial characters of a nation, the economic conditions of development, etc., etc. So long as its enquiry is restricted to the examination of these empirical data, the philosophy of history is evidently

no more than a supplement to the science of history, and must give up its title of philosophical discipline whenever they are included in the province of history proper. As a matter of fact, the current division of the science into the history of civilisation and political history expresses in part, at least, the distinction drawn in earlier times between the philosophy and the science of history.

2. As a rule, however, a metaphysical problem has been assigned to the philosophy of history along with the empirical. An explanation based upon such insufficient data must be not only hypothetical but exceedingly imperfect; and it is therefore necessary to go beyond the operation of the empirical factors and put a metaphysical interpretation upon the course of history. A purely constructive factor thus takes its place among the conditions of historical occurrence. History is conceived of, *e.g.*, as an education of the human race, or as a realisation of the dialectic process which controls the colligation of ideas and concepts, or, from the religious standpoint, as a growth in holiness, manifesting the decrees of God and discovering his purposes. In this sense the philosophy of history is evidently dependent upon metaphysics, upon a definite theory of the universe; and supplements the science of history not by searching out and evaluating empirical factors which its sister-discipline has neglected, but rather by presenting the facts under a new aspect, entirely foreign to historical science.—We have here treated together these two attempts to establish the philosophy of history in an independent position, because they make their appearance together in the history of the discipline.

Representatives of this first view of the aim and province of the philosophy of history are:

J. G. Herder, *Ideen zu einer Philosophie der Geschichte der Menschheit.* 1784–1791.

H. Lotze, *Mikrokosmus. Ideen zur Naturgeschichte und Geschichte der Menschheit.* 4th ed., 3 vols., 1884 ff. (trs., 4th ed., 1894).

C. Hermann, *Philosophie der Geschichte.* 1860.

K. L. Michelet, *Philosophie der Geschichte.* 2 vols., 1879–1881.

R. Rocholl, *Die Philosophie der Geschichte.* 2 vols., 1878–1893. (The first volume contains a critical historical survey of previous contributions to a philosophy of history.)

3. (2) Another view assigns to the philosophy of history the task of laying a philosophic foundation for the science of history. So regarded, it consists in the application of epistemology and logic to a discipline which assuredly offers an unusually rich and fertile field for such investigation. For historical science has to surmount a peculiar difficulty in getting at the facts with which it desires to deal. These facts are, of course, in each special case, some group of past phenomena which refer to human fortunes, human volition or action. Obviously, they are not open to direct examination, but can be reached only by the help of more or less corrupt literary records or other sources of evidence. Hence the historical enquirer needs an extremely circumstantial training before he can begin work upon his real subject-matter; and historical procedure affords an interesting test of logical acumen. Nor is it less valuable, from the standpoint of epistemology, to discuss the value, validity and truth of the insight gained by the historic method. It is more apt to be the case in history than in any other department that scientific investigation leads simply to probability, and not to certainty of result. In the same way the question must be raised, from the philosophical side, as to how far we are justified in supplementing defective records, and the idea of law in history be subjected to a careful analysis. Lastly, special attention should be given to the idea of progress, which is oftentimes accepted as a regulative principle in historical science. Closely connected with it is the idea of development, as the origination of the higher from the lower, of the more perfect from the less perfect, of the more complex from the more simple.—It can hardly be said that the problems which we have here handed over to the philosophy of history have as yet received independent treatment. They are discussed sporadically in various books on logic (especially those of Sigwart and Wundt), in metaphysical treatises, and also in works dealing with the general methodology of the science of

history (*cf.* especially E. Bernheim, *Lehrbuch der historischen Methode*, 2nd ed., 1894).

4. (3) The third view of the philosophy of history, together with a new name to denote it, is found in the 'positive' philosophy of A. Comte (*cf.* § 4. 5). As a 'positivist,' Comte rejects all forms of metaphysical enquiry. Hence his philosophy of history cannot discuss the higher meaning of the course of historical events, or the working of ethical causes in the destinies of the universe, or the rule of a divine providence; but simply a certain group of natural phenomena, which the special science of history can deal with in but fragmentary fashion. It is only society that has a history: not the individual, and not inorganic nature. Comte's philosophy of history thus becomes a theory of the conditions and forms of human society in its present status and past development; a 'sociology' or social physics, divisible into a statics and a dynamics of society. Its method is based upon a comparison or analogy. Society may be regarded as an organism; and the results obtained by the science of animal organisms may accordingly serve as models for a theory of the stages, forms and elements of human society. The social statics emphasises the close connection of all the separate members of the social organism. The social dynamics declares that the human mind is the most important factor in social change, so that the stages or epochs of individual mental evolution are also stages or epochs of historical development. Comte distinguishes three of these stages, the theological, metaphysical and positive; the last is final. The most eminent of Comte's successors in the sociological field is Herbert Spencer (*The Principles of Sociology*, 3rd ed., 1885). Spencer gives a general formula for the process of evolution or development, which purports to be universally applicable. All evolution proceeds from an incoherent homogeneity to a coherent heterogeneity. The analogy between social ('super-organic') life-forms and organic, especially animal types, is carried through in detail. Thus the growth of the cell finds its social parallel in the horde, tribe and race. The various classes of society are further compared with the different structures of the

organism: the army corresponding to the ectoderm, the labouring classes to the endoderm, and the industrial or commercial classes to the mesoderm. And as the ectoderm gives rise to the nervous system, the supreme structure of the animal organism, so the army furnishes the state with leaders, princes or chieftains.

5. The science that has taken shape since Comte's day under the name of sociology is, evidently, not a true philosophy of history. It forms a new supplement to history, comparable with Herder's attempt (2, above) to explain the course of historical occurrence from natural conditions and human endowment. It has also been justly pointed out that sociology has no claim to rank either as the only or as the only genuine philosophy of history. To make society the sole object of historical consideration is every whit as one-sided as to treat exclusively of political events or great personalities. A real philosophy of history must be a discipline which we can put upon the same plane with the philosophies of nature and of law (§§ 7, 9). In that case, it will evidently have to do not with the facts of history themselves, with mental processes and the natural and social influences that determine them, but with the fundamental concepts and ideas presupposed by historical science, and the logical character of the methods which it employs (*cf.* what was said under 3, above). But there is also another problem to be solved. Previous attempts to put a metaphysical interpretation upon the course of history have been unsuccessful, because their authors sought to give an independent exposition of what had already been described, fully and adequately, in history itself. At the same time, there can be no doubt that the results of historical science form an important, indeed an indispensable, part of the foundation of any comprehensive metaphysics. We must go to natural science and psychology for a theory of the existing universe and its shaping in time, when we are looking at things from the side of nature or in the light of individual mental development, but we may not neglect the other and equally valuable material that the science of history provides for the completing and perfecting of our theory. Nothing of any worth can be said as to the significance of a

cosmic evolution, in the highest and widest meaning of the phrase, without knowledge of the history of past ages. A metaphysics thus founded upon history must, of course, shed a reflected light upon the body of facts that form its foundation; but the same thing holds, in precisely the same way, of natural science and psychology. We may talk, if we will, of a higher meaning in history, without changing one iota of the facts established by scientific investigation.

We conclude, then, that the sciences principally concerned, besides psychology, in the philosophy of history, are metaphysics, epistemology and logic.

Under this third heading we may mention the very suggestive work by G. Simmel, *Die Probleme der Geschichtsphilosophie.* 1892. The following books make valuable contributions to the history of the discipline:

R. Flint, *The Philosophy of History in Europe.* I. 1874. (Treats only of French and German investigators). The first part of this vol. has appeared in a 2nd, greatly altered ed., under the title: *Historical Philosophy in France, French Belgium and Switzerland.* 1893.

F. de Rougemont, *Les deux cités; la philosophie de l'histoire aux différerents âges de l'humanité.* 2 vols., 1874. (Contains a very complete bibliography).

R. Fester, *Rousseau und die deutsche Geschichtsphilosophie.* 1890.

P. Barth, *Die Geschichtsphilosophie Hegels und der Hegelianer bis auf Marx und Hartmann.* 1890.

§ 13. *Supplementary and Critical Remarks.*

1. The reader may have been surprised to find in the foregoing Sections no discussion of two other philosophical sciences, which would naturally be classed with the special disciplines: the *philosophy of mathematics* and the *philosophy of language* or of philology. There are two reasons for their omission.

(1) Neither of them is, as a general rule, represented in university lecture courses, while those that we have mentioned form part of the ordinary curriculum at almost every seat of learning.

(2) And the same thing holds of philosophic literature. We find not a little space allotted to mathematics and philology in

logical, epistemological and psychological treatises; but there are hardly any systematic works devoted to the exclusive consideration of their philosophical aspects.—It is, therefore, only a matter of accident, so to say, that the philosophies of mathematics and language do not receive a place in our list of philosophical disciplines. The accident itself is the more striking since essays in these two fields form part of the very earliest material that we possess for a history of philosophy. Pythagoras made a notable beginning in the philosophy of mathematics, and Plato, in his *Cratylus*, laid the foundations of a philosophy of language. Moreover, mathematics and philology were among the first of the special sciences to cut themselves loose from philosophy; and we might, therefore, reasonably have expected that they would have formed the subject of particular and extended philosophical investigation. We shall try to show in what follows why it is that the facts do not correspond to this expectation.

2. (1) The universal applicability of *mathematics* makes it the most general of all the special sciences. Among the attributes of given reality — quality, intensity, spatial and temporal character — there is only one, quality, which is not capable of mathematical treatment; each of the others can be subsumed under the fundamental concept of mathematics, the idea of magnitude. And since quality never occurs alone, since we do not ever find pure qualities among our empirical facts, there is, in principle, nothing which we cannot make the object of mathematical consideration. The possibility of a special application of mathematical method within a given department, however, depends further upon our ability to give a special definition to the general attribute of quantity, *i.e.*, to translate the general idea of magnitude into the more special concept of number or measurable magnitude. Remembering the universal significance of mathematics, as compared with the limited range of the other sciences, we can understand that it very soon came to occupy a peculiar position among them, and was regarded as co-ordinate with philosophy rather than as an object of philosophical investigation.

(2) But this is not all. The logical vigour and unitary structure of mathematics have constituted it since the beginnings of modern philosophy the ideal of all scientific work. Attempts have been made in all earnestness to model the philosophical disciplines after its pattern, in order to assure to them its universal validity and necessity. Here, then, is a second obstacle in the way of an impartial and objective philosophy of mathematics.

(3) Lastly, mathematics seemed to offer but scanty material for philosophical treatment. Its basal concepts were reducible to a comparatively small number; and in geometry, at any rate, the final justification of all its fundamental definitions appeared to reside in pure intuition or perception. Diversity of contents was lost sight of in the interest of formal procedure, and philosophy accordingly found but little to lay hold of in mathematical exposition. But with the increasing differentiation of the mathematical disciplines, the concepts which they employ have grown more numerous and complex; and the time is assuredly not far distant when a philosopher of mathematical training will bring the philosophy of mathematics into systematic form. Even as it is, the ideas of continuity, multiplicity, function, and infinite and infinitesimal magnitude, and the antithesis of geometry and arithmetic or analysis, etc., present a rich field for epistemological, logical and perhaps, too, psychological investigation.—The practical difficulty that confronts the student of this discipline, the mastery of the complex system of mathematical symbols, can here receive no more than bare mention.

3. With the *philosophy of language* the case is a little different. First among the disciplines to which we might look for the philosophical supplement to philology stands the science of logic. For logic, as we have seen (§ 6. 5), is occupied with the general significance of symbols, and especially of linguistic symbols; and the close connection which obtained so long, chiefly through the influence of K. F. Becker, between logic and grammar, would give a positive reason for our choice. Nevertheless, logic cannot help us. In course of time the

difference between the two disciplines was clearly established, and it fell to psychology to furnish the philosophical treatment of philology,—which it did with such entire success that modern essays in the philosophy of language may fairly be classed all together as psychological. Alongside of individual psychology, which has given especial attention to the development of speech in children, there has grown up (chiefly under the impulse of linguistic research) an ethnic psychology (*cf.* § 8. 9), one of whose principal problems is the reference of the various stages in the development of language to general psychological conditions in the history of the race. Here belongs, of course, the vexed question of the origin of language.—Now we have seen (§ 8. 10) that this empirical psychology has already acquired the character of a special science, and may be expected, in the near future, to assume its outward form. Hence we cannot admit that the psychological treatment of linguistic facts will ever lead to a real philosophy of linguistic science. As a matter of fact, however, if we abstract from its relations to psychology, the contents of philology seem to offer no new problem for philosophy; so that a philosophical psychology would be able to meet all the requirements that could be made of a philosophy of language in this meaning of the phrase. On the other hand, the form of philology is as much calculated as its contents to arouse philosophical interest. The various methods which philology, in the general sense, has developed undoubtedly constitute a separate and peculiar field for logical enquiry. Here, however, an objection is raised by the science itself. Some of its most gifted representatives have declared that it is simply an aid to the study of history. And, indeed, there can be no question that textual criticism, exegesis, estimation of authorities, etc., consist simply of a body of rules and facts which every historian must know who has to base his knowledge of past events upon written records; and that language itself forms but one of the many objects of historical investigation. Hence we must hand over this halt of the philosophy of language for treatment by the general philosophy of history (*cf.* § 12. 3).

Here, then, is the explanation of the fact that no attempt at a separate philosophy of language has as yet been made. And the reasons given render it probable that things will remain in the future very much as they are at present.

The omission of the *history of philosophy* from our list of philosophical disciplines hardly calls for special explanation. It must be regarded, of course, as a part of the general science of history, which includes the history of science. It may not, perhaps, be superfluous to insist that only a philosopher who has been trained in historical methods should enter upon research in the history of philosophy.

4. To these supplementary remarks we may add a few words by way of criticism. The survey of the philosophical disciplines which we have undertaken in this Chapter will have sufficed to convince the impartial reader of the justice of our objections to the current definition and classification of philosophy (§§ 2, 3). It cannot have escaped his attention that the sciences now classed together under the general title of philosophy stand upon very different planes. On the one hand we have metaphysics, furnishing a speculative supplement to the positive knowledge of the special sciences; on the other, the science of knowledge, which in its two parts, epistemology and logic, is called upon to set forth and examine the most general contents and the most general form of all scientific thought. By the introduction of natural philosophy and philosophical psychology we see these general disciplines brought into relation with more restricted fields; while ethics, æsthetics, empirical psychology and sociology are one and all engaged in special enquiries, and slowly maturing into independent disciplines. And yet—all alike are 'philosophy'! The facts now appeal to us with increased strength and renewed energy to define philosophy in some different way, and to map out its province upon some more satisfactory principle. And so we may end here with a reference forwards, to the place where we shall endeavour to answer their appeal (Chap. IV).

CHAPTER III.

SCHOOLS OF PHILOSOPHICAL THOUGHT

§ 14. *Classification of Schools of Philosophy.*

1. The criticism of the two preceding Chapters has led us to reject the current idea of philosophy as an unitary body of knowledge, and to distinguish a large number of diverse philosophical problems. It follows that there cannot be any unitary or all-embracing tendency in a man's philosophical thought, in the sense that, *e.g.*, his metaphysical position forthwith determines his procedure in all other philosophical disciplines. We have rather to look for differences of tendency within the separate philosophical sciences; and if we find the same term employed to express points of view in two different disciplines, to interpret it as indicating merely a general resemblance, and not a really close relationship. Thus we hear of 'formalism' both in logic and in æsthetics; but the word 'formal' means something entirely different in the two cases, and we should go very far wrong if we inferred that there was any necessary connection between the sciences. It is true that a philosopher is often characterised off-hand by a single name, as, *e.g.*, an 'individualist' or a 'pantheist.' That, however, merely means that a certain philosophical standpoint occupies a prominent place in his system, or expresses the opinion of the speaker that metaphysics is the most important philosophical discipline, and that one's attitude to it must therefore be taken to indicate one's philosophical attitude in general. The only way to be accurate is always to say in what department of philosophy the particular philosopher belongs to a particular school. By doing

this, we get rid at once of certain inconveniences and errors which arise solely from inaccuracy of linguistic usage; *e.g.*, the bracketing together of materialism as metaphysical theory and materialism as ethical principle. A favourite way of arguing against metaphysical materialism is to insist upon the unworthy estimate of man to which a materialistic principle leads in ethics!

2. We can distinguish schools or tendencies of thought not only in the contents attributed to a given science, but also in the general significance attached to it as a whole. Thus different schools give very different definitions of the problems of logic and psychology and epistemology. Differences of this kind, so far as they are of any considerable importance for modern philosophy, we have already discussed in Chapter II. (§§ 5, 6, 8). Hence we shall confine ourselves in the present Section to differences in the current conceptions of the contents of the philosophical sciences, differences which can be thought of as existing side by side, compatibly with practical agreement as to the significance of each science as a whole.

A difference of opinion in the appreciation or explanation of the same object is evidently indicative of a lack of universally valid knowledge. Metaphysics, of all the scientific disciplines, is the most liable to such differences: for the obvious reason that it travels farthest beyond the empirical determinations of the special sciences, and is at the same time least dependent upon the stage of progress to which any one of them may have attained. Hence we find in metaphysics an extreme variety and persistence of divergent schools. On the other hand, the greatest contrasts of standpoint occur in epistemology. Not only has epistemology to formulate and examine, from the side of contents, the presuppositions of all scientific knowledge (*cf.* § 5); the results at which it arrives are also of influence upon the procedure—indeed, upon the recognition of the possibility—of metaphysics. The best scientific logics give us no ground for the distinction of fundamentally different conceptions. Differences of tendency in natural philosophy and psychology will be considered along with the corresponding differences in metaphysics. There accordingly remains only one other philosophical discipline whose representatives are split up into different camps: ethics.

We thus obtain the following main divisions:—

A. *Metaphysical* schools.
B. *Epistemological* schools.
C. *Ethical* schools.

3. Our classification of *metaphysical* schools can take no account of differences of opinion upon the question of the possibility of the science. It may also disregard the divergent views as to the special methods to be employed in metaphysics. They depend either upon epistemological definitions or upon general theories of the nature of metaphysical enquiry, which we have not here to consider. The only thing left is the contents of metaphysical speculation. This we accept as the basis of classification, and proceed to arrange under five heads. The first two are of a general character, referring to all the principles that can find application in the construction of a theory of the universe. The last three are of a more special type, being concerned with quite definite factors within the total theory.

(1) The first group of metaphysical schools can be classified according to the *number* of principles assumed for a theory of the universe. It is customary to distinguish the various views that can be held upon this question by the terms *monism*, *dualism* and *pluralism*. But as the difference expressed by the first two is at the present day predominantly qualitative, it seems better to make a purely quantitative antithesis, and to speak only of *singularism* and *pluralism*. The former explains or deduces all the phenomena of the universe from one single principle; the latter declares that explanation is impossible without the assumption of a number of independent principles.

(2) A second means of classifying metaphysical schools is afforded by the *quality* of the principles adopted by them. Here we can distinguish principles of *existence* and principles of *occurrence*. As principles of existence we may have matter or mind or both or a fusion of the two—corresponding to the schools of

materialism, *spiritualism*, *dualism* and *monism*. As principles of *occurrence* we have *causality*, the mechanical inter-connection of cause and effect, and *finality*, the colligation of all processes from the point of view of purpose,—corresponding to the metaphysical schools of *mechanism* and *teleology*.

4. The special metaphysical schools may be classified by their attitude to three concepts which played a particularly prominent part in the German philosophy of the eighteenth century: the concepts of a supreme being (existence and attributes), of the freedom of the will and of mind.

(3) The third group may be termed, in general, the *theological*. Within it, metaphysical systems are classified according to their treatment of the idea of God. We can distinguish four typical attitudes; those of *pantheism*, *theism*, *deism* and *atheism*.

(4) The question of the freedom of the will divides metaphysics into two schools. That which accepts and defends it is *indeterminism*, that which opposes it, *determinism*.

(5) A last ground of division is found in the various metaphysical definitions of the nature of mind. The theory of *substantiality* supports, that of *actuality* denies, the existence of a mind-substance. Further, the terms *intellectualism* and *voluntarism* stand for opposing views upon the qualitative character of the fundamental attributes or functions of the mental life. The intellectualist regards thought or ideation as the essential activity of mind; the voluntarist looks upon will as the source and sustaining power of mental existence.

It may be said in general that not more than one of the metaphysical standpoints brought together in a class or group can be represented within a given philosophical system at a given time. They are antithetic, and consequently incompatible. On the other hand, the combination of standpoints which belong to different classes is almost always theoretically possible; and, as a matter of fact, many total systems of metaphysics have been compounded of elements variously chosen from the five groups. A glance at the history of philosophy shows, however, that certain combinations have been preferred. Thus the spiritualist is usually a theist and a believer in the substantiality of mind; the monist as regularly pantheist and determinist, etc. We may infer from this that the different classes are not in reality wholly independent of one another; and, indeed, it would be strange if one's belief concerning the general quality of the principles involved in a theory of the universe did not in some measure affect one's estimation of a special factor. In other words, a man's general philosophical attitude must, within certain limits, determine his attitude to special problems. We shall find this rule exemplified later on, when we come to deal with the philosophical schools in detail.

5. It is easy to see how the different metaphysical categories can be applied to a particular system. We may, however, give a few illustrations.

Spinoza must be termed singularist, monist and mechanist; pantheist, determinist, actualist and intellectualist. These words describe the contents of his metaphysical system in all essential points. Lotze, on the other hand, represents a very modified form of singularism, and is spiritualist, teleologist, theist, indeterminist and substantialist. We cannot speak of him either as intellectualist or voluntarist, since he recognises more than one fundamental attribute or function of mind. It is evident that the theories of the universe held by Spinoza and Lotze are, practically, direct opposites. Herbart and Leibniz stand in closer relation to Lotze, except that both are decided pluralists, as well as determinists and intellectualists. Herbart's metaphysics is a revival of that of Leibniz: tested by our categories, the two prove to be in complete agreement. The differences between the two philosophers are to be found in their attitude to epistemology and ethics, and in the method by which they obtain their metaphysical results.

It might be urged in objection to our classification that there are certain thinkers whose work cannot be subsumed to a category from each of the five classes. Where this is due to the incompleteness of a metaphysical system, the fault cannot, of course, be laid to the door of our schema. Nevertheless, there are theories

—Lotze's theory of mind, *e.g.*—over and above those to which we have given special names, and to them our classification is not adequate. The reason that we do not extend the schema to include them is simply that there are no definite or generally accepted names to express them in philosophical literature; and it would be foreign to our present purpose to add new words to a terminology already complicated enough.

6. In *epistemology* there has been a divergence of opinion upon three principal questions: those of the *origin* of knowledge, of its *validity* or limitations, and of the *nature of its objects* or contents. We find the following schools of thought:

(1) The origin of knowledge is placed by *rationalism* in the human mind, and by *empiricism* in experience. *Criticism* regards both mind and experience as concerned in the origination of knowledge, and attempts to determine the part played by each factor.

(2) *Dogmatism* declares, without examination, that all knowledge is valid. *Scepticism*, on the other hand, denies that any knowledge possesses universal or absolute validity: knowledge is subjective (*subjectivism*) or relative (*relativism*). *Positivism* (*cf.* § 4. 5) restricts the validity of knowledge to the field of immanence or experience; and *criticism* requires us accurately to determine the limits of human knowledge before we speak of transcendence, though it does not regard metaphysical enquiries as wholly impossible or inadmissible.

(3) *Idealism* makes the whole contents of knowledge consist of ideas, *i.e.*, data of consciousness. *Realism* maintains, on the contrary, that there is an objective something existing outside of consciousness. *Phenomenalism* regards the contents of knowledge as phenomena, and thus endeavours to take account of both the idealistic and the realistic factors.

7. Differences in *ethical* systems centre round four great problems of the moral life. The first is the question of the *origin* of morality, in the sense both of moral obligation and of the moral judgment. The others are the questions of the *motives*, the *objects* and the *aims* of moral volition and action.

(1) The *autonomous* ethical systems look for the origin of morality in the acting individual himself; the heteronomous or *authoritative* systems find it in injunctions laid upon the individual from without, whether in the form of religious or of political laws. The origin of the moral judgment and of moral knowledge is placed by *intuitionism* or apriorism in a connate disposition of the human mind; while *empiricism* or evolutionism makes them dependent upon the experience or evolution of the individual and the race.

(2) The *ethics of feeling* or affective ethics defines the motives of moral volition and action, in accordance with their psychological character, as feelings, emotions, etc. The *ethics of reflexion,* on the other hand, sees the impulse to morality in deliberation, a reflective process of the reason or the understanding. A further distinction is drawn within the ethics of reflexion between an ethics of the understanding and an ethics of reason,—where reason is regarded as the higher mental faculty, determining the course of moral endeavour and achievement upon more general grounds.

(3) The objects in which moral purposes are to be realised are declared by *individualism* to be individual men. These are further defined either as the acting subject himself (*egoism*) or as other individuals (*altruism*). *Universalism* opposes this teaching, and affirms that the object of moral endeavour must always be a community or society, *e.g.*, the nation or the state.

(4) The aim of morality is for *subjectivism* the production of a subjective state, that of pleasure or happiness (*hedonism* and *eudæmonism*); for *objectivism,* the attainment of an objective state, a condition of things determinable by objective standards or criteria. The names *perfectionism, evolutionism, naturalism* and *utilitarianism* indicate the various ways in which the definition of this state has been attempted.

8. We may illustrate the working of these new categories by applying them to the philosophical systems instanced just now (*cf.* 5, above). Spinoza, on the epistemological side, proves to be rationalist, dogmatist and realist. His moral system stands midway between an ethics of feeling and an ethics of reflexion.

It is autonomous, egoistic and objectivistic. Lotze, on the other hand, was in epistemology a criticist (in both senses of the word) and a realist; in ethics, an autonomist, intuitionist, adherent of the ethics of feeling, altruist and eudæmonist.

In conclusion, we may note that certain of the expressions which we have defined above are used in different meanings. Thus 'evolutionism' may apply not only to the development of the moral judgment, but also to a particular conception of moral ends. And the same thing is true of 'criticism.' The difficulty cannot be avoided, since the accepted nomenclature puts no other terms at our disposal; and it is far more important, from the point of view of the present book, to describe current linguistic usage than to try and correct its objectionable features. In one single case it seemed well to introduce a new word: objectivism. This was done, however, only in order to bring a number of related theories under their common genus.

The following works may be recommended for the study of the general subject of this Section:—

R. Eucken, *Geschichte und Kritik der Grundbegriffe der Gegenwart.* 1878. Second ed., under the title, *Die Grundbegriffe der Gegenwart.* 1893. (The historical material, which constituted a principal feature of the first edition, and upon which the book depends for its chief value, has unfortunately been greatly curtailed in the second.)

O. Liebmann, *Zur Analysis der Wirklichkeit.* 2nd ed., 1880. (A brilliant and suggestive discussion of problems in epistemology, natural philosophy, psychology, ethics and æsthetics.)

O. Flügel, *Die Probleme der Philosophie und ihre Lösungen.* 3rd ed., 1893. (Herbartian in standpoint.)

W. Windelband, *Geschichte der Philosophie.* 1892. Eng. trs., 1893. (This work gives a history of problems and ideas, as opposed to the usual chronological and biographical mode of treatment.)

NOTE.—F. Paulsen has lately published an essentially different and much simpler classification of ethical schools. He distinguishes (1) the various conceptions of the highest good, the final aim of moral action; and (2) the different definitions of moral judgment. The question of what constitutes the highest good is answered, he thinks, by *hedonism* and *energism* (according to which a certain occupation with the affairs of life possesses an ethical value). The attribute of morality is predicated, by *formalistic* ethics, of all action that corresponds to a moral law or norm; by *teleological* ethics, of all action that attains a determinate end, achieves determinate results. In epistemology, too, Paulsen recognises but four principal schools: those of realistic empiricism, realistic rationalism, idealistic empiricism, and idealistic rationalism. Neither classification appears to be adequate to the facts, and the ethical lays itself open to further criticism by the absence of well-marked lines of division.

A. METAPHYSICAL SCHOOLS.

§ 15. *Singularism and Pluralism.*

1. Singularism is the oldest metaphysical theory of western philosophy. In the earlier Ionian school of natural philosophy Thales chose water, Anaximander the infinite (τὸ ἄπειρον), and Anaximenes air, as the principle from which everything has been derived, or in which the essence of all things consists; and Heraclitus defines fire and the Pythagoreans number in the same way. In every case it is one single principle that is taken as starting-point. Nevertheless, we do not find any explicit consciousness of the necessity or importance of an unitary principle until the time of the Eleatics (Xenophanes, Parmenides, Zeno, Melissus). For them unity is an indispensable attribute of existence, the distinguishing mark of reality as opposed both to the many and to the changing, which are unreal. Moreover, since change and multiplicity are alike data of sense perception, this preference of unity carries with it the belief that reason is the only reliable source of knowledge.—On the other hand, pluralism, too, finds eminent representatives in pre-Socratic philosophy. Empedocles makes the four elements (fire, water, earth and air), and the moving forces of love and hate, principles from which to deduce the things and happenings of the universe: no one of them, he declares, can be reduced to any other, or brought under a still higher principle. The Atomists (Leucippus, Democritus) give up the qualitative differences of the elements in favour of a multitude of merely quantitatively different particles; and Anaxagoras can find only two independent explanatory principles,—matter, crude and chaotic,

which he conceives of as divided up into countless elements; and the ordering and arranging mind.

Plato and Aristotle may be said to combine both views. Singularism holds its own in the theory of a supreme or ultimate creative or impelling agent; pluralism receives expression in the unmediated antithesis of contents and form, matter and idea. Plato undoubtedly inclines more definitely to the side of singularism: the idea of the good or of the divine nature is taken by him as absolute principle of all that is and that occurs. In Aristotle, on the contrary, the pure idea, immaterial form is merely the *primum movens*, and accordingly presupposes something that can be moved. The philosophy of the middle ages vacillates in the same way between the two standpoints, though tending on the whole more towards the Platonic position.

2. The metaphysical systems of modern philosophy, like the mediæval, have not always kept the two views sharply distinct. Descartes, it is true, draws a clear line of division between body and mind, as two absolutely different qualities; yet both alike owe their existence to God, the one real 'substance.' In Spinoza's hands the Cartesian theory becomes a rigorous singularism; thought and extension are two of the infinitely numerous attributes of the divine substance—the only two comprehensible by human knowledge. Leibniz, apart from his confused treatment of the idea of God, is no less decidedly a pluralist. His universe consists of an infinite number of independent individual substances (monads). An explicit preference for a single principle is expressed in the Kantian philosophy, and in its logical developments, the systems of Fichte, Schelling and Hegel. All three endeavour to deduce Kant's system from a supreme principle or highest concept, whether in the form of an original action of the ego (the ego posits itself), or of an absolute indifference or identity, or of absolute existence. Schopenhauer, too, is a singularist, but establishes his position in an entirely different way, setting out to give a positive interpretation of Kant's theory of the thing in itself, and making will the ultimate and only reality. Herbart entered a strong protest against the 'prejudice'

that everything must be deduced from a single principle. What is, he says, must be qualitatively simple, but need not be qualitatively the same. And his explanation of experience leads him to a distinct pluralism, whose ultimate principles, the reals, show an unmistakable likeness to Leibniz' monads. Of quite recent metaphysicians, Lotze, von Hartmann, Fechner and Dühring may be cited as singularists, and Wundt as pluralist. Lotze has succeeded, in some measure, in combining both standpoints; he assumes the existence of independent, individual reals, and explains their interaction by the hypothesis of one all-embracing substance.

3. Singularism has sometimes attempted to justify its standpoint on general grounds; pluralism never. We may distinguish four main arguments for the assumption of a single principle.

(1) That which is *logically most general* must be *one*. Fichte, Schelling and Hegel, in particular, are agreed upon this point. All special ideas must be referable to one highest idea; all special knowledge must be deducible, by a chain of inference, from one supreme proposition. And since, further, there is a perfect parallelism between thought and existence (upon this, also, the three systems are in agreement), a highest idea or supreme proposition must also be the expression of a first principle of all existence or occurrence.

(2) That which is *most fundamental* must be one. Human knowledge, explaining the world by cause and effect, must lead to the assumption of a last cause. This is, roughly stated, the reason given by Plato, Lotze and von Hartmann for the adoption of a single principle.

(3) That which *exists* must, as existing, be one. This is the position of the Eleatics. Dühring propounds a similar theory: the all-inclusive existence must be unitary.

(4) That which is *best* and *most beautiful* must be one. The chief representative of this view is Plato.

It is interesting to note, as was said just now, that pluralism has never attempted to justify its standpoint on general grounds.

4. We have in this fact the expression of a deep-rooted differ-

ence in the character of the two schools of thought. Singularism almost always goes together with a deductive, dialectical, aprioristic procedure; pluralism is as regularly connected with inductive and empirical tendencies. We must not suppose, therefore, that truth is necessarily on the side of the four arguments. If we look at them a little closely, they seem (all but one) to proceed rather from a respect for the superlative degree than from metaphysical conviction. Besides which, singularism confuses the logical subsumption of special to more general concepts with real explanation. The manifold can never be really explained by the simple. The Atomists were quite right when they said that multiplicity of empirical data demands multiplicity of actual existence. For we can adequately explain individual facts only by other individual facts, and particular things only by other particular things. Special changes mean special conditions, and the whole notion of cause and effect presupposes a temporal and quantitative relation which can exist only as between individual and particular processes. Hence, while there is every reason to regard the system of logical concepts as an edifice that culminates in a single idea, that of itself cannot help us to the discovery of real principles which may take the highest place in an explanatory theory of the universe. Reverence for unity, whether ethical, æsthetical or mystical, has nothing at all to do with a scientific metaphysics. And all aprioristic arguments for unity or multiplicity must accordingly be rejected.

Of the other metaphysical schools, pantheism, theism, deism and monism belong to singularism; and dualism (unless connected with some one of these theological views) to pluralism. No other metaphysical theory has any necessary connection with the question of the number of principles requisite for an explanation of the universe.

§ 16. *Materialism.*

1. So many different schools of thought are grouped together under the name of materialism that it seems desirable in the first place to give a brief account of them all, and then to select those

that possess any metaphysical significance. We may distinguish two main forms: *theoretical* and *practical* materialism. Practical materialism is an ethical standpoint, and falls under the fourth category of our classification (§ 14. 7), the category of aim or end. It declares that the material good things of life are the only end worth striving for. Theoretical materialism may be either a regulative principle (§ 4. 3) or a metaphysical standpoint. As regulative principle it simply inculcates the rule that scientific investigation must always proceed as if matter were the only quality of reality, and therefore alone capable of furnishing the explanation of a given fact. This position was maintained, *e.g.*, by Fr. A. Lange, and is held to-day by certain physiologists and psychologists to be essential to their special work. As metaphysical standpoint, materialism appears in a *monistic* (*i.e.*, singularistic: *cf.* § 14. 3) and a *dualistic* form. On the dualistic hypothesis there are two kinds of matter, a coarser and a finer, a more inert and a more mobile; on the monistic, there is but one,—matter is unitary throughout. Finally, the monistic form itself has three subdivisions: *attributive* materialism, which makes mind an attribute of matter; *causal* materialism, which makes it an effect of matter; and *equative* materialism, which looks upon mental processes as really material in character. For convenience' sake we may arrange all these different materialisms in a table as follows:—

Materialism.

Theoretical. Practical.

Regulative Principle. Metaphysical Standpoint.

Dualistic. Monistic.

Attributive. Causal. Equative.

2. We are here concerned only with the metaphysical division of theoretical materialism. Its dualistic branch is confined to the philosophies of the ancient world, where it appears as atomism (founded by Leucippus, further developed by Democritus, and adopted later by the Epicureans). The theory is that the whole

visible universe has arisen by the cohesion of small invisible particles, the atoms. Matter is essentially homogeneous in character, and all differences among phenomena are referable to the size, form and relative position of the atoms. The mind, like everything else, is composed of atoms, which are, however, in its case, very smooth, delicate and round; or, as Lucretius put it in his *De rerum natura*, the smallest, roundest and most mobile that there are. This ancient materialism may be termed dualistic, since it regarded body and mind as composed of different atoms.

The monistic materialism of modern philosophy makes its first appearance upon English soil. Hobbes declares that every real occurrence in the universe is movement. Even sensations and ideas are, at bottom, nothing else than movements of inward parts of the animal body. Later, with increased knowledge of the dependence of psychical states upon the body, materialistic theory takes on a more special form. John Toland, the free-thinker (1670–1721 or 1722), defined thought as a function of the brain, and Robert Hooke, the 'experimental philosopher' († 1703), held that memory was a material storage of ideas in the brain substance. Hooke calculated that the number of ideas acquired by an adult during his lifetime would amount to nearly 2,000,000, and gives us the comforting assurance that the microscope shows the brain to have plenty of room for them all. Pre-Kantian materialism reached its climax, however, in the French philosophy of the eighteenth century. La Mettrie (*L'homme machine*, 1748) endows matter with the power of acquiring motor force and sensation, and designates mind as the cause of this power. Since the mind has its seat (or seats) in the body, it must be extended, and therefore material. It is, indeed, hardly conceivable that matter is able to think; but there are many other things just as hard to understand. A great number of clinical experiences and of facts in comparative anatomy prove the dependence of psychical upon bodily processes, and it is only as part of the brain that mind can exercise its influence upon body. Very much the same ideas recur in the *Système de la nature* by Holbach (1770), the crowning work of this materialistic literature.

The main purpose of the author is to combat all and every form of supernaturalism, *i.e.*, any view which assumes a principle or a world beyond and above the mechanical interconnection of natural, sensible, material things in the physical universe. The materialistic standpoint is here presented in much stricter form than by La Mettrie. Mind is simply body regarded under the aspect of certain functions or powers. No new arguments are alleged, however (*cf.* § 7. 5).

3. The nineteenth century witnessed a revival of materialism, due partly to the decay of Hegel's speculative philosophy and partly to the influence of a number of new observations and experiments on the connection of mind and body. A vehement discussion of these matters at the Natural Science Congress held in Göttingen in 1854 led to the publication of a long series of works, all materialistic in tendency, chief of which are: C. Vogt's *Köhlerglaube und Wissenschaft* (1855), J. Moleschott's *Der Kreislauf des Lebens* (5th ed., 1887), and L. Büchner's *Kraft und Stoff* (16th ed., 1888; trs., 4th Engl. from 15th German ed., 1884). The main difference between the new materialism and its eighteenth century forerunner lies in the fact that it shows some recognition of the need of an epistemological reason for its position. Thus Vogt affirms that the limitations of thought coincide with the limitations of sensible experience, the explanation being that the brain is the organ of mental function. This fact is as certain, he says, as that two and two make four. Nevertheless, our ultimate abstractions from phenomena will never be explicable,—consciousness as little as muscular contraction (!). Here, as in related works, connections are made out in detail between mental capacity and the weight of the brain, the extent of its surface, and the number of its convolutions. The most important work of the whole school, however, is, without any doubt, Moleschott's *Kreislauf*. Its epistemological position is as follows. All existence is existence through attributes; but there is no attribute which does not consist simply of a relation. Hence there can be no difference between the thing-in-itself and the thing-for-us. If we have found out all the attributes of matter that can exert

an influence upon our developed sense organs, then we have grasped the essence of things, and our knowledge, humanly speaking, is absolute. The materialist, Moleschott says, asserts the unity of force and matter, mind and body, God and the world. Thought is a movement, a recomposition of brain substance. It is an extended process, because, as certain phychological experiments—reaction experiments—show, it requires time for its consummation (!). The individual man is the sum of parents and nurse, place and time, air and weather, sound and light, food and clothing. We are the sport of every breath of air that plays upon us.

4. The various statements of Büchner's work are in hopeless confusion. In the first place he declares that force and matter, like mind and body, are merely terms to express two different sides or modes of manifestation of one and the same ultimate reality, whose intimate nature is unknown to us. But this wholly monistic utterance is promptly contradicted by another, to the effect that matter was in existence long before mind, and that mind presupposes the organisation of matter. It is then curious to read, later on, that there is no matter without mind, and that matter is the seat of mental as well as of physical forces. Yet again, mind is defined as the collective expression for the total activity of the brain, just as respiration is a collective expression for the activity of the organs of breathing. How atoms, nerve-cells, and matter set to work to produce sensations and consciousness is a matter of complete indifference: it is enough to know that they do. Not content with this unsurpassed confusion of ideas, the author kindly takes upon himself, in the second place, the remunerative task of distributing mental processes to particular brain ganglia, and packs away reason, imagination, memory, the sense of number, the sense of space, the sense of beauty, and many other things, into their separate cells. He cannot allow the developed consciousness of an adult man more than some 100,000 ideas, and so reaches the pleasing conclusion that the five hundred or thousand million ganglion cells leave full room for new mental constructs (and faculties ?).

At the end of this brief historical survey we may mention the curious form of materialism—a materialism by logical deduction—represented by Ueberweg († 1871). The things of the phenomenal world, Ueberweg says, are our ideas. As things are extended, ideas must be extended also. And as ideas run their course in the mind, mind must be extended. And as, again, what is extended is matter, the mind must be material. There is no doubt that the exact opposite of this conclusion could be logically obtained from precisely the same data.

5. Since our historical exposition of the principal types of materialistic metaphysics has brought to view all the arguments that have been adduced in its favour, and the subforms of the monistic type are never found as pure and as sharply defined as we have made them, we may now, without further delay, attempt the task of a comprehensive criticism of materialism in general. If any metaphysics is justly to be termed dogmatic, it is the materialistic. The arguments and reasons that materialists offer for their faith are extraordinarily feeble. Ancient philosophy was able to cope with the facts, in a certain measure, by its dualism of matters; and attributive and causal monism does not dispute the qualitative peculiarity of mind. But equative materialism, unless it be turned into a monism of a different order (§ 19), is mere naïve absurdity. Identity in idea may be asserted only where the characteristics of the objects or ideas in question can be regarded as identical. But it is an old and a very true observation that the attributes of the 'psychical' differ essentially, if not entirely, from those of the 'physical.' What then becomes of the dictum that mentality *is* a material process? Until quite recently materialism had made no attempt whatsoever to provide itself with an epistemological foundation; and it is one of the results of the Kantian critique of knowledge that at last, in the nineteenth century, some such ventures have been undertaken. But all alike (as can be seen in our quotations from Vogt and Moleschott) leave the real difficulty easily and carelessly on one side. The only fact upon which the materialist can rely for support is the obvious and evident dependence of psychical processes upon physical. But philosophers

of other schools have cast no doubt upon the existence of this connection between the two groups of phenomena; and the fact must consequently be regarded as highly equivocal, not as a sure index of the correctness of materialism. Indeed, the following reasons force us to the conclusion that the materialistic hypothesis is neither the most plausible nor the simplest explanation of the fact.

6. (1) Materialism stands in contradiction to a fundamental law of modern natural science, the law of the conservation of energy; according to which the sum of energy in the universe always remains constant, and the changes that take place all about us are simply changes in the distribution of energy, and involve an absolutely uniform transformation or exchange. The law evidently implies that the series of 'physical' processes is a closed chain, in which there is no place for a new kind of phenomenon: the 'psychical' or 'mental.' Brain processes, *e.g.*, despite their extreme complexity, must be included in the circle of causes and effects, and all the changes produced in the brain substance by outside stimulus conceived of as propagated and diffused in a purely chemical or physical way. A theory of this universal validity leaves the mental side of things 'all in the air'; for how the secondary effect of mentality can be produced without any the least loss of energy upon the physical side, is difficult to say. The only logical thing to do is to co-ordinate mental processes, as representing a special form of energy, with the ordinary chemical, electrical, thermal and mechanical energy, and to assume that the same uniform relation of transformation and exchange obtains between them as between the various 'physical' energies. But apart from the fact that this view is nowhere mentioned, still less worked out in any detail, in materialistic literature, there are several objections to it upon general grounds, all leading to the same conclusion, that the idea of energy as defined by natural science is inapplicable to mental processes.

(2) The idea of matter, which plays so large a part in materialistic thinking, has neither met with such general acceptance nor

admits of such certain proof as to take rank, without further discussion, as a firm and adequate foundation for our direct conscious experience. The conflict between the mechanical and dynamical views of nature (*cf.* § 7. 5) is not yet over; and the latter eliminates the idea of matter altogether. Nor can there be any doubt that it is possible to obtain a consistent explanation of nature on the dynamic hypothesis. But then materialism loses its foothold once and for all.

7. (3) Materialism cannot explain even the simplest psychical process. For it would be requisite that the process should be necessarily deducible from a certain definite group of material processes, given or assumed. But it is so difficult to conceive how a sensation could ever be the necessary and obvious consequence of a movement, that the materialists themselves do not pretend to a single ray of intellectual enlightenment in the matter. It is not true, as they urge when confronted with the argument, that the purely physical nexus is equally inconceivable. In the physical sphere, the necessity of a determinate occurrence can always be demonstrated by some conceptual or perceptual construction. Du Bois-Reymond's eloquent presentation of these old-world truths (*Ueber die Grenzen des Naturerkennens*, 1872 and later) has helped to win acceptance for them in scientific circles, to which philosophy proper makes little appeal.

(4) The idea of a relation of dependence is far more general than that of causal connection. The former implies only that two phenomena, *a* and *b*, are so related that every change in (or of) *a* is followed or accompanied by a corresponding change in (or of) *b*. By 'corresponding' change is meant a change which is qualitatively or quantitatively equivalent to the given change; so that equal or similar processes in (or of) *a* lead to the appearance of qual or similar processes in (or of) *b*, or that greater, less, stronger, weaker, etc., changes on the one side are followed by changes in the same direction on the other. All these conditions are fulfilled, of course, by the relation of cause and effect; but it involves further a definite temporal connection, quite irrelevant to dependence as such, and thus forbids the inversion of the relation, which

is perfectly possible under the less special formula. Hence the assertion of a relation of dependence between psychical and physical processes must be sharply distinguished from the assertion of their causal connection.—Now an impartial observation shows that mind is dependent upon body, and body dependent upon mind. The unprejudiced investigator will, therefore, be content with the general idea of functional relation, and make no attempt to apply the more special law of causal connection in this particular field. Materialism, on the contrary, starts out with the assumption of the special relation, unmindful of the difference between cause and dependence, and blind to the extreme one-sidedness of its position.

8. (5) Epistemologically, materialism is guilty of a misunderstanding of the ultimate character of human experience. 'Subjective' and 'objective,' 'mind' and 'matter,' are not given *a priori* as independent magnitudes or qualities; what we have to begin with is an undifferentiated whole. This is the 'datum of experience,' and it is only by fairly complicated processes that we rise from it to the conceptual distinction between subject and object (*cf.* § 26). But materialism, in its search for the sole and only ground of existence, the essential reality of things, is not even satisfied to take this first result of conceptual abstraction, but chooses what we may call an abstraction of the second order, the idea of 'matter.' For 'objective' and 'material' are not by any means convertible terms. The 'objective' element in the datum of experience is simply the element which is not dependent upon the experiencing individual; *e.g.*, certain spatial and temporal attributes or relations. The idea of matter presupposes a common substrate of all these processes. Instead, therefore, of taking account of the full contents of original experience, materialism has raised a secondary product of conceptual abstraction to the rank of a metaphysical principle.

(6) To the materialist, however, matter is not an 'idea' at all, but a self-evident reality. He talks of the atoms as if they could be perceived by the senses, and regards matter as the seat of forces which operate upon us, etc. We have the word of sober

thinkers, who have attained to eminence in natural science, that this pictorial application of the idea of matter and its parts may be very useful, provided that it does not usurp the place of a true explanatory principle. The atoms would then be merely figures of speech, valuable just so far as they helped to simplify one's total conception of the interconnection of natural phenomena. But the correct idea of matter and its parts cannot be made pictorial, since it depends upon a twice repeated abstraction from the original data of perception. And so it comes about, as Mach says, that the atoms have been unhesitatingly endowed with certain attributes which contradict all previous observation. Materialism, that is, is all too ready to confuse the figurative idea of corporeal particles with the abstract idea of atoms.

9. (7) The sole purpose in the formation of the concept of matter is, as we have seen, to hypostatise the objective element in the datum of experience. There is no intention of paying the slightest attention to its subjective side. This is the epistemological reason for holding to the closed series of causally connected physical processes, as defined by the law of the conservation of energy. But the subjective element in the datum of experience is an ultimate character in human experience in general. Tones, colours and the rest of the qualities of sense,—processes of thought, acts of the will, feelings and emotions,—all alike are under all circumstances and in all their parts among the given things of experience itself. Matter, on the other hand, is an abstraction of the second order. How, now, can any connection such as that required by materialism, whether in its attributive or causal form, obtain between an original contents of experience and this abstract idea It is much as if one should try to establish a causal or attributive relation between a good action and the concept of morality. The relation can exist only when the phenomena brought into connection are processes of the same order, or at least stand upon the same level of abstraction.

It follows from this discussion that materialism is not only a very hypothetical, but also an exceedingly improbable metaphysical explanation of the world-whole. It has now lost all standing in philosophical circles, but still enjoys a considerable vogue among physiologists and alienists, and is often used as a catchword, in the sense of a well-substantiated scientific theory, in the ordinary conversation of the educated classes. This is why we have offered so extended a criticism of its metaphysical pretensions.

In conclusion we may mention the admirable work of F. A. Lange: *Geschichte des Materialismus und Kritik seiner Bedeutung in der Gegenwart* (3rd ed., 2 vols., 1876-77; 5th ed. [popular edition without notes], 1896; Eng. trs., 1892).

§ 17. *Spiritualism.*

1. Spiritualism, the direct metaphysical antithesis of materialism, appears much later than its rival in the history of philosophy. The only philosophical doctrine of antiquity that could possibly be termed spiritualistic—the Platonic theory of ideas—does not belong to spiritualism in the strict meaning of the word, since the 'idea' was simply the reality in the concept, and did not denote anything originally mental, a simple contents of internal experience. We may, therefore, regard Leibniz as the first exponent of spiritualism. According to the Leibnizian epistemology, metaphysics, like mathematics, must pursue a deductive method, must set out from what is simplest, what is absolutely clear and certain. The impressions of sense do not meet these requirements, since they give no clear information at all as to the origination of the qualities contained in them. Hence we must begin every philosophical enquiry with definitions, formed in accordance with the laws of identity and contradiction. Leibniz' own metaphysical system is an instance in point: in all its most important aspects it is developed from the definition of *substance.*

Descartes had defined substance as the being which so exists that it needs no other being for its existence, and concluded from this that God alone can properly be called substance. Yet it seemed to him that matter and mind, the *res extensa* and the *res cogitans*, might also fitly be termed substance, since only God, and not any other being, was necessary to their existence. Spinoza objected to this lax use of terms, and asserting the material as well as the conceptual independence of substance, reserved the name for God. He defined substance as that which exists in itself, and is conceived by itself, *i.e.*, as that the idea of which does not presuppose the idea of any other being, as its necessary source and origin.

2. Leibniz' definition is practically the same with that of Descartes. It runs as follows: *substantia est ens per se existens.* But while his predecessors had maintained the unity of substance, Leibniz combines with their definition the hypothesis of an infinite multiplicity of substances. Now that alone can exist by itself which has the power of action; so that force, self-activity, is the essential mark of substance, and substance itself must be something immaterial, unextended. Following Giordano Bruno († 1600), Leibniz calls these substances, the independent units of the sum of existence, *monads.* They are the true atoms, as opposed to the phenomenal atoms of natural science; they are the simple elements in everything complex, and therefore indivisible and indestructible; metaphysical points, as opposed to material or mathematical. Further: since their essence consists in self-activity, they cannot receive any impression, nothing can penetrate them; and the apparent interaction of processes in the visible world depends solely upon a wise fore-ordination, the 'pre-established harmony,' in virtue of which the states of all substances correspond to one another without exerting any mutual influence. This limitation, again, helps us to a more exact definition of the activity which we must assume to be present in substances. It will consist in a *repraesentare, i.e.*, in an idea or representation. Ancient philosophy had been wont to conceive of sense perception as a copy of the external world, and the conception is one that has appealed to the popular consciousness in all ages. Leibniz makes use of it here, in working out the details of his metaphysics,—supplementing it, however, by the mathematical idea of representation. He is thus led to the view that every monad ideates or represents the whole universe, and is in this sense a microcosm, a mirror of the all, *une concentration de l'univers.* Yet again: since the idea is a mental act, the essence

of the monad is a psychical quality. Things extended or corporeal are thus reduced to the level of mere phenomena, whose underlying reality is to be found in a multiplicity of unextended substances. But not every monad mirrors the universe with equal clearness; there are as many monads as there are degrees of clearness of the ideating activity.

3. The spiritualistic hypothesis then lapsed till it was revived in very much the same form by Herbart. He sets out from a general definition of the idea of existence. Being consists for him in absolute position, which is equally exclusive of relation and of negation. Now it is clear that a multiplicity of existential qualities would introduce a relative element into the idea of existence; whence it follows that existence must be conceived of as perfectly simple in character. Such a view, however, stands in contradiction to the experiential idea of a thing with many attributes. Reconciliation, without violence done to the facts of experience, is only possible on the hypothesis of a multiplicity of existences, each of absolutely single nature. These are Herbart's reals,—incorporeal existences like Leibniz' monads, but indefinable as regards their simple quality. The relations in which the reals stand to one another are those of disturbance, which they undergo, and of self-preservation, which they originate: every self-preservation cancels a disturbance "in such a way that it does not occur at all." Now in the Herbartian psychology the idea figures as the sole process in which our conscious mental life finds expression; so that the self-preservations of the mental real may be regarded as ideas. At this point Herbart's spiritualism is plainly less rigorous than that of Leibniz: Herbart does not attempt to define the nature of the self-preservations of the reals constituting 'body,' or the simple quality of any real.

Lotze is far less reserved in his attitude to the spiritualistic theory. He defines existence as a standing in relations, or a capacity to do and to suffer. Relations, however, are only conceivable on the assumption of an unity which holds all existences together. Lotze accordingly looks upon individual things as modifications of an absolute, or a substance. He further asserts that things can be regarded as independent units only if we attribute to them a mental quality, thought of as analogous to our own consciousness.

4. In a certain sense we may term Wundt, too, a spiritualist. Setting out from a common source, the original reality of the object of idea (our 'datum of experience'; *cf.* § 26), scientific and psychological enquiry diverge to follow different paths. The ultimate unit to which we are brought by a metaphysical consideration of the results of natural science is the atom, as merely quantitatively or formally defined. On the other hand, a parallel consideration of the range of psychological fact leads to the assumption of an ultimate unit of a qualitative character, which we call will. The problem of ontological metaphysics is to reunite these divergent paths, and so obtain a conceptual definition of the original reality. We arrive at a will-atom as the essential unit of all existence. The purely formal determination of the atom-aspect of the unit is, however, unessential.

The spiritualistic mode of thought is also found, quite frequently, outside the circle of philosophers *von Fach*. In such cases it is ordinarily connected with the epistemological form of idealism (*cf.* § 26). For if we have made up our mind that the quality of all experience must be conceived of as idea, we may very easily go on to read this mental or spiritual process into the concepts employed in scientific investigation, and so to give even 'material' existence a spiritual contents. Berkeley is the typical representative of this point of view: his 'immaterialism' or 'psychism' recognised none but psychical substances, spirits. Sometimes judgments of value play a part in the scheme of thought; mental processes being regarded as the more important, indeed as alone really valuable, while 'material' processes are reduced to the level of an unimportant and worthless mode of phenomenal existence. Spiritualism in metaphysics makes special appeal to those who hold a dynamic theory in natural philosophy (*cf.* § 7. 5). If the atoms are simply centres of force, and consequently unextended points, it is not difficult to believe that they can be adequately and exhaustively defined by some psychical quality.

Attempts have also been made to demonstrate the validity of spiritualism by arguments from analogy. Thus Schopenhauer declares that it is only in ourselves that we can perceive the thing-in-itself as well as the phenomenon. It is therefore only from the analogy of our own nature that we can determine what, in the existences outside of us, corresponds to the phenomena that we think in space and time. Hence the universe as phenomenon is a sum of ideas; but the universe as thing-in-itself is will.

5. The principal thesis of spiritualistic metaphysics admits of very much simpler formulation than that of materialism. It is that all empirically given processes, the material or corporeal in particular, are referable to a mental existence or process. The quality of this latter is defined on the analogy of our own consciousness, and conceived of as a more or less perfect expression of personal mental experience, varying with the degree of spontaneity and independent action manifested by natural objects. The more precise formulation, in its turn, allows us to make our critique of spiritualism much briefer and less complicated than was possible in the case of materialism.

(1) It is very evident that *psychology* can be brought into complete harmony with a spiritualistic metaphysics. One objection, it is true, has been advanced. A spiritualistic interpretation of the universe, it is said, leaves the existence of other centres of consciousness, outside ourselves, unexplained; nay, more, it makes them inexplicable. But there seems to be no reason why a particular metaphysical interpretation of the movements of other individuals from which we are wont to infer their inner or psychical existence should imperil the conclusion that analogy has suggested. The facts themselves are not altered in any way by interpretation; we have merely to strip them of the scientific concepts in which they are ordinarily expressed, and clothe them in the new raiment of the spiritualistic hypothesis. Hence objections to spiritualism can be raised, if at all, only from the side of natural science or epistemology.

(2) But again, the store of ideas, laws and methods which has been laid up by *scientific* investigators will suffer no change at the

hands of spiritualism. It is a matter of indifference whether we keep to the idea of material atoms and a mechanical connection between them, or attempt to modify it by positing a spiritual contents, in which we suppose their essential nature to consist. For in the latter case, as in the former, we must assume the existence of all the relations and the truth of all the rules whose universal validity has been established by the observation and calculation of natural science.

6. (3) Very much the same thing may be said from the point of view of *epistemology*. The phenomena of consciousness form the entire contents of all 'data of experience.' There is no one concrete experience which cannot be regarded as sensation or idea or feeling, *i.e.*, as mental process; and the 'objective' side of things consists simply of certain spatial or temporal attributes and relations of experiences which are customarily referred to formal concepts like those of 'matter' and 'energy.' If now a special meaning is read into these terms by the substitution of a spiritual existence for the 'material,' we seem to get, in place of mere magnitudes without quality, a definable contents in its full and complete reality.—True, we may go very far wrong in an attempt to reconcile a spiritualistic metaphysics with the teachings of epistemology: *cf.*, *e.g.*, the unfounded assertion that idealism is the necessary or self-evident (!) starting-point for any philosophical explanation of the universe (see § 26).

We conclude, then, that the possibility of spiritualism must be conceded. It will, therefore, take rank above materialism, as not subject to direct disproof either by epistemology or by the special sciences concerned,—psychology and natural science. This does not mean, however, that it is preferable to all other possible metaphysical theories. On the contrary, when we try to apply it in detail, we are met by many and considerable difficulties. We pass to a brief consideration of them in what follows.

7. (1) In the first place, we must note that the spiritualistic interpretation of scientific concepts is extremely arbitrary. (*a*) Nothing compels us to believe that there lies dormant and concealed in the elements of matter a peculiar existence which we

must conceive of on the analogy of our own consciousness. The forces which are supposed to be concentrated in the atoms stand in relation only to their changes of position, *i.e.*, are simply the conditions of those transformations which are rendered perceptible by the movement of physical bodies. (*b*) Moreover, the idea of force is often regarded at the present day as superfluous, and replaced by an exact statement of the spatial and temporal relations of masses to one another. (*c*) Lastly, there is no trace of any intimate connection between the physical relations and the relations ascertained by psychology to obtain among mental processes. Hence the results of natural science itself neither demand nor suggest the spiritualistic interpretation of natural processes.

(2) A further difficulty confronts us when we ask for some definite description of the mental existence which spiritualism ascribes to the material elements. Leibniz says that the capacity of representation (ideation) is the inner aspect of natural phenomena; Schopenhauer, that it is will; while on a third view the whole series of events which manifest themselves in our individual experience must be transferred *mutatis mutandis* to physical bodies and their constituent parts. Here, again, the ideas of natural science give us no indication that one or other of these possibilities is necessarily true in fact.

8. (3) Nor does psychology afford any support to the spiritualistic hypothesis. It teaches that our personal mental life is connected with an extremely complicated part of the physical organism—not at all that it is packed away in the ultimate material particles of the body. Modern physiological psychology does not place the seat of consciousness or mind in a point, or even in a cell of the brain: the immediate conditions of mental processes are situated in different quarters of the cerebrum, probably in the cerebral cortex. Hence there is no sort of precedent or analogy for the view that every atom represents a mental existence of the kind known to us in human consciousness. And if we descend with the comparative psychologist to the lowest levels of animal life, where a last trace of mentality may be suspected or conjectured, we are still brought to a halt at the cell or the cell-nucleus; there

is no warrant for placing the supposed rudiment of consciousness in the atom. As for the inorganic world, the scientifically-trained judgment finds no empirical reason whatever for endowing it with mental attributes.

(4) Finally, epistemology has neither facts nor arguments in favour of spiritualism. Epistemologically regarded, mental existence is merely one aspect of the data of experience, however completely it may coincide with their qualitative contents. The direct matter-of-fact of experience is not exclusively subjective or mental. Moreover, spiritualism makes two entirely arbitrary epistemological assumptions. (*a*) It asserts the independent existence of the atoms, *i.e*, of matter, the substrate of objective phenomena; and (*b*) it affirms that these hypostatised realities are spiritual or mental in nature.

LITERATURE.

E. Vacherot, *Le nouveau spiritualisme*. 1884. (Attempts to put spiritualism upon a basis of natural philosophy, and to justify it by a critical discussion of other schools of philosophic thought.)

NOTE.—Spiritualism is sometimes called *idealism*. This is due, in part, to the close connection which obtains between epistemological idealism and metaphysical spiritualism.—In our own day *spiritism* is fond of parading under the nobler name of spiritualism.

§ 18. *Dualism*.

1. The dualist looks upon mind and matter, the subjective and the objective, as two separate and independent existences. His view is that of the 'healthy human understanding,' and of the Christian dogmatist of the middle ages and the present time. It appeared comparatively early in the history of philosophy.

Anaxagoras was the most pronounced dualist among the pre-Socratics (*cf.* § 15. 1). He definitely distinguishes νοῦς, the mental principle, from the σπέρματα or ὁμοιομερῆ, the innumerable ultimate material elements. Mind brings order and movement into what is in itself inert and chaotic matter; it has the attributes of self-subsistence, simplicity, independence and self-identity. The two greatest philosophers of antiquity may also be termed dualists. Plato separates matter (ὕλη) from idea (εἶδος), the non-existent and empty from existence with its wealth of contents, sensible particularity from the real that finds expression in the generic idea. There is also a further difference, a difference of value, between them, which makes the metaphysical distinction all the sharper. In Aristotle we have the same antithesis, though the separation of its terms is not so radical as in Plato; it is expressed in the concepts of matter and form. Every individual being (οὐσία) is, in its concrete reality, formed matter; matter alone is not capable of existence, nor—divinity excepted—can there be a pure form. The two determinations stand to one another as possibility and realisation, as potentiality and actuality (δύναμις and ἐνέργεια). Thus mind is defined as the 'entelechy' or realisation of the body. Divinity is pure form, and νοῦς, as in Plato, is raised above all the other faculties of the human mind by the predicate of immortality. In mediæval philosophy this dualism holds its own, both in metaphysics and in ethics.

2. There is a great difference between ancient and modern dualism. The dualism of ancient philosophy looks upon body and mind as the terms in one out of a whole number of valid antitheses, using them merely to illustrate the more general contrast of matter and form. Their relationship, that is, does not constitute a dualism, in virtue of any peculiar feature or import: they simply furnish an instance of dualism in its more general aspect. Descartes is the founder of modern dualism, and the typical exponent of dualistic metaphysics in modern philosophy. He makes the conceptual distinction of *corpus* and *mens* fundamental for metaphysics. The 'corporeal' is universally characterised by extension, the 'mental' by thought. Hence there are two substances: a *res extensa* and a *res cogitans* (*cf.* § 17. 1), which exist independently, but stand in reciprocal relation to each other. How interaction between two completely dissimilar substances can be possible Descartes does not go on to explain. Later philosophers attempt to fill in this gap in his system. Among them the *Occasionalists* (Arnold Geulincx,

† 1669) deserve special mention. Occasionalism regards a real interaction between existences so fundamentally different as impossible. The appearance of interaction is produced by the direct action of God *(concursu Dei).* Thus the ideas which we think we receive from the external world through excitation of the organs of sense are really shaped by God in conformity with material things, and the movements of our body which seem to arise from a definite volition are regulated by Him in accordance with the mental intuition. Mind and body are, therefore, each of them only the accidental or apparent cause of changes occurring in the other, *causae per occasionem.* They are but the opportunity, the occasion of the working of the true cause, which is God.

It is remarkable that from that time to this—apart, of course, from modern representatives of mediæval philosophy—there has hardly appeared a single vigorous or thorough-going exposition of the dualistic theory. At present, the standpoint is generally discredited as inadequate to the problem of interaction. In popular thought, however, it has still no rival beyond materialism (§ 16. 9); and we must also conclude, judging from the phraseology which they universally employ, whether with or without 'reservation,' that it is the dominant view in the empirical disciplines of psychology and natural science.

3. This difference between the trend of thought in philosophy and in the special sciences and the popular consciousness cannot, of course, be allowed to pass as final or inevitable until the reason alleged for it—the impossibility of a dualistic solution of the problem of interaction in the form of a logical and consistent interpretation of the facts—is demonstrated beyond the reach of question. It is urged, as an insuperable difficulty in the way of dualistic explanation, that the law of cause and effect is necessarily inapplicable to two entirely disparate processes. But we must then ask whether qualitative likeness is, as a matter of fact, the invariable precondition of causal connection. And the answer seems to be that the causal law says nothing at all as to the likeness or unlikeness of the processes that stand in the relation of cause and effect. On the other hand, to dispute the applica

bility of the principle of causation to disparate processes, and then to deny, on that ground, that interaction is possible between corporeal and mental phenomena, as dualism defines them, looks very much like a *circulus in probando:* for body and mind furnish the only instance of disparity, in the required sense of the word.

As for mental phenomena themselves, no more objection is raised to their causal interconnection than to that of physical processes. It is truly a strange rule that is based upon one single instance, and then held to be valid simply in order that this single instance may be brought under it! The empirical reasons for the idea of causation are given in the temporal succession and qualitative or quantitative equivalence of phenomena (*cf.* § 16. 7). It is evident from this that only changes, processes, can be causally related; and that the modification which they undergo in a particular case must correspond both in direction and in magnitude, if there is to be any talk of causal connection between them. But causal equivalence has nothing whatever to do with likeness or unlikeness of kind. We believe in the interaction of bodily and mental processes because we see that a more intensive sensation follows upon a stronger excitation of sense, and a more vigorous movement upon a more vehement impulse of the will; and our belief is not affected in the least by the difference that undeniably exists between excitation and sensation or intention and movement.

4. The rightness of this view can be shown in another way. The processes of the material and mental worlds evince different degrees of qualitative likeness. Yet there is no corresponding difference in the degree of confidence with which we subsume them to the law of cause and effect. Mechanical, electrical and chemical processes may all be causally interconnected; nor has the very much greater difference between feelings, ideas and volitions prevented psychologists from attempting their causal explanation. True, objections have frequently been raised against the causal interrelation of psychical processes, the principle of psychical causation: but the reason is not that there is any question of their essential similarity, but merely that the law of

equivalence does not seem to allow of exact application in the conscious sphere.

We may, then, be allowed to dispute the validity of this venerable argument against a dualistic metaphysics. And if we are asked, in our turn, to show something of the mechanism of the causal nexus, to say just how it is that the cause produces the effect, we can answer with Hume and Lotze that the demand is a demand for the impossible. The actual working of the causal law is everywhere hidden from us,—even in the material realm, where its operation seems so entirely a matter of course. We must also note that the belief that the cause *produces* the effect implies a metaphysical interpretation of the empirical facts. All that experience gives us is succession and equivalence.

Dualism has sometimes been attacked from the standpoint of epistemological idealism (*cf.* § 26), upon the ground that it entirely overlooks the fact that what are called 'material' things are given only in the form of ideas. We cannot here enter in detail upon the proof of the erroneousness of this statement. We may say, however, that it has no more weight as an argument against dualism than it had as an argument in support of spiritualism (*cf.* § 17. 6).

5. Psychology has no quarrel with metaphysical dualism. This is sufficiently clear from the circumstance that metaphysicians of very various schools use a dualistic terminology when they are dealing with psychological topics. With natural science, however, the case seems to be different. The hypothesis of interaction between two different substances, or, at least, two independent processes, appears to conflict with one of the fundamental laws of modern science—the law of the conservation of energy. We have already mentioned this law (*cf.* § 16. 6) in our criticism of metaphysical materialism; and it seems to tell with equal force against dualism. But we must remember that materialism derives mental processes from physical, *i.e.*, affirms a purely one-sided dependence of mind upon matter, whereas dualism assumes the interaction of the two. Hence the difficulty is by no means the same. We need only posit, as modern psychology does, an equivalence of mental and

material processes. That granted, it follows that the amount of energy lost upon the physical side in the origination of a corresponding amount of mental energy will be replaced by the subsequent transformation of the mental back again into a new form of material energy. It will then make no difference whether or not a given quantum of mental energy is interpolated into the course of material processes; the law of the conservation of energy, in its ordinary acceptation, is not touched at all. We shall be obliged, finally, to credit the temporal succession of mental and material processes; but we may assuredly do so without contradicting any fact of experience or any requirement of empirical science. Dualism may, then, be regarded at the present time as a possible metaphysical interpretation of experiential facts and scientific knowledge.

§ 19. *Monism.*

1. There can be little doubt that a monistic theory of the universe is that most generally accepted to-day, whether in scientific circles or among psychologists and metaphysicians. It appears in two principal forms. Either mind and matter are two 'sides' of one and the same existence which is constituted by them, or they are modes of manifestation of an unitary existence, which in itself is separate and distinct from them. We may characterise these two forms as *concrete* and *abstract* monism. Abstract monism falls, again, into two divisions, according as the unitary existence is regarded as accurately *definable* or as absolutely *unknown*. Besides these three fairly determinate forms of monistic metaphysics, we find the term 'monism' used, especially in popular parlance, as the equivalent of materialism. On the other hand, we sometimes meet with the phrase 'spiritualistic monism.' This difference of usage is partly due to the fact that monism is not as a rule distinguished from singularism (*cf.* § 14. 3), so that it may either denote a peculiar qualitative definition of existence, or simply indicate the number of principles employed for that definition

(1) Concrete monism is one of the very oldest metaphysical theories. It occurs as *animism* or *hylozoism*, in connection with a kind of dualism, among quite primitive races. All nature is endowed with mind, on the analogy of the human individual. There is not the slightest recognition either of the difference between mechanical uniformity and the operation of psychical motives, or of the significance of a closed causal series. The arbitrary action of the individual is carried over to nature, and all sorts of natural phenomena pressed into the service of the theory, as signs of spontaneity and self-originated movement. Hylozoism is also the doctrine of the earliest Greek philosophers. Here, too, we have a confused mixture of monistic and dualistic thought.

2. No attempt at a consistent working out of this concrete monism appears among the later developments of philosophy. Since mankind has learned that the organic and the inorganic are two separate provinces, that uniformity in material processes takes a different form from uniformity in psychical, and that we can speak of mind only where we may posit consciousness,—since this time, animism, and its useless generality of a mind in nature, have given place to some other type of metaphysical theory of existence. Now and again a hint of it occurs, as when the materialists put the unity of mind and matter upon the same plane with that of matter and force. But these scattered traces of loose thinking are not enough to make us hesitate in declaring that concrete animism has practically disappeared from modern philosophy. As a matter of fact, it does not solve, but merely states, a problem. The unity of material and mental existence which it is concerned to uphold is nothing more than an empirically given interconnection; whereas the explanation of this interconnection is the very task upon which metaphysics has to bend its energies. Animism must accordingly be considered merely as a stage of transition, and not as a final system. In this sense, it may still find a certain acceptance, as it does in Fechner and Wundt. When these philosophers assert that mind is the inner unity of that which, regarded from the outside, we call body, and so go on to define mind and body as two different sides of a single

existence which they together constitute, we have before us an exposition of concrete monism. Reading further, however, we arrive at the theory that mental existence furnishes an exhaustive expression for this unitary reality of things, and so witness the transformation of animism into spiritualism (§ 17. 4).

3. (2) Abstract monism has played a far more important part in the development of philosophic systems. Spinoza is its first typical exponent. Spinoza's one infinite substance, God or *causa sui*, is possessed of innumerable attributes. Only two of them, however, are accessible to human knowledge: extension and thought. Each of these finds expression in particular 'modes.' Thus the various physical bodies are modes of the attribute of extent, and the different individual minds modes of the attribute of thought. But since divine existence is possessed of a countless number of other attributes, its true nature remains unknown to us. We thus obtain the second sub-form (1, above) of abstract monism, according to which the common substrate of matter and mind is not exactly definable. On this theory there cannot, of course, be interaction, but only parallelism, with essential identity of the corresponding processes. Hence Spinoza's famous saying: *Ordo et connexio idearum idem est ac ordo et connexio rerum.* Every 'event' is, in its full significance, a process, conceived of as running its course within the one substance, God. Our perception of it in mind or body is limited, one-sided, fragmentary.

Many modern philosophers take up this monistic attitude to the universe. If they do not speak of innumerable attributes of the original unity, they still firmly maintain that its nature is unknown, and that we obtain knowledge of its reality only from the parallel forms of external and internal occurrence. Herbert Spencer, *e.g.*, is a 'monist' in this sense of the term. His agnosticism (*cf.* § 4. 5) is simply a disclaimer of all attempts to define the original reality. Fechner, too, vacillates between this position and that of spiritualism.

4. The other sub-form of abstract monism (the first in 1, above) is much bolder, taking upon itself to define the unity of mental and material, or, as it prefers to say, of the ideal and real aspects

Fichte, Schelling and Hegel are its typical representatives. Fichte makes the absolute ego, or (in his later and simpler terminology) the absolute, the single source from which an individual ego and non-ego develope,—makes it, in brief, his one metaphysical principle. Schelling, on the other hand, regards absolute identity or indifference as the original existence. From the self-knowledge possessed by the absolute arises the antithesis of subject and object; but the difference between them cannot be more than quantitative, since their qualitative identity must not be disturbed. Individual things are, therefore, differences or powers of this quantitative sort; and even the contrast of real and ideal must be interpreted as simply formal or quantitative, not a difference of kind. Hegel's absolute appears at first in the indefinite form of 'being.' By the operation of the dialectic process the concept receives more and more of contents, until finally the nature of the absolute or God is laid bare in the particular definitions to which the impetuous onrush of the method leads. The special forms of absolute existence are nature and mind. A very similar standpoint has been worked out in recent years by von Hartmann, for whom the 'unconscious' is the quality of the absolute. Lotze, too, may be regarded as a monist, since he identifies his all-embracing substance (needed to explain the possibility of interaction among individual things), in the religious sense, with the idea of God, and endows it with ethical attributes; so that the original being is not only creative substance, but also moral ideal, and guide of historical development.

5. In attempting to arrive at a critical estimate of metaphysical monism, we may rule its concrete form out of the discussion. Concrete monism is, without any doubt, merely a disguised dualism. It offers no real explanation of the way in which mental and material hold together. It expresses the facts somewhat differently from dualism, without really gaining an iota by its formulation. With abstract monism, on the other hand, the case is very different. The derivation of the two modes of phenomena from a single existence, known or unknown, seems to render their course in time and their parallelism more intelligible. We shall accordingly

consider in what follows whether (and how far) this form of monism is in a position to furnish an adequate or satisfactory solution of the great problem which the special sciences give up. We need not, clearly, expect any opposition to it from the side of epistemology. It fully recognises the reality of the two-sided 'datum of experience'; it simply supplements experience by the hypothesis of an existence which underlies both sides or aspects. Nevertheless, it has to run the gauntlet of numerous objections, some purely logical, some psychological and scientific. We give the chief of these in the appended summary.

(1) Abstract monism is guilty of a two-fold 'transcendence.' In the first place, it indefinitely extends the limits of the mental sphere; in the second, it hypostatises a known or unknown unity of mental and corporeal. There is nothing in experience to necessitate the taking of either step; so that we cannot but raise a logical objection to the theory—an objection which may well take the form of the old scholastic rule: *principia praeter necessitatem non sunt multiplicanda.*

6. (2) The interpretation which abstract monism has to offer of the interaction of mind and body is neither the easiest nor the most obvious. Recourse is had to it only when the simple idea of interaction, in the strict meaning of the term which is suggested by experience, seems to break down; monism is then a last resort, a house of refuge from the supposed difficulties of dualism. But the monistic interpretation is not by any means, as its champions strangely believe, an obvious deduction from experiential facts. Granted that one and the same thing has two different 'sides' or modes of manifestation, it does not follow of necessity that these evince precisely parallel changes. *A priori* there are two other possibilities; the 'sides' may be altogether independent of each other (*cf.* form and quality, or intensity and duration of some concrete experience), or an inverse relation may obtain between them (as between the two component parts of a sphere of constant volume, where increase of one is accompanied by decrease in the other, and *vice versâ*). There is consequently no reason why the particular relation between body and mind that we find in experi-

ence should follow from the assumptions of abstract monism. And if the monistic theory needs bolstering by secondary hypotheses in order to make the given appear as the only possible relation, it becomes very much more complicated than a straightforward dualism. Fechner makes use on occasion of the figure of a circle. One who stood within the circle would always and necessarily obtain a different view of it from one who stood outside. To which we may add that, despite the difference of standpoint, any change in the size of the area or form of the periphery would be a change for both observers. But, even as thus amplified, the figure (which, of course, cannot be regarded as the only adequate representation of monism in general) is of no great service; it offers no explanation of the equivalence of material and mental. Lastly, to assert the essential identity of the two sides is simply to fall into the absurdities of equative materialism, which received its deserts in a previous Section (§ 16. 5).

7. (3) But monism professes to expound not merely the determinate relation of the individual mind and the animal body that belongs to it, but also a general relation between the outer and inner sides of all the elements of the universe. The consequence is that the distinction between the psychical as conscious process and all the purporting 'unconscious' processes, which the history of psychology shows to have been won with so much pains and labour, goes completely by the board. Paulsen, who makes a most eloquent appeal for a monistic metaphysics, does not scruple to extend the idea of mind to include the unconscious. He seems entirely to overlook the fact that such a procedure makes a scientific psychology absolutely impossible. If psychology is to be a science, it must take the form of an empirical, experiential discipline. This fantastic extension of the idea of the psychical bars the way completely to any exact formulation of a science of the psychical.

(4) It is sometimes supposed that justice will be done to all the facts if we posit an unbroken mental series as the counterpart of the known continuity of material processes. But we have seen

that there is an inherent difficulty in the notion of psychical causation (*cf.* § 18. 4): a difficulty which leaves it at least very doubtful whether the desired end can be regarded as attainable, even in imagination, by this hypothetical extension of psychical values. If no causal connection is discoverable among the facts of the internal perception as given in experience, any attempt to extend the meaning of the phrase 'mental processes' must be declared hopeless from the outset. They cannot be defined except on the analogy of the facts of consciousness.

8. (5) But abstract monism also comes into collision with the teachings of empirical natural science. It completely ignores the line of division between the organic and the inorganic worlds, though no theory of development has as yet brought the two together. Now it is plain that no knowing subject can establish the presence of mental processes in the things or creatures outside of him except by analogical inference. And his inference becomes the more uncertain the less similarity there is between human expressive movements and the expressive movements of other creatures. Push the analogical expression as we will, it seems, from everything that we know at present, to be brought to a full and final stop at the elementary organism, the cell. The difference between the reaction of the cell to stimuli and the purely physico-chemical change of one inorganic body under the influence of another is so fundamental that the metaphysics which ignores it stands convicted, at the very least, of a disregard of facts.

We cannot, therefore, bring ourselves to believe that monism offers the most plausible metaphysical interpretation of existence. The result of our criticism of the different metaphysical schools so far has rather been to show that, as things are, dualism can lay claim to possess the greatest probability, since it accords best of all the metaphysical theories with the special sciences, and can also best meet the requirements of epistemology and logic. Æsthetical or ethical disinclination to a multiplicity of principles cannot under any circumstances furnish a theoretical argument against it (*cf.* § 15. 4). The least degree of probability, on the other hand, resides, if our criticism is sound, in the hypothesis of materialism.

Spiritualism would stand next to dualism in the order of probability. In most monistic metaphysics the monism tends, as a matter of fact, to shade off into spiritualism.

NOTE.—The term monism (doctrine of unity) has also been employed for the theory of the coincidence of God and the world, or *pantheism* (*cf.* § 22). And in epistemology we often hear to-day of a monism, in the sense of a belief in the original unity of the contents of knowledge, as contradistinguished from the dualistic separation of idea and object (*cf.* § 26).—There is no want of literature upon monism, but so great a lack of any thorough historical and systematic treatment of the position, that it seems best to make no mention here of publications in which it is discussed.

§ 20. *Mechanism and Teleology.*

1. Mechanism takes for its general principle of occurrence the blind and necessary connection of cause and effect, as typified in 'natural' causation. The point of view is called 'mechanistic' because all connections of this kind can be regarded in the last resort as laws of motion, and the science of the laws of motion is termed mechanics. Mechanism evidently stands in close relation to materialism (*cf.* § 16), and is, as a matter of fact, always found along with materialism in the history of philosophy. This is true of the very earliest form of materialism, the atomism of the ancient Greek philosophers. Leucippus and Democritus conceive of all occurrence under the form of processes of movement, consisting partly in a free fall of the atoms, partly in the modification produced in this by mutual pressure or impact. In modern philosophy, Hobbes (§ 2. 5) and the author of the *Système de la nature* (§ 16. 2) are equally convinced of the universal validity of mechanism. However, it is not only materialists who support the theory; it has found favour with monists as well (*cf.* § 19). Spinoza, *e.g.*, is as staunch a champion of mechanism as Hobbes. There is no free will to interrupt the connection of cause and effect; nor is there any end or purpose in things by which the course of events is directed. For Spinoza, however,

the mechanism of cause and effect coincides further with the logical relation of reason and inference; and thus arises the confusion between thought and existence which is so characteristic of his philosophy.

2. A similarly exclusive formulation of teleological metaphysics is not to be discovered in the history of philosophy. Wherever the teleological principle is accepted, mechanism, too, receives recognition as one, though only a subordinate, form of occurrence. We see this, *e.g.*, in Plato, the first indubitable teleologist in metaphysical history. In his view, everything has arisen and everything developes in accordance with purposes, prototypes of things, 'ideas.' But at the same time his estimate of the immediate occasion of each separate phase or stage of progress proceeds strictly by way of cause and effect. The antithesis of idea and matter is also expressed in the statement that the realm of ideas is governed by reason and purpose, but the material domain by a blind necessity.

The co-ordination of the two forms of occurrence appears much more clearly and precisely in Aristotle. On the one hand we find change in the natural world in the form of movement through space; this is subject to a purely mechanical uniformity. On the other, we have to conceive of the goal of all development as a growth of form, of energy, of the actual principle. In this way a teleological uniformity is superimposed upon the mechanical. Nature does not act without purpose, but turns everything to some useful end; and this general purposiveness can be explained only upon the hypothesis that nature itself makes towards a definite goal, or works for the accomplishment of a definite purpose. Hence mechanical causes, though indispensable conditions of, or aids to, the realisation of this purpose, must not be regarded as 'causes' in the strict sense of the word. The real causes are the *causae finales*.

The Aristotelian teleology is typical of a whole series of similar theories. Leibniz, *e.g.*, essays to reconcile mechanism and teleology in the same way; and in the present century Lotze is the exponent of an essentially similar position.

3. Kant was the first to attempt an analysis of the idea of purpose by a critical and empirical method, and to test its applicability to natural phenomena. His *Kritik der Urtheilskraft* treats of the teleological as well as of the æsthetic judgment (*cf.* § 10. 3). He describes the purposiveness of a natural object as both objective and internal or immanent: it consists in the congruence of the object with its idea, or the determination of the parts by the whole. The teleological view of nature is first suggested by the organism, all of whose members and functions are of service for the preservation of the individual and the race, and whose various constituent parts are constantly acting and reacting one upon another. From the organism it is extended over the whole of nature, which can also be regarded as a purposive system. The goal of natural development at large is the moral subject; for it is not till we arrive at morality that the question 'To what end?' ceases to have a meaning. The teleological view does not conflict with the mechanical if we are careful to make the idea of purpose a regulative (*cf.* § 4. 3) and not a constitutive principle. As a subjective maxim of the faculty of judgment, teleology will, therefore, find its most useful application in cases where a mechanical interpretation is not (or not at present) possible. The two views will accordingly supplement, and even assist each other, —teleology serving as an heuristic principle of causal investigation. To an intellect higher than our own the difference between the two standpoints would entirely disappear. Modern logicians, especially Sigwart and Wundt, define the relation between finality and causality in very much the same way.

4. The cause of mechanism rose considerably in philosophical favour when the phenomena of life were declared to be one and all capable of mechanical interpretation. Descartes had paved the way for this view by his assertion that animals are automata or machines. But his theory was opposed by a *vitalistic* hypothesis, which looked upon all the phenomena of life as ruled by a peculiar principle—the 'vital force,' as it was termed—and thus drew a sharp line of division between the living and the lifeless or 'mechanical.' Schelling's natural philosophy, in particular, uses

this 'organic' theory to explain the development and forms of the animal kingdom. But the 'vital force' was rather a hindrance than an aid to scientific investigation. As a principle of explanation it was just as useless in the organic field as the various mental faculties of the eighteenth century psychology proved to be in the field of mind. It was, therefore, a great step in advance when modern physiologists, with Lotze at their head, made mechanism a regulative principle in the study of the processes of life. Almost simultaneously with this revulsion against vitalism in physiology came the introduction of mechanistic ideas into psychology. The old mental faculties were finally abandoned, and Herbart embarked upon no less an undertaking than the writing of a mechanics of mind (*cf.* § 8. 7). Not long after, the belief, still widely current, that the manifestation of a transcendent purpose could be observed in the development of the animal series, was destroyed by the Darwinian theory of descent. Not by any economical limitation to the changes that lead to a desired end, so the theory tells us, but by a course of the most lavish extravagance, does the animal kingdom come by slow degrees to wear the garb of purpose. He alone is of influence for further development who can survive in the struggle for existence; and he alone can survive in that struggle whose organisation is in a high degree purposive. But this purposive organisation is merely a special case among many others, and realised only through accidental variation in the different members of a family or species.—In quite recent times, however, there has been a revival of vitalistic tendencies. The internal conditions of development do not receive their due recognition at the hands of the Darwinians, and the problem of life is still as far from a solution as it was a hundred years ago.

5. They are but superficial observers and wholly lacking in historical knowledge who declare with so much emphasis that teleology has lost its right to existence as mechanism has grown. Leibniz believed in a far wider dominion of mechanical laws than we can prove for them to-day, and Kant saw clearly enough what the main course of modern progress would be. Lotze, too, despite his brilliant criticism of the doctrine of 'vital force,' and his

purely mechanical conception of organic life, was a teleologist from beginning to end. It must then be possible somehow to reconcile the two interpretations of natural occurrence. To test this conclusion we will try to find out a little more definitely what is meant by mechanism and teleology, or causality and finality.

(1) We understand by *causality* a relation of dependence of such a character that one member of it, the cause, must be conceived of as invariably preceding the other member, the effect, in time (*cf.* §§ 16. 7; 18. 3). This definition does not say that the relation between two processes which may be called cause and effect is wholly unequivocal. True, we assume that one and the same cause must always produce a quite definite effect (the reader will not forget, of course, that there are cases in which different circumstances co-operate to produce an observed effect). But the converse of the proposition, that one and the same effect can only be produced by one equally constant cause, has by no means the same claim to universal validity. On the contrary, we are taught by a whole series of facts that disparate processes may produce the same effect. We can, therefore, as a general rule, easily infer effects, assuming definite causes to be given, but cannot so certainly argue from a given effect to the causes which must have led to it.

6. In the realm of inanimate nature we are enabled to overcome this difficulty, owing to the uniform character which the causal relation there assumes. Astronomy, physics and chemistry can accordingly infer causes from given effects as definitely and confidently as they can derive effects from causes. But in the organic world the case is very different. Here it is always the effect that is given,—whether we term it 'life' or the 'preservation of the individual' or the 'preservation of the species' or 'form.' The factors which produce the effect are, on the other hand, so manifold and so inconstant that we can never argue with any certainty to a *particular* causal connection. A simple mechanistic theory of vital phenomena is consequently both impracticable and valueless, however sure we may be that, at bottom, organic processes are as universally subject as inorganic to the law of cause and effect.

(2) *Finality*, too, is a relation of dependence, so that it does not stand in absolute opposition to causality. Its two terms are the end and the means; and as strict a connection is assumed to obtain between them as between cause and effect. Human voluntary action looks towards ends, and realises them by appropriately chosen means. The first peculiarity of this procedure is, then, the anticipation of an effect: it is essential to an idea of purpose that the effect be foreseen, and the idea itself starts the causal series whose end or goal is judged to be the anticipated effect. Secondly, however, it nearly always implies a choice between various means or paths, all of which lead to the same end. Such means, as referred to the effect that is producible by them, are termed *purposive*. And we further distinguish degrees of purposiveness according to the greater or less degree of certainty, rapidity and ease with which the different possible means can produce the particular effect.

7. The parallel idea of degrees within the causal relation is entirely foreign to the mechanistic theory. This confines itself to the unequivocal, quite definite causal connections, in which one thing is simply 'cause,' and another simply 'effect.' On the other hand, it is of the very essence of the teleological standpoint to assume a great variety of means and contrivances, all leading, though not all with equal directness, to one and the same end. We must not suppose, however, that anticipation of the effect, which seems to be possible only to a thinking and willing creature, is one of its necessary preconditions. For it is where our actions show the nearest approach to an unequivocal causal connection (habitual or impulsive actions) that teleological considerations are least in evidence; although even here purposive ideas are not wanting. Nor must we think that it is necessary for the teleological judgment that the causal connection of means and end be completely known; it is enough if we have an empirical series or regular arrangement of processes. Mechanism and teleology are thus seen to supplement each other in a very useful way.

8. Fuller justice would be done to both theories if they were

not opposed to one another under the names of 'causality' and 'finality.' Causality should rather rank as the superior concept, to which mechanism and finality are alike subordinate: mechanism being defined as 'unequivocally determined' and finality as 'equivocally determined causality.' The idea of purpose leads to a metaphysical transcendence only if we assume, in every case of its application to natural phenomena, the same anticipation of the effect that appears in human voluntary action. If we assert, *e.g.*, that every organism possesses ideas of end, whereby it must regulate its actions, or if we conceive of the universe as ruled by a supreme intelligence, which lays down its own ends and realises them in the series of natural occurrences, then we are undoubtedly guilty of introducing a metaphysical transcendence. It is to be noted, however, that while the former of these hypotheses is opposed to the facts of experience, the latter is easily harmonised with the results of the special sciences. This is true even if we do not venture, with Kant, to define the end towards which the whole course of nature trends. Indeed, the real difficulties of a theological appendix to a theory of the universe arise simply from the strange attempts that have been made to define the ends which a divine intelligence may have proposed to itself in the government of the world.—It follows from our whole discussion that 'purposeless,' in the strict sense of the word, must either mean 'mechanical,' or refer to some teleologically wrong relation that we have assumed to obtain between certain natural processes or arrangements.

9. It may be objected to the foregoing account of the mechanistic and teleological theories that it does not bring to light the real difference between them. Even in the inorganic sphere, in the domain of physical and chemical processes pure and simple, the same effect can be produced in a great variety of ways. A particular temperature, *e.g.*, can be brought about by friction, by radiation and by the electric current.

(1) Really, however, the effect in all these cases is not a constant phenomenon, always realised under the most varied

conditions, but as transient and accidental, if one may use those terms, as the causes which give rise to it.

(2) Moreover, the phenomenon of self-preservation has no true analogue in the inorganic sphere, where a complex is not marked off or protected from its surroundings, and where, consequently, we cannot stress any single function of the totality of interconnected parts and processes as determined by or determining all the rest. Nor do we find in the inanimate world the characteristic process of vicarious function, the substitution of one special function for another.

(3) Finally, it is not correct to say in the inorganic sphere that the effect is better known than the cause, still less that it is the only thing given. The effect is never anything more than a transition point, which is just about as accessible to human observation as its conditions.—We see from all these reasons why it is that the teleological view is applied only to the organic world, or why, if extended to the great whole of nature, it is valid only for certain aspects, in certain principles.

There can be no doubt, however, that judgments of value have their part to play alongside of the purely theoretical arguments. Life and the preservation of individual or species seem more valuable than death and annihilation; and it is almost a matter of course to us to regard them as the effects which are to be realised by all possible means. We have purposely steered our discussion clear of this point of view, because we are here concerned only with the theoretical question, and the facts themselves furnish us with matter enough to explain and justify the distinction drawn between mechanism and teleology. It cannot be denied that the teleological hypothesis has been and may be advantageously employed by the science of life as an heuristic principle, and a principle of explanation of complex phenomena: it cannot be denied that the introduction of a similar conception in the sciences of inanimate nature has too often resulted in grave error. To understand this we must appeal to the interconnection of the facts themselves, not to any scale of values that may have been applied to the facts.

LITERATURE.

C. Sigwart, *Der Kampf gegen den Zweck.* In the *Kleine Schriften.* Vol. II., 2nd ed., 1889.

P. Janet, *Les causes finales.* 2nd ed., 1882.

F. Erhardt, *Mechanismus und Teleologie.* 1890.

E. König, *Die Entwicklung des Causalproblems.* 2 vols., 1888-90.

§ 21. *Determinism and Indeterminism.*

1. The antithesis of determinism and indeterminism bears a certain relationship to that of mechanism and teleology. Determinism asserts the universal validity of the causal connection, reduces everything to cause and effect, condition and consequence, motive and action; indeterminism, relying upon certain facts of the moral life, assumes that 'free' acts, acts not causally conditioned, are at least possible. Nevertheless, the relation between the two antitheses is not very close. Mechanism and teleology can both be harmonised with a causal theory; and as a matter of fact the history of philosophy shows us not only mechanists but a number of teleologists too among the adherents of determinism. The one obvious connection is that of mechanism and determinism. Indeed, the mechanists are apt to let their determinism rise to *fatalism*, which holds that the world is a closed and immutable chain of causes and effects, beyond the reach of modification by any action of the individual, and that everything that happens has been predetermined and calculated out, as if by some great mathematical formula. The author of the *Système de la nature* (*cf.* § 16. 2), *e.g.*, seeks strongly to impress upon his reader the value of the fatalistic theory. To combat it we need only call to mind the arguments of the preceding Section (§ 20. 6ff.). We saw there that there were connections in the world other than those of mere mechanical causation; and it follows that we cannot ignore all the various ways in which the action of separate individuals may help to determine what we call the course of events. Indeterminism is ordinarily affirmed only in regard to the *human* will, because it is only there that the psychological process of choice plays any important part, and that the moral

and legal ideas of merit and guilt, responsibility and accountability, can find application.

2. The problem of the freedom of the will received no large share of attention in ancient philosophy. The questions raised and answered by the Greek philosophers were questions of good and bad, not of merit and demerit. They did not, as a rule, place the ideal of moral action so high as to make it seem unattainable, or realisable only in a few fortunate cases; and so their ethics had no need to consider the painful contrast of action and intention, when with all desire for the highest good a man falls far short of its achievement. But the antithesis of will and deed was inevitable. Historically, it is a product of Christianity (*cf.* § 9. 4 f.). Ever since it appeared, the conflict of determinism and indeterminism has coloured the whole history of philosophy. The principal stages in the controversy will be considered in the following paragraphs.

We find in Spinoza a vigorous denial of the freedom of the will: his mechanistic metaphysics leads him, of course, to a clear-cut determinism. The feeling of freedom which we experience in our actions is simply due to ignorance of the causes. Just as all the properties of a triangle follow from the nature of the figure, so the whole behaviour of every living creature is the necessary consequence of its nature. Leibniz' determinism takes a slightly different form. He distinguishes between mechanical constraint and determination by motives. Motives can no more influence human volition and action by way of mechanical compulsion than a geometrical proposition can compel a man to recognise its truth. They move us without compelling us (*inclinent sans nécessiter*). The articles of faith put forth by the philosophy of the illumination and its rational religion included belief in the freedom of the will, along with that in the immortality of the soul and the existence of God. The adherents of this school tried to prove the possibility of free will by figures and analogies. Thus Tetens (*cf.* § 8. 7) compares the will to a steel spring. The direction in which it works depends upon the objects which accident has placed around it, but the force of its action is an original and native character. In the case of the will, even the direction of resolve is self-determined. Just as the water can run out of a full vessel only at the place where an opening is made, but for the outflow to happen there must already have been a pressure of the water exerted upon that particular point, so the will is to be conceived of as potentially active in the direction in which its force is actually manifested upon the occasion of some accidental circumstance.

3. Kant places indeterminism upon a new and different basis (*cf.* § 9. 8). The fact from which his ethics sets out is the moral law, the categorical imperative, with its peremptory demand for unconditional obedience. A fact of this kind would be unintelligible, he says, if we were not able at every moment to postulate the possibility of the law's fulfilment. Since, now, the universal rule of causal connection in the world of experience renders any such absolute possibility inconceivable, we must hold that the requirements of freedom are realised in the world of the transcendent, of the thing-in-itself. In other words, the will, in itself, is free; but the will as phenomenon (as object of experience) is woven into the inviolable network of cause and effect. Schopenhauer has framed a very similar theory. He, too, takes his stand upon the distinction between phenomena, with their limitations of space, time and causality, and the invisible, inconceivable world of things in themselves. He dates the freedom of the will, however, from the moment of the first decision taken by the developing individual. The character of the individual is thereby determined for all succeeding time: his actions proceed from the empirical causality of an unchangeable character. Herbart, on the other hand, declares that determinism is the only tenable position, since no other admits of any ordered system of human education, or prevents the dissolution of all things into arbitrariness and unreason. Lotze, however, returns to indeterminism. We cannot speak of a moral judgment of human actions, of accountability and responsibility, unless we assume a freedom of the will. Freedom

is an inexplicable fact: but we must and can prove that it is harmonisable with the empirical connection of cause and effect. Determinism is the dominant theory in the psychology, metaphysics and ethics of the present day, although indeterminism still holds its own in criminal jurisprudence, theological dogmatics and popular opinion.

4. The problem of the freedom of the will can be considered under three different aspects: metaphysical, psychological and ethical. We must note, in the first place, that no one would have thought of proposing any such exception to the general law of causal connection if definite facts of the moral life had not seemed to demand it. For the *metaphysical* considerations upon which indeterminism is based are both precarious and inadequate. Metaphysicians affirm and attempt to prove the possibility of freedom, but that is all: and the way in which that is done is neither scientifically nor logically satisfactory. They either call metaphors to their assistance, or posit two contrasting worlds,—a sphere of phenomena and a sphere of things in themselves. Freedom lies beyond the borders of knowledge or demonstration. It would not be freedom, in the true sense of the word, if it were necessarily deducible from given assumptions, or could be brought within the scope of some more general uniformity. The argument is sometimes urged that necessity is simply a product of our understanding, of that by which we know the world, and that the world itself has no part or lot in it. The reply is that it is impossible to say anything of the things that exist independently of our apprehension or estimation. Either we dispense with any kind of positive definition of things in themselves: in which case we leave no room for freedom; or we look upon them as knowable: in which case an uniformity of connection among them is inevitable. Moreover, this antithesis of phenomenon and thing-in-itself can never justify freedom in the special sense of freedom of the will; and it is only with this that the moralist and the metaphysician who has entered his service are concerned: they care nothing for a freedom which should be shared by all things alike, the falling stone as well as the choosing will.

Nor is the case very different with the *psychological* arguments for indeterminism. The fact from which the psychological theory sets out is that of choice between various actions which appear equally possible. But introspection often shows that there was really a quite definite reason why the particular motive should prove effectual; and we are but following an accepted scientific plan if, in cases where perception or memory is not conscious of this preponderance of definite reasons, we nevertheless infer by analogy that the reasons must have been there.

5. Our internal experience is throughout of so fragmentary a character that this inference does not really present the least difficulty. What we ordinarily call 'character,' *e.g.*, is not a sum of clearly analysable processes, but a force in which the entire course of an individual development is concentrated. The little of it that comes to the surface of consciousness hardly helps us even to guess at its full wealth of contents and energy. And the incongruity thus shown to exist between internal experience and its substrate is further evidenced by another undeniable fact of our mental life, viz., its high degree of independence of external or accidental influences. The simplest instance of our power to resist the constraint of the external world is that of following and holding by the attention a contents in itself weak and inconsiderable, despite the presence of other and far stronger stimuli. The scholar's absorption in mental work, and the poet's engagement in artistic production, close the door of consciousness, so that external occurrences of incomparably greater intensity may appeal in vain for notice. Fatalism entirely overlooks these facts; and determinism is not inclined, as a rule, to give them the emphasis that they deserve. They are clear evidence of freedom in the sense of independence of external influences. At the same time, this freedom is evidently not identical with the freedom affirmed by indeterminism. This freedom shows itself in cases where there can be no question whatsoever of a legal or ethical judgment (*e.g.*, in animals); and it certainly never means independence of all reasons. On the other hand, it is this freedom that we have in mind when we say that it is the task of reflection or reason to

direct the volition and action of mankind. Experience shows that the control of external circumstance extends over a wide range of conduct, though its limits are very different in different individuals; so that we cannot entertain any doubt as to the possibility of 'free' decisions in this empirical meaning of 'freedom.' Where a special interest or feeling of value is present to enhance the strength of the subjective motives, they may be regarded, under normal psychological conditions, as practically irresistible.

6. The *ethical* judgments which indeterminism invokes are the judgments of merit and guilt (*cf.* § 9. 11). The resolution of the good will, which might have resolved differently, is meritorious; the resolution of the bad will, which might have resolved differently, is blameworthy. In both cases it is the addition "which might have resolved differently" that contains the characteristic assumption of freedom: the predicates 'good' and 'bad,' which simply express a *quality* of will, have nothing to do with the question at issue. We can speak of actions as good or bad without being obliged to assume that they are undetermined. We desire to lay the greater emphasis upon this fact since, in our own opinion, the two attributes represent the two extremes of moral value. The consideration of different possibilities always presupposes a certain internal struggle; and we would not award the palm of highest morality to him who can only bring himself to good resolve by victory over rival tendencies. Rather is a noble simplicity of goodness, that seems the necessary outgrowth of the inward nature, the highest goal of morality in man. We may suppose, too, that the goodness which springs into being without struggle against baseness or indifference loses nothing of its inherent force, whereas a meritorious deed always implies a loss of moral energy. On the other hand, the ideas of merit and guilt give us our sole means of estimating the *intensity* of the moral will; and both in daily life and in the court of justice the degree of criminal or virtuous endeavour is judged by the quality, number and strength of the motives opposing a determinate voluntary action. The significance of the two con-

cepts in this connection is generally overlooked; as a matter of fact, it makes them very important factors in moral appreciation.

7. Indeterminism, however, lays stress upon the statement that the agent might have decided otherwise than he did, and appeals to the old definition of necessity, which says that that is necessary whose opposite is impossible. If, now, something else than what actually happened was possible, the event cannot be called necessary; and as we are not able to conceive of causal connection without this attitude of necessity, cannot either have been causally conditioned. The reply is that the idea of possibility does not in any way contradict the idea of necessity, and that consequently the definition of necessity formulated by Ch. Wolff cannot be universally valid. A thing is 'possible' when certain, but not all, of its conditions are realised, and when not it alone, but many other things are dependent upon those particular conditions. Thus an occurrence is not unequivocally determined by the enumeration of its general conditions. We must know other 'special' conditions besides, if we are to be able to say that just this and nothing else will take place. Hence the necessity of one particular process is perfectly compatible with the possibility of various other processes. For to say that other events are possible is simply to abstract in thought from the special conditions by which that which actually occurs is adequately and unambiguously explained. A thing can only be declared impossible when no single condition of its appearance is present. We can therefore (and rules are given for it in the logics) argue from a fact to its possibility, and from the necessity of a fact to its reality,—which, of course, includes possibility and a great deal more. On the other hand, it would be quite wrong to deduce any kind of impossibility—say, the impossibility of the opposite—from a necessity. We are, on the contrary (to return to our special question) fully justified in maintaining the possibility of a different action from that actually performed, since every process of choice points to conditions (motives) which, if they had been present alone or in greater strength, would undoubtedly have diverted the activity into a different channel.

8. The conclusion of this logical argument is, then, that the moral judgments, which are concentrated, so to speak, in the ideas of merit and guilt, are entirely compatible with the full determination of the resolves actually taken by the will. Those who know anything of the complexity of the psychophysical factors concerned in voluntary action will readily admit that our bodily and mental organisation contains the possibility of very various actions indeed. Moreover, the fact of choice proves to superfluity that we can aim at a great variety of ends. It is, therefore, impossible to dispute the validity of the assertion that the agent might have acted otherwise than he did. The same result follows from the ideas, more important in law than in ethics, of responsibility and accountability. That every man is the doer of his own deeds, and, a normal constitution presupposed, has a much greater share than accidental external circumstances in the performance of an action, is a truth that we may gather, without need of further explanation or confirmation, from the preceding discussion. The freedom, *i.e.*, which the judge attributes to the criminal, is not the freedom of indeterminism, but independence of external determinants to action, and a mind in which considerations of the importance of the law of the state or of morality have free play and full force. If any other kind of freedom were intended, it would be absurd to try and determine the age of responsibility; and if the will were unconditioned, it could not be affected by intoxication and insanity, which are universally regarded as lessening the gravity of an offence, and as relieving the agent of accountability. On the other hand, the assumption of an unmotived and unregulated resolve does away with any kind of stability or continuity in internal development or in the relations of a man to his fellows. Indeterminism really aims a blow at the moral and legal judgment of mankind.

9. Lastly, no support can be found for indeterminism in the denial of a strict psychical causality (*cf.* § 18. 4). For this does not mean that there is no uniformity at all in the sphere of mind: it does not mean, therefore, that the choosing will is unconditioned. The psychologist defends his practice of using certain physical

processes as an aid to a scientific knowledge of the mental life by asserting that a direct causal connection among the phenomena of consciousness cannot be demonstrated. Thus the power of the will to resist the encroachment of accidental stimuli, even when intensive (*cf.* § 21. 5),—an undeniable fact of experience,—would remain completely inexplicable if we should insist on looking to introspection alone to furnish us with a means of explanation. For ethics and criminal law, however, it is entirely indifferent whether the fact be referred exclusively to definite conscious processes, or also to something unconscious, something given in the psychophysical organisation, behind conscious processes. The denial of a special psychical causality is, therefore, of no importance whatever for the question of the freedom of the will. On the other hand, Leibniz is undoubtedly right when he points out the difference between mechanical constraint and psychical motivisation. The process of choice and our independence of external determinants to action show little trace indeed of the uniformity and simplicity of the causal connection as posited by mechanism (*cf.* § 20).

LITERATURE.

C. Gutberlet, *Die Willensfreiheit und ihre Gegner.* 1893. (Written from the libertarian standpoint).

J. H. Scholten, *Der freie Wille.* Trs. into German by Manchot. 1874. (Defends determinism).

M. W. Drobisch, *Die moralische Statistik und die menschliche Willensfreiheit.* 1867. (Deterministic in the Herbartian sense).

Fr. J. Mach, *Die Willensfreiheit des Menschen.* 1887. New (titular) ed., 1894. (Takes neutral ground).

L. Traeger, *Wille, Determinismus, Strafe.* 1895. (Deterministic. Treats more particularly of practical questions, which it handles very ably).

§ 22. *The Theological Schools in Metaphysics.*

1. Metaphysicians are also divided into hostile camps by their attitude toward the questions connected with the idea of God. The theories whose philosophical aspect we have here to consider are those of *theism*, *deism*, *pantheism* and *atheism*. The first three, which make the idea of God positive, are included under the

general name of *monotheism*. In the history of religion we meet with other forms of belief, such as *fetichism* and *polytheism;* but these have never found support or representation in a philosophical metaphysics, and so need not be discussed in the present connection. Certain minor divisions may be distinguished, however, within the four principal schools, and especially under the somewhat vague rubric of pantheism.

The various theological beliefs are pretty closely related to the more general metaphysical theories (§ 14. 3). Theism ordinarily goes along with spiritualism and dualism; pantheism has an affinity to monism; and atheism is a natural consequence of materialism. The theist is, of course, always teleologist as well. It is clear even from this summary description that deism is the most colourless view of all; it harmonises with the greatest number of general theories. Practically, it is equivalent to atheism. For if we merely postulate a divine being to serve as the final cause of the world, we cannot take up any religious or ethical attitude to him, except that of an indefinite reverence. Theism and pantheism, on the other hand, rarely receive detailed treatment within the limits of theoretical philosophy. They acquire their real meaning from the moral attributes which are predicated of the divine being as highest ethical ideal, and from the religious attitude of veneration, worship, etc., which mankind takes up towards it.

2. Theism is the belief which has the longest list of names attached to it in the history of philosophy. To mention only the greatest, Plato and Aristotle among the ancients, and Descartes, Leibniz, Kant, Herbart and Lotze among the moderns, all represent some form of theistic metaphysics. The common element in all the different systems is the conception of a personal being, who is the cause of the world and the director of its course in time. Where attempts have been made to formulate a more definite idea of the qualities of this being, they have always arisen from some practical religious interest. Thus we are accustomed to speak of God as all-powerful, all-wise and all-good; but the last attribute is, really, entirely foreign to theoretical

philosophy. The two other predicates may, however, be looked upon as postulates of metaphysical knowledge, since they indicate characteristics which must be present if the being who is characterised is to be judged adequate to his task in the universe. The emphasis laid by certain writers—Chr. H. Weisse († 1866), H. Ulrici († 1884), and J. H. Fichte († 1879)—upon the part played by ethics in the construction of a theistic metaphysics has won for their doctrine the name of *ethical theism*. The arguments upon which a given theism is based are, naturally, dependent upon the special metaphysical views of its author. They are not the same for Plato as for Aristotle, for Descartes as for Leibniz, for Kant as for Herbart or Lotze.

It is usual to bring together the principal arguments for theism urged by the different philosophers under the title of 'proofs of the existence of God.' We may distinguish an ontological, a cosmological, a teleological (physico-theological), a logical and a moral proof. Another proof ordinarily added to the list—the proof *e consensu gentium*—need not be considered here, as it is valid only from the point of view of deism. There is, however, hardly a single one of the remaining five, with the exception of the moral proof, that applies exclusively to theism; they serve the cause of deism and pantheism every whit as well.

3. (1) The various forms of the *ontological* proof need not be separately discussed here. They all reduce, in essentials, to an inference of existence from idea. One form, *e.g.*, starts out from the idea of God as the *ens perfectissimum*, and then argues that absolute perfection is not compatible with non-existence. Existence, *i.e.*, is a necessary attribute of the idea of an all-perfect being. Descartes and Leibniz are fully agreed upon this view. True, Leibniz declares, as against Descartes, that the first thing to do is to prove the idea of a most real or most perfect being to be free from all inherent contradiction; but this does not touch the essential part of the argument. If the idea is free from contradiction, *i.e.*, possible, the reality of the object which it designates follows just as necessarily for him as for Descartes.

The pre-Kantian philosophers of the eighteenth century (Crusius, *e.g.*, in Germany and Hume in England) raised valid objections to the ontological argument. Kant, whose criticism of the proofs of the existence of God has won him the title of 'the all-destroyer,' simply put these objections in more comprehensive form, giving them a general epistemological reference. Existence, he says, is never one attribute of an idea along with others. It is a predicate which we can apply only to objects of possible experience or perception, and does not add any new determination to the idea of those objects. There is, therefore, no difference between the possible and the actual in the sense that the conceptual contents of the former lack one attribute (the *complementum possibilitatis*) which attaches to that of the former: conceptually considered, the two are exactly alike. Hence we may argue without more ado from the possibility of an idea to its existence, but not to the reality or existence of the object that corresponds to it.

4. Hegel gave a peculiar turn to the ontological proof. The absolute being at once idea and existence, it follows as a matter of course that the thought of God has its real counterpart. As thus formulated, the validity of the ontological argument stands and falls with the validity of the Hegelian principle of panlogism. And unfortunately that principle is wrong. Lotze adduces a logical consideration, which, though he does not regard it as constituting an actual proof, follows a line of thought similar to that of the ontological argument. If the greatest did not *exist*, he says, the *greatest* would not exist; and it is inconceivable that the greatest thing conceivable should not *exist*. Persuasive as the word-play is, however, we need not spend time to show that it does not take us beyond the circle of our own thoughts or of the conceivable: it does not demonstrate existence. Closely akin to the ontological argument is Descartes' view that our thought can give rise only to what is adequate to us or it. But this always wears the character of finitude, limitation, imperfection. If, now, we form the idea of an infinite, perfect being, the idea cannot be a product of our own thinking, but must issue from a reality which corresponds to it. And the truth of God then becomes, in its turn, the warrant for the truth of our thought.

(2) Related to this, again, is the *logical* proof offered by Trendelenburg († 1872). Human thought knows itself as finite thought, but still strives to surmount every barrier. It knows itself dependent upon things, yet proceeds as if they were determinable by it alone. This assurance would be self-contradictory, if truth were not postulated in the real, or conceivability in things. Thought would be but the play of chance or the boldness of despair, if God, the truth, were not the common source and the band of union between thought and things. Here, too, it is not difficult to see where the spring is made from conceivability or truth to its objective guarantee in a true being. It would really be much more correct to say: since all human understanding and knowledge are adapted only to the given or the properties of the given, they can find natural and legitimate application only within the limits of the given. If we seek to go beyond these limits, we may come to new words and definitions, but cannot come to a larger measure of understanding.

5. (3) The *cosmological* proof argues from the fact that the world exists to a final cause of the world, in order to avoid the assumption of the eternity of matter or motion. Aristotle found a typical expression for this proof in his demand for a *primum movens*; and Plato had previously emphasised the creative activity of God. The proof constantly recurs in modern philosophy, though no new reasons are adduced in support of it. The search for causes brings to light more and more remote conditions of the course of the universe. Then, finally, our knowledge of things comes to a standstill; we are face to face with something which cannot be explained. But facts which cannot be deduced from other facts bear the stamp of chance or accident upon them. If, then, we assert that matter and its movements cannot be further explained, we have reached in them a fact which is in the air, so to say,—a fact which is causeless. And if we further attempt to remove this last fact from the realm of chance, we are led to the assumption of a being who can be defined as creator of the world, *causa sui*, absolute intellect, etc.

(*a*) This proof, too, received very thorough refutation at the hands of Kant. Causality, he says, is a category applicable only to phenomena, to the empirically possible. It cannot carry us beyond the range of given fact, to a transcendent cause of the world. Furthermore, although the idea of chance is valid for the individual fact of experience, it does not follow from this that the whole universe may be regarded as a mere accident, which must have its necessary cause in a being outside of itself.

(*b*) It is also to be noted that the cosmological proof does not furnish any argument for theism, but rather suggests a simple deism. Theoretically, too, nothing is gained for knowledge by this step beyond the last given fact of the universe. Whether we stop short at the eternity of matter and motion, or regard both as the work of a divine being, is indifferent for theory; for an actual derivation of the world from the creative activity of God would seem to be impossible, and his definition as *causa sui* gives our thought a purely arbitrary resting-place.

(*c*) But, finally, the ceaseless advance of causal enquiry into the conditions of the given points merely to the observance of a regulative principle (§ 4. 3), by which we are forbidden to pause here or there in our search, and taught to regard every resting-place as provisional, a place to recruit our strength for still further investigation.

6. (4) The *teleological* proof argues from the purposive arrangement of the universe or of nature to a creator who frames and realises purposes. And since purposes admit of empirical demonstration only as ideas in a mind, this creator must be further conceived of as intellect. The teleological proof appears in ancient philosophy, and is declared by Kant to be at once the clearest of all and the worthiest of consideration. It also furnished Herbart with the starting-point for his discussions in the field of the philosophy of religion. But, like the two preceding, it must be judged to be inadequate. In the first place, as Kant shows, we can argue from it only to an architect, a planner of the universe; for the purposiveness of nature is manifested in its form, not in its contents. Secondly, Kant says, the teleological hypothesis is a subjective, regulative principle, and cannot be employed for

transcendent conclusions. Lastly, it is doubtful (*cf.* § 20. 7) whether we may interpret a teleological theory to mean that an intellect furnished with purposive ideas is the necessary presupposition of an explanation of the world. Empirically, it is only the phenomena of life that suggest the idea of a purposive arrangement of parts and functions; the teleological proof, on the other hand, regards the whole of nature as a system of purposes. Here again, then, we cannot really speak of a 'proof.'

It has sometimes been urged that although no one of these arguments is sufficient in itself, nevertheless, all taken together deserve the title of proof. The plea does not hold, if only for the reason that the 'proofs' are by no means independent, but (as Kant pointed out) really presuppose one another. The cosmological proof refers back to the ontological, and the teleological to both the others. And if the foundation is insecure, that which is built upon the foundation must surely be insecure also.

7. (5) The *moral* proof of the existence of God argues either from the existence of an absolute moral law to a lawgiver, or from the incongruity of virtue and happiness to an all-good and all-powerful being who is able to harmonise them. But (*a*) the fact of an absolute moral law is by no means assured or universally valid; and (*b*) attempts have been made of late, and made with success, to explain moral norms from an evolutionary standpoint. Either of these objections is sufficient to rob the inference of a personal lawgiver of any binding force that it may seem to possess. In any event, however, the empirical incongruity between an existence in accordance with moral requirements and a life which completely satisfies the desires of the individual cannot be regarded as an adequate reason for the postulate of a divine justice. For (*a*) the argument simply implies a wish to see virtue rewarded with all the good things of life; and there have been times when the one certain indication of moral character has been found in the avoidance of 'happiness,' in contempt of these same good things. Moreover, (*b*) the inference involves a twofold transcendence. The proposed reconciliation requires not only a personal God, but the immortality of the individual as well.

The result of all this discussion, then, is entirely negative. No one of the five 'proofs' of the existence of God deserves its title; and the five together accomplish no more than each can do alone. On the other hand, nothing that we have said touches the question of the *possibility* of the ideas which culminate in theism, and of the *practical* interests which may lead to a theistic hypothesis, although they neither possess nor need to possess any theoretical validity. Theism did not grow up on the soil of a theoretical metaphysics, but had its source in religious motives, and as a theory of the universe has always been shaped by religious ideas. And no religion has allowed the demand for an explanation of the world to determine its theistic theory.

8. The first beginnings of *deism* can be traced back to Herbert of Cherbury († 1648). He wished to win recognition for a natural religion, a religion demanded and justified by reason, as contradistinguished from the historical religion that had authority for its foundation. No religion can lay claim to these titles unless it has found universal acceptance (by the *consensus omnium*). The concept of religion—that is, the common element in all its forms—is made the criterion of its truth. The contents of the ideas thus obtained are set forth by the author in five propositions, which are declared to be truly catholic, *i.e.*, universally valid principles. They affirm the existence of a supreme being, and the duty of worshipping him; assert that virtue and piety are the most important parts of the *cultus divinus;* accept the ideas of repentance and retribution; and profess expectation of reward and punishment in a future life. The founder of deism also held the strange belief, which persisted even into the eighteenth century, that primitive religion embodied this pure universal idea, and that the specific characters of the historical religions have come into being through the cunning and deception of individual men.

Deism was made much more definite by John Locke. He denied that there was any universal agreement as to the idea and worship of a divine being, and explained the concept of deity as formed by the combination and enhancement of the most estimable qualities of man. He based the existence of God upon the cosmological argument. The principal representatives of deism after Locke were J. Toland (*cf.* § 16. 2) and M. Tindal. From their time on it also found adherents in France and Germany. F. M. A. de Voltaire († 1778) and H. S. Reimarus († 1768) may be regarded as its most prominent exponents in the two countries.

Deism, which has found enthusiastic disciples in our own century (*e.g.*, Thomas Buckle, † 1862), rests in part upon the same arguments as theism. God is a transcendent being, supramundane, the creator of the universe: but he has ordered everything so well that any later interference in the course of events is not only unnecessary, but would seem to be incompatible with his dignity. There can be no doubt that, practically regarded, deism comes very near to atheism; for a personal attitude to a being who does not interfere in the course of the world can manifest itself only in quite general forms of veneration. Deism can no more be proven than theism, and the disadvantage under which it labours in consequence of its practical unfruitfulness has been the most important factor in its gradual disappearance. The world, it says, would be badly made, and God not a perfect being, if he were obliged constantly to devote himself to the control and improvement of the course of events. Naturally, it is especially hostile to miracles. But if the deist were consistent in his idea of God—whom he endows with attributes which are but faintly shadowed forth in man—he would have to confess that he can know absolutely nothing of God's purposes and intentions in the creation of the world, or of what is compatible or incompatible with his dignity.

9. *Pantheism*, on the other hand, is very widely held at the present day. It is the form of theology which appeals most strongly to the scientific adherents of monism (§ 19. 1). Hence, in view of the great variety of opinions included under the title of monism, we shall be apt to infer a corresponding diversity of pantheistic theories. We may, as a matter of fact,

distinguish between *particular* and *universal* pantheism, basing the distinction upon the different contents of the idea of God. Universal pantheism identifies the idea of God with that of the all, of the universe, without any further specification. Particular pantheism lays emphasis upon some definite aspect or attribute of the all, and of its connection with the idea of God. Thus the materialists who affirm the unity of God and the world hold a *naturalistic* pantheism, *i.e.*, a pantheism which regards external nature as the equivalent of the idea of God. The Stoics look upon the inner being of the world or the world-soul as God: theirs is a *spiritualistic* pantheism. J. G. Fichte's system, again, is an *ethical* pantheism; for him the moral order that runs through the universe represents the divine being. Hegel's belief that the absolute idea reflects the being of God is a *logical* pantheism. K. Chr. Fr. Krause (*cf.* § 9. 12) has tried to reconcile theism and pantheism in a *panentheism*, which places God at once above the world and in the world. And so on: the list does not by any means include all the different forms that pantheism has taken. Monism seems to owe its special attractiveness to a sort of kaleidoscopic variety; and the confused multiformity of pantheism is surely one of the chief reasons that it has found so many supporters in an age averse as the present is to keen and accurate thought.

10. Universal pantheism has found historical expression in two principal forms: in the philosophy of the Eleatics and of Spinoza. Xenophanes and Parmenides identify existence with the idea of God; and as there is nothing outside of or beyond existence, God is the universe. And Spinoza does not hesitate to speak (as Giordano Bruno spoke before him: *cf.* § 17. 2) of *deus sive natura.* He distinguishes a *natura naturans* and a *natura naturata* as two sides or aspects of this single nature. God is the creative principle, and the world the created, passive.—Universal pantheism is also found, more or less explicit, in treatises upon æsthetics and the philosophy of religion. The positive sensations or feelings which arise in consciousness when one is lost in contemplation of nature or of a work of art are interpreted as a resignation of self

to the universe, a renunciation of personality, the merging of the individual in his environment, so that he ceases, as it were, to be an individual, and becomes simply a part of the world. The frame of mind is wholesome enough, no doubt; but it does not furnish a sufficient reason for the acceptance of pantheistic doctrines. Atheism and theism are perfectly well able to explain the appearance of the sensations and feelings in question.

But this apart, pantheism has no better arguments to offer in defence of its position than theism had. We need not criticise what it has to say in detail, since the objections that we raised against the closely related theory of monism (*cf.* § 19) apply with very little change in the present connection. From the point of view of practical needs and interests, pantheism is far less satisfactory than theism; we cannot conceive of a personal, moral, or religious relation to the universe or an aspect of it, except in a very confused and fanciful way.

11. The final outcome of our discussion seems, then, to be a rejection of all the proofs for the existence of God, *i.e.*, an atheism. But we have merely wished to show that the necessity of the idea of God cannot be demonstrated by any theoretical argument, and that there is nothing in scientific investigation that necessarily takes us to it. It does not follow that there are no other reasons for rounding off our theory of the universe by a theological concept. And, as a matter of fact, all those who have included a positive definition of God within the limits of their philosophical system have laid the main emphasis upon the religious or ethical consequences which follow from it. Atheism, as set forth by L. Feuerbach († 1872) or by E. Dühring, is theoretically incontrovertible. But its inability to satisfy mankind, with all their ideals of moral conduct and all their religious needs, is reason enough for transcending or supplementing the powerlessness of theory to cope with it. And, after all, even when metaphysics has demonstrated or admitted that a particular theology cannot be proven, it has still a not unimportant task to perform: it must show the *possibility* of combining a theological hypothesis with all that we know of the universe from other

sources. That is a sorry kind of book-keeping which sets down the items of belief upon one page and the items of knowledge on the other, and never comes to any settlement or adjustment of the two. And we shall not break free of it till we have brought the assumptions or requirements of our moral and religious life into harmony with the results of theoretical knowledge. It is natural that the attempts at reconciliation, past and present, should occupy themselves for the most part with theistic doctrine: theism is the form of theology that accords best with our practical interests.

LITERATURE.

J. H. Fichte, *Die theistische Weltansicht und ihre Berechtigung.* 1873.

A. Drews, *Die deutsche Speculation seit Kant mit besonderer Rücksicht auf das Wesen des Absoluten und die Persönlichkeit Gottes.* 2 vols., 1893. 2nd ed., 1895. (The various philosophers are criticised from the standpoint of E. von Hartmann. The statement of their views is not always objective and just).

Cf. also the literature cited under § 11 (the philosophy of religion).

§ 23. *The Psychological Schools in Metaphysics.*

1. In the most recent works on psychology we find a twofold antithesis of metaphysical theories. On the one hand there is difference of opinion as to the nature of mind. The theory of *substantiality* posits a substance underlying the individual mental processes; the theory of *actuality* gives the name of mind to the sum total of mental processes themselves, as actually and immediately given in experience. In the second place there is difference of opinion as to the essential quality of the 'psychical.' *Intellectualism* asserts that the intellectual processes of perception, idea, thought, are the source or foundation of all the others. *Voluntarism* declares, on the contrary, that the phenomena of will, *i.e.*, impulses, passions, emotions, feelings, are the determining and primary elements of our inner experience.

The first attribute of *mind-substance* is the first attribute of substance in general,—stability. All the various 'states' of mind are phenomena or accidents of the permanent substance. Secondly, the existence of the mind-substance is self-constituted independent of other existences. It stands in reciprocal relation to them, but can return, so to speak, of its own initiative, anything that it suffers at their hands. Thirdly, the mind-substance is indestructible, and consequently immortal. Fourthly, it is often defined as a simple existence, *i.e.*, as something not compounded of parts, and therefore indivisible, unextended and immaterial; and also as something whose peculiar and intrinsic quality is incompatible with any kind of multiplicity. As against all this, the *actuality* theory affirms that the unitary connection of actual mental processes forming our experience at a particular moment *is* the mind, and that we have no right to speak of a vehicle of the separate phenomena of feeling, thinking, willing, etc., if we mean anything more than just this interweaving of them into a single general whole.

2. Descartes is the real founder of the theory of substantiality. Ancient philosophy identified the mind with the vital principle, and therefore did not draw so sharp a distinction between the material and the psychical. It was not till Descartes separated thinking substance from extended substance (*cf.* § 18. 2) that the idea of a mind-substance took clear and definite form. It recurs in Leibniz, but in a different dress (*cf.* § 17. 1, 2). The mind is there a monad, and stands in close connection with the many other monads that make up its body. These two views dominated the psychology of the eighteenth century. The notion that mind is a substance, and, as such, immortal and self-constituted, had been so completely assimilated by the general consciousness of the period, that it needed all the force of Kant's criticism to bring the transcendence of the theory into clear light. Among the metaphysicians of more recent times Herbart and Lotze are adherents of substantiality. Herbart makes the mind a real, the simple quality of which we do not know; our experiences, the ideas that cross the threshold of consciousness, are the efforts whereby this real preserves itself in its interaction with other existences (*cf.* § 17. 3). Lotze says: "The fact of the unity of consciousness is also *eo ipso* the fact of the existence of a substance." Every mind, however is "that which it gives itself out to be;

an unity that lives in definite ideas, feelings and efforts." Mind substance, that is, is not a mysterious essence behind the rich contents of our inner experience, but the unification of the inner experience. Here Lotze's view approaches very nearly to the theory of actuality, differing from it in little more than name.

3. The theory of actuality occupies a much less important place in the history of philosophy. It is only quite recently that actuality has been explicitly opposed to substantiality. We may trace its first beginnings in Hume's doctrine that there is no occasion to hypostatise an individual psychical being; indeed, that the idea of a mental substance is wholly inconceivable, and the self or mind to be regarded simply as a bundle or aggregate of perceptions. In our own time the theory of actuality has been carefully worked out and elaborately explained by Wundt (who gave it its name) and Paulsen. The constructive part of it takes the form of a criticism of the opposing view. This is legitimate, since actuality affirms nothing but what is already given in experience: it does not constitute a metaphysics, in the strict sense of the term; whereas substantiality is really a metaphysics of psychology, criticism or rejection of which would seem to lead at once to the acceptance of the rival, empirical view. In what follows we have brought together the various points made by Wundt and Paulsen against substantiality. We add brief metacritical remarks, the gist of which is that the severity with which substantiality has been handled is very far from being deserved. The first four paragraphs refer to Paulsen, the last three to Wundt.

(1) A mind-substance, we are told, is not an object of perception. Now of this there can be no doubt: but then the atoms cannot either be perceived, and the unconscious processes which Paulsen does not hesitate to accept never come within the range of possible experience. True, it might be replied that though the atoms are not perceptible, still, complexes of atoms are; and the simple which gives rise to the complex must naturally be conceived of as equally existent. But in the case of mind, precisely the reverse might hold. Here it is the elements that are open to

observation, the sensations and feelings that are experienced; the substantial unity which is required to make the connection of all these elements intelligible might lie outside of the field of perception.

4. (2) We are told, again, that no idea can be formed of the connection between the mind-substance and the psychical processes of experience. But neither can an idea be formed of the connection between psychical and physical phenomena which is assumed by monism. Moreover, Paulsen defines the mind as "the multiplicity of mental processes brought together *in some inexplicable way* to form a unity." So that the theory of actuality cannot, for its part, help us to understand the connection between the whole of mind and the individual mental elements.

(3) We are told, once more, that the attributes of a mind-substance consist simply of negations. But self-constitution and stability are not negative predicates. And on the other hand the properties attributed to matter (with the exception of the empirical relations of bodies to one another) are in great part of a purely negative character.

(4) The theory of substantiality declares that the occurrence of mere acts or functions in the absence of any vehicle or substrate is inconceivable. The theory of actuality replies that the difficulty disappears when we remember that a mental act, *e.g.*, a feeling, never occurs alone, but always in connection with a whole mental life. As if a number of acts could serve as the substrate of each individual act in the number! The theory comes to this: that various simultaneous mental processes, which together simply give us more of the same experience that is given by each one alone, are able somehow to acquire a unifying function in virtue of which every individual process may be related to the whole. Now either we have here the old substance idea in a changed form (and this is suggested by Paulsen's "in some inexplicable way"), or the inconceivability which substantiality ascribes to actuality is left, after the explanation, just where it was before. We may note that the question has been raised, in this connection, whether the mind-

substance itself would not need a further support or substrate. It is answered by a reference to the attribute of self-dependence or self-constitution, which has always been involved in the idea of subtantiality.

5. (5) We are told, further, that the distinction of phenomenon and thing-in-itself, first drawn by Kant, and later adopted practically without change by Herbart, has no significance for the inner experience. There, we apprehend things exactly as they are; so that there is no reason why we should posit a mental substance to play the part of the thing-in-itself, and oppose it to our particular psychical experiences. Now we freely admit that the distinction of phenomenon and thing-in-itself has no special application in the sphere of psychological experience. We go farther, and declare that it is wrong wherever it is applied. But on the other hand, this distinction was not the primary, still less the only, influence in the formation of the idea of a mind-substance. Descartes and Leibniz spoke of mind-substance in the old days before Kant; and Lotze defends the theory upon quite other grounds. There is absolute agreement among a wide circle of psychologists at the present day, that some sort of supplement of what we call inner experience is necessary if we are to obtain a definite scientific idea of its field or subject-matter. The assumption of unconscious psychical excitations, and the endowment of particular psychical functions with properties and forces of which we get at most but slight indications in introspection, come under the same heading with the hypothesis of a mind-substance: all alike are attempts to satisfy this requirement of a supplement or completion of the conscious inner life. To rule out mind-substance, and introduce in its place the idea of a psychophysical substance—obtained by the ascription of mental characteristics to material substance—is not the way to reach a more fruitful or better-grounded theory (*cf.* the previous discussion of § 19).

6. (6) It is said, too, that there is an inconsistency in the definition of the mind-substance, which is made at once stable and subject to change. But no one who has adopted the theory

of substantiality attributes changeableness to the mind-substance. Every substance has accidents, phenomena, modes of expression, etc., predicated of it; and so here the changes which actually take place in our mental life are referred to the empirically given phenomena of the mind-substance.

(7) Lastly, it is said that the hypothesis of a mind-substance is not even useful for holding together the facts of experience. To which we may reply that no metaphysical hypothesis is useful for that purpose. Metaphysical theory simply supplements the results of scientific enquiry. Empirical psychology must, of course, always be kept perfectly free from any admixture of the substance idea in its description and explanation of facts. To say that the mind feels, thinks, wills, etc., does not give us the least insight into the origin and mechanism of these activities. But the philosopher who is concerned with the question of the connection of psychical and physical phenomena, and who comes to the conclusion (as we did on what seemed good grounds: *cf.* §§ 18, 19) that dualism furnishes him with the most probable answer, will hardly be able to avoid recognising the independence of psychical existence and postulating for it a substantial underlying unity

It must be noted that our criticism of actuality does not carry with it a profession of faith in the rival theory of substantiality. But it seemed desirable to show that the objections urged against the latter are not by any means of the nature of constraining arguments, and that consequently we must concede the *possibility* of substantiality, after as before.

7. The antithesis of intellectualism and voluntarism, like that of substantiality and actuality, did not become precise and explicit until quite recently. There is no trace of it in ancient philosophy, as no attempt was there made to reduce the properties of the mind to a single essential function. Here, as before, the first impulse comes from Descartes: thought is the one characteristic attribute of mind-substance. Spinoza followed Descartes, except that he regarded the individual mind not as substance, but merely as a mode of the attribute of thought (*cf.* § 19. 3). A similar intellectualistic theory was propounded by Leibniz and worked out by his

school. The universal activity of all monads is the activity of ideation or representation (*cf.* § 17. 2). But the colourless generality of this concept made it possible to endow the mind with a faculty of desire alongside of and co-ordinate with the faculty of knowledge. With the recognition of the faculty of feeling as a third *facultas* (*cf.* § 10. 2) the simple intellectualistic schema finally broke down. We thus find no strict formulation of the theory until it was revived by Herbart. For him, ideas are the only true vehicles of conscious occurrence. The feelings of pleasantness and unpleasantness arise from the relations of reinforcement and inhibition (or arrest) that obtain among them; and the impression of desire or aversion is produced by the rise of an idea in consciousness in face of certain obstacles or the opposition which it offers to rival ideas that would force it down. Feeling and will are, that is, merely by-products of the ideating forces, not independent and co-ordinate phenomena. This standpoint has not always been very vigorously insisted on by the Herbartians, but, on the other hand, has never been entirely given up. They accordingly represent the intellectualism of the present day.

8. The first hint of voluntarism appears in Kant, where it is a consequence of his ethical metaphysics. If freedom is necessary for the intelligibility of the absolute character of the moral law, then the thing-in-itself of our mental life must be a free will (*cf.* § 9. 8). Schopenhauer, however, was the first to expand this thesis to a general theory of the universe. For him the thing-in-itself is always will, wherever it occurs, whether in external nature or in the inner life; and intellect is simply an instrument ready to the hands of will. Sometimes, but only in man, this secondary function frees itself from the dominion of will, and most completely in the state of passionless æsthetic enjoyment (*cf.* § 10. 6). Quite recently, Wundt and Paulsen have made an especially noteworthy attempt to put voluntarism upon a psychological basis. Here, again, we will give the separate arguments of both thinkers, one by one, and append short critical comments to them. The first three are Paulsen's, the last Wundt's.

(1) First of all we are told to look at the importance of will in the universal and individual development of the mental life. We cannot attribute any form of ideas, *i.e.*, any intellectual processes, to the lowest organisms: they seem to be controlled by sheer blind compulsion. Impulse is, therefore, taken as the basal function of the inner life. So in the child it is the life of will that first makes its appearance, and only gradually that the activities of intelligence supervene upon it, in ever-increasing complexity. To this we have to reply that the idea of development, methodologically considered, would lead us to posit an undifferentiated whole as the source of mental functions, and not a phenomenon which has acquired its specific differentia in the adult mental life. We must accordingly attribute to the lowest organisms an indefinable total something, of psychical character, out of which both intellectual and impulsive or volitional processes emerge by slow degrees in the course of evolution, until they become the distinguishable and co-ordinate states that we know. The mental life of the newly-born infant, we believe, on the other hand, to contain from the first not only desires and feelings but also a number of special sensations.

9. (2) But even in the developed mental life, we are told further, will is the primary and determining factor. Will sets the final goal of every man's life; and will originates and holds to all the special purposes that are realised by individual actions. Will also directs the attention, and chooses among the different stimuli to which consciousness is exposed. Interest, a phenomenon of will, decides which of our experiences are to be stored away in memory and which forgotten. And the direction and trend of the course of ideas itself are governed by will, so that even our theoretical knowledge and judgments constantly betray its influence. To all of which the reply is that what is here described as will is not the simple impulse, the blind compulsion, that came before any differentiation of the mental processes. This will does not act blindly, without reason; it is determined always by more or less complicated motives and reflections. Hence we might assert with equal truth that the really primary

and determining factor in our mental life is not will, but that which occasions the will's activity.

(3) The statement that voluntarism can be harmonised with a spiritualistic metaphysics, while intellectualism cannot, is sufficiently disproved by a reference to history. Leibniz' metaphysics is spiritualistic, in spite of its intellectualism. Moreover, there is the third possibility to be taken into account, that intellectualism and voluntarism are alike one-sided and consequently incorrect. Lotze's spiritualism tends towards this view (*cf.* § 14. 5). Lastly, however, in the light of the objections that we have raised against spiritualism (§ 17), we should not be able to admit that this incompatibility, were it proven to exist, had any value as an argument against intellectualism.

10. (4) The ideas are declared to be subsidiary, not independent activities, and consequently incapable of explaining the unity that, as a matter of fact, characterises our mental life. Moreover, their changes are so uncertain, and their connections so fragmentary, as to make them altogether unsuited for the discharge of an unifying function. And the feelings share this character with the ideas. The will is, therefore, the only thing left to which we can appeal; and its qualitative constancy renders it eminently fitted for the task assigned to it. But this qualitatively constant will is generally rejected by psychologists as an abstraction which does not correspond to the facts. Moreover, the unity of our mental life, or of our personality or character, is not a simple fact of experience, but itself a reflexion upon the facts, and wears the appearance of an immediate experience simply because it is familiar to the popular consciousness. The unity of the personality is really a hypothesis, based not so much upon any simple and constant psychical quality as upon (1) the perception of a thorough-going interconnection of our separate mental acts, mediated by the association of ideas; (2) the continuity of our mental development, which does not admit of sudden and violent transitions, of the co-existence of incompatible states of mind, etc.; and (3) the constancy of the sensory background of our mental life, *i.e.*, of the bodily form in which we are clothed.

The result of our critique of voluntarism[1] is not by any means a proof of the correctness of intellectualism, but merely the knowledge that no one of the elementary processes of our mental life can be regarded as 'primary' in any absolute and exclusive sense. Intellectualism and voluntarism are, therefore, both alike in the wrong.

LITERATURE.

O. Flügel, *Die Seelenfrage.* 2nd ed., 1890. (For the author's standpoint, *cf.* the literature to § 14.)

J. H. Witte, *Das Wesen der Seele und die Natur der geistigen Vorgänge im Lichte der Philosophie seit Kant und iher grundlegenden Theorien historisch-kritisch dargestellt.* 1888. (The writer is an adherent, but not a skilful advocate of the substantiality theory.)

Cf. also the literature cited under § 8, and especially W. Volkmann, *Psychologie.* Vol. I.

B. EPISTEMOLOGICAL SCHOOLS.

§ 24. *Rationalism, Empiricism and Criticism.*

1. The problem now before us is that of the origin of knowledge. *Rationalism* (also called *apriorism*) affirms that reason, a connate mental faculty, is the fountain of all true knowledge, and, more especially, the sole source and warrant of the two most important attributes of knowledge—necessity and universal validity. *Empiricism*, on the other hand, derives all knowledge from experience, and designates the mind or intellect prior to perception a *tabula rasa*. If it makes external experience, the experience mediated by the sense organs, primary and all-determining, it is called *sensualism*. Lastly, *criticism* attempts to reconcile the opposing claims of both the other schools. It explains knowledge as the resultant of a formal factor, deducible from the nature of the knowing intellect, and a material factor, constituted by the

[1] We have here discussed voluntarism only in its metaphysical form. The methodological voluntarism represented by Wundt in his later books (*Logik* ii. 2 and *Outlines of Psychology*) is something essentially different. It simply declares that will processes are the typical processes of the mental life, and that all the rest must therefore be explained by reference to them.

sensations of sense-perception. If either of these factors is lacking, we can have no real knowledge. It is wholly impossible, in particular, to derive facts of any scientific significance from pure reason, as rationalism asserts. The relation between rationalism and empiricism is of such a kind that empiricism completely excludes rationalism, but not *vice versâ*. Rationalism simply denies that universally valid and necessary knowledge can be obtained from experience. It grants that a great mass of detailed knowledge comes from experience. Empiricism, on the contrary, will hear nothing of a creative reason which is to colligate concepts or intuitions *a priori* and put the stamp of truth and adequacy upon knowledge in general.

2. These epistemological differences did not play an important part in ancient philosophy. Our knowledge of pre-Socratic epistemology is very scanty; but the Eleatics seem to have been radical, and the atomists moderate rationalists. Plato, too, undoubtedly inclines to rationalism, though he gives no clear formulation of its leading characteristics. Aristotle's system, the great compromise of the ancient world, is suggestive of criticism; but matter and form mean very different things for him from what they mean for Kant, the founder of critical epistemology. In modern philosophy, on the other hand, the division of schools is sharply marked. Continental philosophy has been exclusively rationalistic, English philosophy as exclusively empirical. Francis Bacon, with whom English empiricism began, shows, it is true, some of the most pronounced features of rationalistic thought; and we should not do justice to the philosophy of Hobbes if we termed it a pure empiricism. It was Locke who gave the theory its decisive and characteristic form. His attack upon all innate ideas or principles, whether in the field of theoretical knowledge or in the domain of practical moral injunctions, was the first open avowal of disbelief in the competency of pure reason to furnish any sort of *a priori* certainty. Hume and John Stuart Mill have followed Locke very closely. The principal names on the rationalistic side are those of Descartes, Spinoza, Leibniz and Wolff. All these philosophers agree that the best part of our

knowledge proceeds from the mind itself. Leibniz, *e.g.*, opposes the *vérités de raison* to the *vérités de fait*. The truths of reason are eternal, universally valid and necessary; their fundamental law is the principle of identity. The truths of fact are merely accidental, and rest upon the principle of sufficient reason or of purpose.

3. Kant distinguishes, as Lambert had done before him (*Neues Organon*, 1764), between the matter and the form of knowledge. He is thus able to reconcile rationalism and empiricism, and to transcend the older antithesis of understanding and sensibility. The senses are capable of giving real scientific knowledge, since they, equally with the understanding, are ruled by *a priori* forms. These are the forms of space and time, which ensure the necessity and universal validity of mathematical intuition. At the present day, the three epistemological standpoints are neither so sharply opposed nor so variously formulated as in the past history of philosophy. Of rationalism we may say that it has ceased to exist as a separate theory. Criticism and empiricism still stand in opposition to each other; but criticism has given up one of the most important of its original tenets, viz., the *a priori* in the sense of the connate, of an ultimate subjective disposition. Modern adherents of criticism have nearly all changed the definition of the *a priori* to mean simply that part or aspect of knowledge whose validity is independent of individual experience. The chief names in the critical school, outside of the 'Neo-Kantians' in the narrower sense (*cf.* § 4. 5), are those of W. Windelband, A. Riehl (*cf.* § 5. 10) and O. Liebmann (*cf.* § 14. 8).

4. In examining the epistemological theories we shall have (1) to weigh the arguments upon which they stand, and (2) to raise and answer the general question whether hypotheses as to the origin of knowledge can properly be termed 'epistemological theories' at all. *Rationalism* declares that the necessity and universal validity of certain propositions is indisputable evidence of their apriority, and looks upon mathematics and mathematical natural science, with their deductive method and array of definitions and axioms, as the models of all true science. We may reply (1) that the *a priori* in the sense of innate dispositions,

ideas, knowledge, or what not—in other words, the subjectivity of the *a priori*—is no guarantee either of necessity or of universal validity. Mathematics and natural science try to rid their results, as far as possible, of any sort of subjective addition, and can lay claim to universal validity only on the assumption that their contents are exclusively objective. Moreover, there are subjective states or processes which are quite universal, and still have no power at all to put the stamp of necessity and universal validity (in the ordinary meaning of the terms) upon the knowledge of which they are the condition. Thus it is a quite universal optical illusion that, other things equal, vertical lines seem longer than horizontal lines of the same objective length. But no one would think of using this fact as the basis of a necessary or universally valid system of knowledge. We must accordingly conclude that the subjective as such has nothing to do with knowledge of this kind. (Criticism is open to the same objection, so far as it uses the *a priori* in the same way.) Again, (2) if the principle of identity is the only principle that runs through the innate 'truths of reason,' progress in the rational sphere must consist in the development of identical propositions, and knowledge in the exercise of formal reasoning. The conclusion is evidently in conflict both with the facts and with the desire or intention, if one may use the words, of our impulse to know. (3) Lastly, we may notice that it is extraordinarily difficult to draw a satisfactory line of division between the *a priori* and *a posteriori*, and that the rationalistic attempt to include transcendent definitions among the functions of the *a priori* has ended in total failure.

5. *Empiricism* takes its stand upon the undeniable fact that as experience increases all departments of knowledge increase also. It explains the necessary character of certain propositions, as contradistinguished from certain others, by the nature of the psychological processes involved in their formation. Hume, *e.g.*, gives an explanation of this sort for the law of cause and effect. When one process constantly follows another process in consciousness, a strong and enduring association is set up between them. There grows up, in consequence, what we may call a subjective

constraint to reproduce the idea of the one process whenever the idea of the other is present in consciousness. This subjective compulsion is the condition of the necessity which characterises connection by cause and effect. The theory can, of course, be extended to other laws and concepts.

There can be no doubt, however, that it is inadequate to its problem.

(1) There is no need to collect a number of repeated experiences in order that we may apply the law of causality to observed phenomena. The scientific worker can demonstrate the causal nexus by a few suitable variations of a single case; and frequent repetition adds nothing to the stability of the connection, and nothing essential to the certainty of its demonstration. It follows, obviously enough, that an association due to frequent experience is not the prime factor in the causal relation.

(2) The same thing may be shown in a different way. The necessity of the causal connection shows no mark whatsoever of a subjective constraint to the reproduction of ideas. Its necessity is not psychological but logical, resting upon the connection of the concepts.

(3) Empiricism has not been altogether fortunate, in other respects, in its explanation of the general facts of human knowledge. When the empiricist speaks cautiously of a 'belief' in the universal validity of certain truths or axioms, instead of simply affirming it, he forgets that the propositions in question are not universally valid because everyone recognises their validity, but because their validity is entirely independent of the recognition of any particular individual.

6. *Criticism* meets with no better success than rationalism and empiricism when it essays to determine the origin of knowledge, and of the constituents of knowledge. As a matter of fact, the whole question of the sources of knowledge is not epistemological but psychological, and must be approached by psychological methods. The psychologist is interested to discover from what processes an universal proposition has developed, what part of it has been contributed by sense-perception and what by thought

or imagination, etc., etc. But to the science of knowledge, to a *Wissenschaftslehre*, the psychological evolution of a bit of knowledge is wholly indifferent. We defined epistemology (*cf.* § 5. 7 f.) as a science of the most general contents of human knowledge. Its business is evidently not with the historical or psychological derivation of knowledge; all that it has to do is to furnish a systematic analysis of the most general contents of knowledge. Really, therefore, rationalism, empiricism and criticism, although tradition allows them the right of citizenship in the realm of epistemology, represent *psychological* theories or standpoints, and should be banished from the company of epistemological schools. On the other hand, universal validity and necessity are attributes of knowledge which are materially and formally conditioned and materially and formally determinable, and thus fall in part within the province of *logic*. There it must be shown by what logical operations we arrive at universal and necessary propositions. Lastly, *epistemology* must tell us what forms of knowledge possess this distinguishing character, that they are valid independently of the recognition or attitude of individuals, *i.e.*, universally valid, and what are valid independently of individual observation or experience, *i.e.*, necessary. The predicate of universality refers to the relation of knowledge to the knowing subject; the predicate of necessity to the relation of knowledge to the object or contents known. We can see at once, when we compare these remarks with the definition of psychology given earlier in the book (§ 8. 5), that both the logical and the epistemological enquiries lie altogether outside of the psychological domain, and that the attempts made to solve the problem of the origin of knowledge by the three schools whose positions we have reviewed—rationalism, empiricism and (historical) criticism—do not and cannot lead to any satisfactory conclusion.

LITERATURE.

C. Göring, *System der kritischen Philosophie.* 2 vols., 1874–75. (Incomplete. The author is a positivist.)

NOTE.—Rationalism is used in a wider sense to denote the exclusive recognition of what is conceded by reason, or proven by the understanding. Thus a criticism of church dogma, which made rationality or demonstrability its sole criterion of truth, would be called 'rationalistic,' in this meaning of the word. The name of *supernaturalism* or *irrationalism* is given to the opposite standpoint, which posits superrational realities (unattainable by the natural light of human knowledge, but known by a special function of 'faith' or 'presentiment' or 'intuition'), or an equally superrational source of knowledge (revelation).

§ 25. *Dogmatism, Scepticism, Positivism and Criticism.*

1. Since the time of Kant the word *dogmatic* has been used to characterise any philosophical statement or system which has not been preceded by an epistemological enquiry into the degree of certainty or range of validity of the assumptions which underlie it. In this general sense, the investigations of the special sciences are also dogmatic. All that is required by them is a special 'technical' criticism,—an estimation, *e.g.*, of the probability of an historical event, or of the limits of error in a series of experimental observations. The epistemological test may be allowed to lapse altogether; in the first place because it can be applied to the whole company of the special sciences, once and for all, in a general discussion of their presuppositions, and further because an enquiry which moves wholly within the limits of possible experience is not apt to raise peculiar difficulties of an epistemological kind. Hence we hardly speak of dogmatism except in philosophical matters. The term is used more especially to denote the schools which think it unnecessary to draw a line of division between experiential knowledge and definitions of transcendent objects. Dogmatism in this narrower sense, that is, is a theory which sets no limits to human knowledge. It is at once the emptiest and the most pretentious conception of the capabilities of our knowing faculty. It is accordingly most generally found in connection with rationalism. For if all true knowledge comes from pure reason, it has no external or objective limits. The dogmatists therefore figured very largely among the rationalists of the seventeenth and eighteenth centuries. The

worst of them all is Spinoza, who does not offer the slightest epistemological justification of his deductive procedure, but comes upon the scene with a whole number of the most dubious definitions and axioms ready-made. Descartes and Leibniz were also dogmatists; and chiefly for the reason that they were rationalists.

2. Dogmatism, in the specific meaning of the word, is not confined to modern philosophy. Plato and Aristotle were no more concerned to draw epistemological distinctions of degrees of certainty than were the rationalists of the seventeenth century. But the dogmatism of antiquity was due to a lack of scientific knowledge. The universal validity of a statement of empirical fact had not as yet taken stand above more or less uncertain conjecture as to the nature of the transcendent. The problem of the limits of human knowledge does not arise, therefore, until the steady progress of mathematical and scientific enquiry forces upon men's notice the difference between it and the confused and contradictory essays of metaphysics.

Empiricism, too, has at first a taint of dogmatism. Defining experience as the sole source of knowledge, it assumes without further argument that knowledge cannot pass beyond the limits of experience. Sometimes, indeed, it confounds the spheres of immanence and transcendence as impartially as rationalism itself. Even in Locke the absence of any clear idea as to the range of empiristic validity can be easily demonstrated. Hume is the first to give definite expression to the view that scientific statements and metaphysical opinions cannot be placed upon the same level, and that positivism is the natural complement of empiricism.

Since Kant's comprehensive criticism of the dogmatic position, dogmatism proper has practically disappeared from philosophy. A modern philosopher, setting out to construct a metaphysics, would probably declare his right to dogmatic procedure, but at the same time would not blink the fact that the definition of the transcendent is incomparably less certain than the results of investigation within the special sciences. We may say, therefore, that dogmatism as a pseudo-epistemological position has now a merely historical interest.

3. If dogmatism sets no limits to knowledge, *scepticism* sets no limits to ignorance. Absolute scepticism affirms that it cannot affirm anything. It cannot even say with Socrates that it knows that it knows nothing; any claim to knowledge seems to it to be unjustifiable presumption. Many arguments have been brought forward in its defence, but we need here consider only the two most important, which are characteristic of two different sceptical schools—the schools of *relativism* and *subjectivism.* The relativists declare (1) that all our knowledge is relative, *i.e.*, dependent upon the particular circumstances under which we chanced to acquire it; and, consequently, that it is valid, if at all, only for a particular place or time, under particular conditions, etc. They point out further (2) that every act of knowledge must be relative, since it always presupposes a relation between the knowing subject and the particular object of knowledge; so that we are never able really to grasp anything actual or objective, anything that exists independently of all relation to ourselves. The subjectivists (1) lay an even greater emphasis upon the part played by the knowing subject in the acquisition of knowledge. What is known can never possess more than subjective significance, because it is valid only for the individual who has come to know it. (2) They also make much of the difficulties which stand in the way of the particular act of perception, and which (they say) render it impossible for us to get a trustworthy view of things. (3) Again, they tell us to look at our proofs and inferences, and see how inconclusive they are and must be. Every argument has presuppositions, and assumes the validity of some other argument; that, in turn, assumes the validity of others, and so on. However far back we follow the chain of reasoning, we can always travel further still; so that we either go on for ever, or come to an arbitrary standstill at some proposition whose uncertainty throws doubt upon our entire deduction. (4) And lastly, they assert that every statement may be converted into its contrary or contradictory. This, however, is simply a natural consequence of sceptism, not a new argument in its favour.

4. Scepticism ran a brilliant and uninterrupted course in ancient

philosophy. It owed its success partly to the peculiar pleasure that the Greeks took in the exercise of dialectic, and partly to the circumstance that there was as yet no scientific knowledge, in the strict sense of the phrase, to show the emptiness of the philosophic word-play. It is usual to distinguish three successive schools of scepticism: the *Pyrrhonists*, the sceptics of the *academy*, and the *younger* sceptics. Pyrrho of Elis (*ca.* 300 B.C.) was the founder of the first. From the very beginning emphasis is laid upon the practical advantages of a sceptical theory. He who knows nothing certainly cannot be disturbed by any doubt; and he who is never positive in judgment finds the fullest happiness. Happiness is peace of mind, *ἀταραξία*. The most famous of the later sceptics are Ænesidemus of Cnossus (in the first century B.C.) and the physician Sextus Empiricus (about 200 A.D.). Ænesidemus brings ten reasons (*τρόποι*) to disprove the possibility of knowledge: they were soon afterwards reduced to five, and then to two. The whole theory reaches its culmination in the works of Sextus Empiricus.

Modern scepticism, or all of it that is worth mentioning, is confined almost exclusively to French philosophy. M. de Montaigne († 1592) figured as the champion of relativism, more especially in the moral sphere; and P. Charron († 1603) and P Bayle († 1706) tried to make a place in philosophy for religious faith by a sceptical denial of all certainty in the field of theoretical knowledge. In later times, theology has often attempted to explain away the difference between scientific knowledge and religious faith, or at least to show that those points in a scientific theory which cannot be harmonised with traditional religious ideas are doubtful and disputable. We often find Hume called a sceptic. But, though he applied the name to himself, we must not forget that his scepticism extends only to the peculiar knowledge of reason, and that he is by no means concerned to deny the right of the facts of life and of sensible experience to our acceptance and belief. In 1792 there appeared a work entitled *Ænesidemus*, written (as was shown later) by G. E. Schulze († 1833). Its scepticism, again, is a limited scepticism, extending only to the critical philosophy of Kant and C. L. Reinhold. It made no disciples.

5. Scepticism has thus died out as an epistemological theory. If its method is used at all by modern philosophers, it is only incidentally and for some definite purpose. And, indeed, the sceptical standpoint cannot be made consistent except by the complete renunciation of the right to judgment or assertion. Even the statement that we cannot know anything, and the reasons alleged for it, must be adjudged dogmatic from the point of view of a radical scepticism. He who holds that nothing is demonstrable will not attempt to demonstrate that he can know nothing. In other words, scepticism in its absolute form is self-destructive. On the other hand—and this is the great advantage that it has over dogmatism—its method possesses a very high degree of value in all departments of scientific investigation. Many of the ideas that 'occur' to us, and many of the observations that we make are wholly lacking in the permanent value and universal validity that would entitle them to rank as scientific results. Hence what Hume called the 'academic doubt' is a necessary concomitant of all honest zeal for knowledge. It prompts to manifold variation of conditions, to repeated consideration, to unceasing test and trial. Under this aspect scepticism is an important part of the education of every investigator. And its methodical advantages will be especially fruitful in metaphysics, where it teaches the enquirer rightly to appreciate the worth of reasons and the force of arguments, and so helps him to take the concepts and theories of previous systems at their true value. Finally, scepticism brings out more clearly than any other attitude the difference between a theoretical assumption and a practical guarantee of the justice or truth of a given statement. A comparatively simple train of sceptical reasoning shows that no theoretical assurance is, in the last resort, beyond the reach of doubt, and that consequently the influences which constrain us to believe must be sought in the sphere of volition and action.

6. *Positivism* and *criticism* are at one in the opinion that human knowledge has limits or degrees of certainty, and that the range of universally valid knowledge is co-extensive with

the sphere of possible experience. While enquiry is confined to this sphere, it is able, in theory, to attain results of an evidential or necessary character. Ideas, for both schools, are not self-existent magnitudes, whose combinations furnish new knowledge, independently of experience: they are simply aids to the arrangement and connection of facts, and possess no contents of their own apart from the various perceptions to which they may be applied. Hence we can never argue from concepts, as such, to realities.

At this point the views of positivism and criticism diverge. Positivism disputes not only the certainty, but also the possibility or right of existence of every metaphysics. Criticism, on the other hand, accepts metaphysics as an 'irrepressible' need of human reason, as a natural disposition educated by criticism of knowledge.

7. Laas (§ 4. 5) calls the sophist Protagoras the first positivist. But his famous saying that "Man is the measure of all things" is much more like relativistic scepticism than positivism. The limitation of knowledge by the Epicureans, too, had its root rather in practical than in theoretical reasons. What is worth knowing, on their view, is not what is certain but what seems necessary for the furtherance of life. Hume, following in the footsteps of Bacon and Locke, was the first to reach a really positivistic standpoint (*cf.* especially the "Treatise on Human Nature," 1739–40). His pitiless analysis of metaphysical attempts to extend the sphere of knowledge beyond experience deprives them of even the semblance of success.

The phrase 'positive philosophy' was introduced by A. Comte. The purpose of all the sciences, he says, is to give us a prevision, whereby we may acquire the mastery over things, over the course of events in the world; and all knowledge is knowledge of the real laws of natural occurrence, and rests exclusively upon experience. This positive standpoint cannot be reached till thought has passed through a theological and a metaphysical phase. Neither theology nor metaphysics is founded in knowledge, and for this reason neither has had any considerable influence upon human purposive action. Philosophy, however, must take as its task the systematisation of the separate sciences; it must organise them more perfectly, and so make them better adapted for their practical purpose. The name of positivist may also be applied to John Stuart Mill, Herbert Spencer (whose philosophy is usually termed agnosticism, because it asserts the unknowability of the transcendent), E. Laas, A. Riehl, and, in a certain sense, E. Dühring and R. Avenarius (*cf.* § 4. 5).

8. Kant is the founder of criticism, in this as in the other meaning of the term. His critique of metaphysics was not intended to prove its total impossibility, but simply to rebuke its dogmatic presumption and contest the scientific value of its results. For apart from the fact that he recognises an irresistible metaphysical impulse, which is constantly urging us to transcend the limits of possible experience, Kant frequently inclines, even in the course of his critical discussion, to admit at least the possibility of certain metaphysical assumptions, and to conduct proofs by purely theoretical methods. The one secure foundation upon which to rest transcendental speculation he finds in the moral subject; and so comes himself (as seen above: *cf.* §§ 4. 3; 9. 8) to an ethical metaphysics. This standpoint holds its own, practically unchanged, at the present day. Philosophers of different schools accept the Kantian view of the possibility of a metaphysics.

And, as a matter of fact, the truth seems to be with criticism rather than with positivism. If there is a need for a final and comprehensive theory of the universe, erected upon the basis of the special sciences, it can be satisfied only by a metaphysics. Metaphysical theory can give up the dogmatic form, without losing any essential part of its significance. It will be a bridge uniting theory and practice; and what it lacks in theoretical necessity or certainty, it will regain by its combination of all the conclusions of all the sciences into a serviceable picture of the universe. Positivism, which refuses to follow this method, is thereby guilty of dogmatic pretensions. Moreover, it has never been very rigorously worked out; many of its representatives have given it an illegitimate extension by transcendent speculations, and also satisfied their personal need for a theory of the universe by a metaphysics meant, at least, for private use. But it is difficult to see why the metaphysical ideas which prove acceptable to an eminent thinker, after careful weighing of the results of scientific enquiry and of all the various theories, should be withheld from others, merely because they are not adequate to the strictest canons of scientific demonstration. So we shall remain firm in our opinion (*cf.* § 4. 6), that metaphysics is both possible and desirable as a supplement and completion of the special sciences; and that its great task is to move between theory and practice, experience and hope, reason and feeling,—weighing probabilities, balancing arguments, reconciling differences.

LITERATURE.

J. F. I. Tafel, *Geschichte und Kritik des Skepticismus und Irrationalismus.* 1834.

H. Gruber, *Auguste Comte, der Begründer des Positivismus.* 1889. *Der Positivismus vom Tode Auguste Comte's bis auf unsere Tage.* 1891. (Written from the standpoint of Roman Catholicism).

J. Halleux, *Les principes du positivisme contemporain.* 1896.

§ 26. *Idealism, Realism and Phenomenalism.*

1. *Idealism* lays it down that everything knowable, every object of experience, is in its proper or original nature a contents of consciousness. If it defines this contents as a purely subjective process in the mind of an individual, it takes the special form of *subjective* idealism or *solipsism.* If on the other hand it simply says in general terms that experience always consists of ideas, or that consciousness is an universal attribute or form of the contents of knowledge, without adding any reference to a subject to whom ideas and consciousness belong, it is *objective* idealism. Kant's *transcendental* idealism is quite different from either of these standpoints. It affirms that the formal elements of human knowledge (space and time as forms of perception; the categories of multiplicity, causality, possibility, etc., as root-concepts of the understanding) are an original possession of the

mind; but looks upon the material elements as given, and interprets them in a realistic way. The characteristic feature of *realism* is the recognition of an external world, not dependent for its existence upon the ideas or states of consciousness of the knowing subject. The contents of experience are regarded not as simply subjective signs, but as signs or effects of something objective. Differences in the definition of this 'objective' lead to the distinction of naïve and critical realism. *Naïve* realism is the view of the great mass of civilised humanity; things or objects are really just what they are perceived to be. *Critical* realism is naïve realism corrected by natural science; one of its chief tenets, therefore, is the law of the subjectivity of the qualities of sense (*cf.* § 7. 4). Besides this *scientific* critical realism, however, there are other definitions of the objective, all of which arrogate to themselves the name of critical realism. Lastly, *phenomenalism* is the theory which terms the formed material of knowledge a 'phenomenon,' *i.e.*, something both subjectively and objectively conditioned. The special phase of it which appears in Kant has not won its way to general recognition, but its fundamental idea still finds adherents.

2. No philosopher has worked out a logically consistent theory of subjective idealism. It is customary to cite Berkeley and J. G. Fichte as representatives of the school. Berkeley (*A Treatise concerning the Principles of Human Knowledge*, 1710) certainly says that the existence of things consists in their perception, and so writes the equation *esse = percipi*. But he did not stop short at this definition. Finding sense-perceptions independent of the subject in whose consciousness they arise, he is led to seek their explanation in a divine mind. He also assumes the existence of a number of minds, all supposed to be, like our own, the vehicles of ideas (*cf.* § 17. 4). The point of departure for Fichte's philosophy, theoretical and practical (*i.e.*, for the universal 'science of knowledge'), lies in the idea of an absolute ego, which is by no means to be identified with the individual self of an empirical subject. This absolute, which is constructed in order to bring together epistemology and ethics,

is endowed with an unconscious productive imagination, whereby the ego sets up an antithetic non-ego, or rather separates into a finite ('divisible') ego and non-ego. The moral necessity that human action be directed upon some purposive object gives the true reason for the recognition of reals in the sphere of the non-ego: they are the objects of the moral will, goals or aims of its endeavour. Here too, therefore, the theory of subjective idealism is not worked out with logical consistency. It might be said, however, that the later developments of the theory, which compel us to give up its first idealistic formulation, are really metaphysical amplifications of the epistemological standpoint, which in itself is still necessary and inevitable. As a matter of fact, most philosophers of the present day believe that we must begin with the statement: 'All the contents of knowledge is, *in the first instance*, nothing but my idea'; while many are of Schopenhauer's opinion that it is theoretically incontrovertible. There is also a disposition to play it off against materialism, phrasing it, perhaps, in some such way as that psychical processes alone are given, in the first instance, and that their reality is consequently more real than that of material processes (*cf.* § 17. 4).

3. This phrase "in the first instance," as employed by subjective idealism, may mean one of two things.

(1) It may be interpreted, purely psychologically, to signify that subjective states, and the reference of all our experiences to our ego, come earlier in the course of individual mental development than objective processes or the reference of experiences to external things. Now, even if this psychological conception were correct, it could not be looked upon as decisive for the epistemological position; the original subjectivity, in spite of its inevitableness, might be wrong, or at least one-sided,—an idea to be gradually replaced or corrected by the results of a more exact criticism. Regarded in the light of modern knowledge of mental evolution, however, it is very evidently incorrect. All that we know of child-psychology points to a complete parallelism in the origin and development of the consciousness of the internal and external worlds. Indeed, it cannot be otherwise; the ego and the

non-ego together comprise the entire contents of possible experience, so that if either of them is limited it must be by the other. It is therefore absurd to speak of an ego and its states without at the same time positing a non-ego by which the contents of the described experience is limited to the ego. We can say definitely, however, that the first experience of a child is neither subjective nor objective. It is what we have called (*cf.* § 16. 8) the 'datum of experience,' and accordingly contains no reference either to an ego or to the objects outside of the ego. The process by which the antithesis of subject and object comes into being is extremely gradual, and the antithesis itself is constantly receiving addition and correction as scientific enquiry advances (*cf.* § 8. 5). But always and everywhere subjective and objective go together, the one limiting and determining the other.

4. (2) The 'first' may indicate a logical, not a chronological priority. Subjective idealism then sets out from the apparently self-evident statement that everything which can be experienced must be denominated idea. Idea, however, is never given us otherwise than as a state or process of a mind, a subject. It follows that everything which can be experienced is an idea of an (more particularly of my) ego. Granted the premises, no exception can be taken to the conclusion, which may accordingly be justly urged as against the objective idealism that neglects to draw it. But (*a*) the presupposition of the whole theory, that everything which can be experienced is idea, must be called in question. It assumes, without giving reasons, that the characterisation of the contents of experience as ideas is a full and complete definition. Nevertheless, the simple fact of the existence and range of natural science is enough to prove that the element of idea in the datum of experience is not the only element that we can find there. (*b*) The logical form of subjective idealism falls into further error in that it exalts what can evidently be meant to designate only one side or attribute of possible experience into the characteristic mark of its entire contents. 'Idea,' 'perception,' 'consciousness,' 'sensation,' etc., are psychological concepts, and refer merely to certain elements or factors in pure experience, all of which are

capable of exact definition. Nor is anything gained if we write 'the psychical' for 'idea,' and say that 'the psychical' is, in the first instance, all that is given. For the concept of the psychical introduces a very large abstraction indeed (*cf.* § 8. 5). It is formed by abstracting from certain sides or attributes of reality, and considering only that aspect of it which stands in functional relation (relation of dependence) to an experiencing subject.

(3) Finally, it is not clear how one could advance from the standpoint of subjective idealism to the recognition of an objective world, of a non-ego, etc. If anything that we experience is simply our idea, then there is really no possibility and no necessity of postulating or defining anything trans-subjective. If, on the other hand, the words 'idea,' 'consciousness,' 'psychical,' etc., are used to mean something different from what they mean in current scientific work, things are thrown into unnecessary confusion by the terminological inaccuracy.

5. Plato's philosophical system might perhaps be termed an objective idealism, in the sense that he makes the idea the logical or conceptual element, the essence of things, without any reference to a subject. But his epistemology is so much mixed with metaphysics that we can hardly separate it out, and give it a definite name. True objective idealism first appears in the post-Kantian philosophers, and more especially in Hegel. For Hegel, the absolute idea includes all existence, and the dialectic method, a purely logical process, determines the origin of all reality. Even here, however, the idealism is not purely epistemological. Nor does it become epistemological until quite modern times, in the hands of W. Schuppe, A. von Leclair, J. Rehmke and others, the exponents of what is called 'epistemological monism' (*cf.* § 19, *Note*). The school affirms that consciousness or thought is the general character of all existence; there is no existence that was not thought, and no thought that did not think an existing thing. Now, this idea of 'consciousness' admits of only two interpretations. Either consciousness is the ordinary consciousness of psychology, or it is something new, to which the name of consciousness is not usually given. In the former event,

objective idealism is open to precisely the same objection that we urged against subjective. It takes a *pars pro toto.* If, on the other hand, the word consciousness means something more general, something like what we have called the 'datum of experience,' or what others have termed pure experience or the object of idea, then the previous objection does not hold, but another does: the objection, *i.e.*, that an expression which has its acknowledged place in scientific nomenclature is applied in a wrong and misleading context. Or if, once more—and this is what the epistemological monists would themselves say—consciousness is an unitary idea, bringing out what is common to the objective and the subjective as concrete phenomena, then we must ask what the use of the abstraction is, where there is no intention of proceeding further to the construction of an Hegelian metaphysics. The empty concept of consciousness or thought cannot create an unity: the unity which it is meant to create is given, as a fact, in the datum of experience or the object of idea.

6. Naïve realism considers the object as the original, and the idea as its copy, and accordingly places the two in a relation of likeness or similarity. Things are grey or coloured, dull or resonant, rough or smooth, of this or that extent and duration, just as ideas are. We find the same conception of the world in the oldest Greek philosophy. To explain the relation between object and idea it was assumed that particles are given off by the object, and produce images or copies, which affect our sense-organs. The difficulties in which the theory necessarily becomes involved do not appeal to the mind of the practical man. In the first place, he is inclined to objectify his perceptions, *i.e.*, entirely to overlook their ideational character. Secondly, however, in every individual case different sense-qualities can be contrasted with one another—taste with touch, *e.g.*, or smell with sight—and then the one group be ascribed to the idea, and the other to the object.

The principal reasons which have led to the hypothesis of objects outside of us are the following.

(1) The evident difference between the idea of memory or imagination, as it is called, and the idea of perception, produced

by the direct action of sensory stimuli. The two kinds of idea differ primarily in intensity, but, as a rule, show qualitative differences also; and while memory and imagination are subject to the influence of will, sensations set up by external stimulus appear to come and go without regard to us at all. A realistic theory is well fitted to explain this difference: it parallels the dependence of reproduction (memory and imagination) upon will by a dependence of peripheral sensations upon stimuli or objects.

7. (2) It is felt further that an explanation is required for the constancy of what is perceptible by the senses, in spite of pauses intervening between the individual acts of perception. It was from this point of view, *e.g.*, that John Stuart Mill tried to justify the assumption of an external world. It rests, he says, upon the presupposition of a "permanent possibility" of perception. The pauses in perception, that is, are conceived of as filled up by existing things, which possess the same character when they lie outside the range of perception that they have when they fall within it.

(3) Lastly, it is felt that justice must be done to the independent relations of the contents of experience to one another, and more especially their relations in space and time, none of which we can derive from the subject, from ourselves. The assumption of self-existent objects, in which changes go on and which stand in the required relations, is again made use of to explain the independent character of the phenomena.

It is not necessary, though we set out with these considerations, to proceed straight to naïve realism. That is only one, and the most obvious and simple theory of the nature of the reals which correspond to our perceptions. It is accepted in the common usages and intercourse of life for the sole reason that the theoretical difficulties which at once arise to overthrow it are, as a rule, entirely irrelevant for our practical relations with the external world. But we cannot take the very first step in scientific reflexion without stopping our ears to the *vox populi*, and exchanging the old theory for a new, in which the objective is conceived of as essentially different from the idea in which it appears to us. The reasons are briefly as follows.

8. (1) How are we to picture the nature of the object during pauses in perception? Does it sound when no one is listening, or is it coloured while no one is looking? (*a*) It evidently cannot be right to ascribe to objects when they are not objects of our idea the properties which we know only by virtue of this idea. (*b*) We know that those born blind are ignorant of the colour or brightness of objects, and that those born deaf are ignorant of auditory qualities. Nevertheless, they are able to form an idea of things, of objects; and though the idea lacks certain sense-qualities as its characteristics or concrete basis, it need not on this account be any less adequate than that formed by the normal individual. (*c*) Lastly, the sensible character of an object, as Galilei remarked long ago, is not to be counted among its necessary characteristics, the attributes which are necessarily implied in its idea (*cf.* § 7. 4).

(2) The dependence of the impression which we receive from the object, but not of the object itself, upon all sorts of circumstances which are of influence in perception, compels us to draw a qualitative distinction between object and idea. Differences of illumination make a thing look very different: its brightness varies with the intensity of the incident light, and in the twilight its colour disappears altogether. Furthermore, the thing looks very different according to the position which we take up to it in space; and its apparent size changes with change of the distance between it and us who observe it. All these are variations that we cannot place to the account of the object as such, and that therefore constrain us to look upon the idea as something essentially different from the thing about which it informs us.

(3) The fact of the stimulus limen and the difference limen leads us to the same conclusion. 'Stimulus limen' is the phrase used by experimental psychology for the just noticeable stimulus; 'difference limen' is the just noticeable difference between stimuli. Their values are determined in the following way. We take a stimulus or a stimulus difference, and gradually

increase it until it is noticed or cognised by an observer who is unacquainted with the objective conditions of the experiment. The method presupposes the existence of stimuli and stimulus differences which cannot be perceived. It follows, of course, that the object must be different from the idea.

9. (4) Finally, the manifold objective appliances which natural science has gradually perfected in order to a more exact determination of its subject-matter show how wide is the difference between our perception of things and the things themselves. Microscope and telescope, instruments of measurement, direct and indirect, weights and numbers, all alike are constantly emphasising the discrepancy between our impressions and the corresponding objects. So the naïve realism of the *vox populi* passes over, by a sort of internal necessity, to the critical realism of natural science. The doctrine of the subjectivity of the qualities of sense is but a beginning, though in the right direction. Even as regards the spatial and temporal character of the contents of experience, we must distinguish between what appears in idea and what is present in reality (*cf.* § 5. 2).

Scientific realism, in its ordinary form, looks upon the world as composed of atoms of ponderable and imponderable matter, ruled by all kinds of forces, and subjected to spatial and temporal change. This conception was worked out, in all essential points, by Isaac Newton. But it, again, cannot be taken as "wisdom's final word." It does not give by any means the only possible account of the nature of objects.

(1) The controversy between the mechanical and the dynamical views of nature still continues. The mechanist defines the atoms as material extended particles; his opponent makes them centres of force, unextended points of reference for the effects of force (*cf.* § 7. 5).

(2) It has not yet been decided whether space is discretely or continuously filled. The atoms may be separated from one another by empty space, or matter may be an interconnected whole, subject to displacement or change of density in its various parts, but never suffering disruption of its direct connection

10. (3) In quite recent times attempts have been made to eliminate the ideas of matter and mass altogether, and to substitute for them that of energy, the capacity of producing effects. In this way, again, we should get a very different view of the universe from that offered by the usual scientific realism.

(4) Lastly, high scientific authorities have admitted that matter, atoms, etc., are only pictorial aids to thought, models or constructions of things, provisional means of explanation (*cf.* § 16. 8). It is not the purpose of natural science, they say, to establish objective entities: it has the more modest task of exhibiting or describing, in as simple form as possible, the perceptible processes of nature. And they accordingly refuse to read any realistic meaning whatever into scientific concepts. When we attempt to obtain a pictorial idea of small particles, *e.g.*, moving in space, or of a strain or pressure or blow which they give or receive, we are inevitably led away from the *concepts* of the atoms and of their mutual relations. These concepts, which inform us merely of spatial or temporal characteristics, and may perhaps involve the assumption of qualities unknown, true *qualitates occultæ*, are on their side incapable of representation in idea. All that they give us, therefore, is the bare thought that their objects exist; and since (as we have seen: 9, above) the thought of existence may be formulated in various, equally possible ways, the positive definitions of scientific realism cannot be accepted as valid without long and careful examination. It is the duty of the metaphysics of nature to tell us what ideas we may most properly entertain as to the nature of objective reality.

It is not necessary to enter here upon a discussion of other and far more dubious forms of critical realism. But we may add one general remark, by way of appreciation of it as an epistemological theory. It is this: that epistemology is not competent to decide upon the *existence* of a conceptually necessary reality. When it has determined the character of the subjective and the objective, with due regard to the quality of the original contents of experience, it has done all that we can demand of it. To set up an existing reality as the counterpart of these concepts is to take a step into the realm of metaphysics.

11. The phenomenalism which follows from this limitation of the epistemological domain is not the phenomenalism of Kant. The Kantian epistemology holds, and holds correctly, not only that we cannot say anything definite about the quality of things-in-themselves, but also that we do not even know whether or not they exist. Nevertheless, it distinctly assumes their existence, and makes them the causes of our sensations or of the material aspect of phenomena. Furthermore, Kant's hypothesis of the subjectivity, with its corollary of the necessity, of the forms of perception and categories, and his view of the objective determination and contingency of the contents of perception, are neither of them in conformity with modern theory. It is only in general outline, therefore, that we can accept the Kantian phenomenalism. We agree with it that a subjectively conditioned and an objectively conditioned are to be distinguished in pure, actual experience; and we agree that this experience itself cannot be adequately described either as subjective or as objective. Wundt, Avenarius, Mach, and many others—despite wide divergences of opinion on certain points—are at one in the view that all experience is at first wholly indifferent, but that it presents two different sides or contexts, which necessarily lead to its separation into a subjective and an objective factor. So much of the original contents of experience (Wundt's object of idea, our datum of experience) as is dependent upon a knowing subject we call the subjectively conditioned, or simply the subjective or the psychical. We have no right to call the data of experience conscious processes,—ideas, perceptions, sensations, etc.,—except so far as they show this subjective side. On the other hand, that element in the same original contents of experience which is dependent upon other objects in space is the objectively conditioned, the objective or external. We have, again, no right to call the data of experience objects or things, without qualification, except in so far as we are directing our attention to these objective relations of dependence.

Since, however, a real separation of the two sides is impracticable—natural science having to determine in each individual case, by all sorts of laborious methods, what is actually given in nature, *i.e.*, truly objective—we are obliged in practice to define the whole of a particular experience as conscious process or as object (*cf.* § 8. 5).

12. The terms 'subject' and 'object,' however, are not entirely free of ambiguity. It will be well, therefore, briefly to pass in review the different meanings which may attach to them.

The antithesis of ego and external world, subject and object, is brought about, in the first place, by the discrimination of our own body (more particularly of our body as seen) from other bodies in space. As thus produced, it goes along with a special form of subjectification and objectification. The parts, attributes and states or activities of our own body are made subjective, and the parts, attributes, states or activities of other bodies objectified. By 'attribute' or 'state' is here meant anything that is spatially or temporally connected with a body as its point of reference, or that can be regarded as the emanation or effect of that body. The latter definition gradually becomes the more important, so that finally nothing is subjectified, *e.g.*, that does not stand in a relation of dependence to our own body or its physical properties.

Gradually, however, the antithesis takes on a different meaning. Theoretically, there is no reason for marking off our own body, as an individual spatial form, from the other bodies in space, and setting it over against them as ego against external world. Our own body may itself be regarded as a datum of experience, and considered under the two rubrics of subject and object. The new concept of subject then connects with the existence of processes which are always subjectified and never objectified,—feelings, acts of will, thoughts, images of fancy. All these states are characterised by a total lack of any objective side, in the earlier sense of the term. They therefore constitute the nucleus of a new concept of subject; and the subjectification of a contents of experience now means its assignment to a position within the connection of merely subjectified contents.

13. Objectification, too, must now mean simply a special relation of the contents to one another, not a relation to determinate objects, marked off in a class by themselves. We may call the relation that obtains between the subjectified constituents an *association*, and that which holds between the objectified processes a *mechanical connection*. In its final and most abstract form, the concept of subjectification will then mean the apprehension of a contents as member of an associative connection; and objectification, in the same way, will mean the apprehension of a process as member of a mechanical connection. This new concept of the subjective need make no change in our definition of the problem of psychology (*cf.* § 8. 5). For 'membership in an associative connection' is precisely the same, so far as contents is concerned, with 'dependence upon the body of the experiencing subject.' Formally regarded, however, the new concept labours under a disadvantage: it does not place any exact instrument or method at the disposal of the scientific enquirer. Hence, for scientific purposes, psychology will do well to retain the older definition of the subjective, which, if epistemologically less exact, is in contents identical with the new.

Literature.

E. von Hartmann, *Das Grundproblem der Erkenntnisstheorie.* 1889.

H. Schwarz, *Das Wahrnehmungsproblem.* 1892.

E. König, *Ueber die letzten Fragen der Erkenntnisstheorie und einen Gegensatz des transcendentalen Idealismus und Realismus.* In the *Zeitschrift für Philosophie und philosophische Kritik.* Vols. 103 and 104.

Cf. also, for the epistemological schools in general, the works cited under § 5.

Note.—As early as Schopenhauer we find complaint of the misuse of the word idealism. In popular parlance it is used as a term of respect for any attempt to rise above the ordinary, average, every-day level. In philosophical terminology we hear of metaphysical, epistemological, ethical and æsthetical idealism and realism. O. Willmann's *Geschichte des Idealismus* (2 vols., 1894–96) apparently means to treat of idealism in this comprehensive way.

G. W. F. Hegel's system is often called an *absolute idealism*. Herbart's philosophy, again, is termed realistic, because in his metaphysics he designates the ultimate elements of existence 'reals.' The *transcendental realism* of E. von Hartmann affirms that things in themselves come under the forms of perception (space and time) and the categories, and so paves the way for their metaphysical determination.

C. ETHICAL SCHOOLS.

§ 27. *Theories of the Origin of Morality.*

(*a*) THE AUTHORITATIVE AND THE AUTONOMOUS MORAL SYSTEMS.

1. The heteronomous theory of morality refers the moral obligation of the individual to external precepts, rules or laws. Either God (the church) or the state may be looked upon as law-giver. It is not always clear, however, where the line is drawn by the heteronomists between statement of historical fact and ethical hypothesis; so that the reader must regard it as an open question whether the authors whom we quote as representing the theory would derive moral action in the individual case from the authority of state or church. Socrates, as we saw, speaks of two different sources of morality: the written law of man and the unwritten law of God (*cf.* § 9. 2). Theological ethics is especially inclined towards heteronomy, tracing moral obligation to the will of God and its revelation. The stricter form of the theory maintains that a thing is good and right simply because God wills it, and that if God should will otherwise morality would necessarily assume a different character. In a modified form it declares that human reason is capable in itself of discovering what is good and right, though it is a matter for rejoicing that the interests of human knowledge harmonise as they do with the divine will. On the side of political heteronomy the first writer to mention is Hobbes (*cf.* § 9. 7). He accepts the absolutism of the state in all departments, and accordingly gives it the right to determine the nature and direction of human action. True, he also concedes the validity of a natural moral law and of the commands of God: but both alike are so largely dependent upon individual interpreta-

tion that they cannot possess the same universal validity and power as the laws of the state. J. H. Kirchmann († 1884) has recently taken up a similar position.

2. The hypothesis that the origin of moral obligation is to be looked for in social or political or religious (ecclesiastical) sanctions may serve all the purposes of an historical enquiry. But it is not an historical enquiry that the heteronomists are engaged upon. The essential point of difference between autonomy and heteronomy is this: autonomy finds the origin and sanction of the moral conduct of the individual in spontaneous, independent thoughts and impulses; heteronomy in constraining precepts, whose validity is derived from obedience and submission, not from a free recognition of their rightness. And there can be no doubt that a heteronomy of this kind is often realised in practice. The man who refrains from a crime because it is forbidden and punished by the state does not feel a direct moral obligation to keep from criminal action; and the man who tries to order his life in accordance with moral standards for the sake of pleasing God or satisfying the precepts of the church is, like the criminal, merely bowing his will to an external authority. On the other hand, there seems to be as little doubt that our moral judgment decides in favour of autonomy. The first thing that we require of a moral action is that it arise from inner freedom, and not at the hest of some extraneous consideration.

We consequently distinguish very definitely between legal enactments, rules of propriety in social intercourse, the etiquette of professional conduct, etc., on the one hand, and moral duty on the other. That duty and propriety may and should prompt to precisely the same mode of behaviour does not lessen the difference between them in the smallest degree. Autonomy, then, is the natural standpoint of ethics; and it is readily intelligible that, apart from the few authors we have cited (and not all even of these are wholly consistent in their heteronomy), the moral systems both of ancient and modern times are throughout autonomous in character. We need not, therefore, give a special list of them here.

(*b*) Apriorism and Empiricism.

3. We found two opposing views of the origin of knowledge (§ 24), rationalism and empiricism. This epistemological difference has its ethical parallel in the antithesis of apriorism, or, as it is also called, *nativism* or *intuitionism*, and empiricism, which in its modern and specialised form is termed *evolutionism*. We may say, if we will, that the question here at issue is the question of the origin of *conscience*, understanding by 'conscience' the source of moral judgment within us, whether passed upon our own actions or upon those of others. The apriorists look upon conscience as an original, innate activity, which can be known only by intuition; the empiricists seek to refer it to experience or to a gradual process of development. In ethics, as in epistemology, therefore, it is a question of psychogenesis, of historical psychology, that stands in the forefront of the battle of the schools. The apriorists, however, hold further that the obligatory force of moral norms and the universal validity of moral judgments compel us to regard them as an innate possession or at least a necessary development of the practical reason (*cf.* § 9. 8). Hence nativism in ethics goes along with rationalism in epistemology. Descartes, Leibniz, and the school of Leibniz, were all apriorists. Kant, too, combines apriorism and rationalism. The moral law with its categorical imperative is a given fact, which can be understood only if we recognise its *a priori* character. Conscience is the function whereby judgment compares an action with the moral law; so that it may be termed "the representative of the moral law in the empirical consciousness of mankind." As such, it is incumbent on it not only to judge of human actions, but also to influence choice by warning and admonition.

4. The intuitionist aspect of apriorism is most prominent in English ethics. The intuitionists place moral ideas or judgments upon the same level with mathematical axioms or the laws of nature. The mathematician and the physicist declare that their first principles neither require nor admit of proof; the moralist declines in the same way to popularise his intuitions or fit them

for general recognition by any process of demonstration. It makes no great difference to the theory that some of its adherents offer a satisfactory psychological account of the nativistic character of morality, explaining that it becomes conscious by the fact of social intercourse, but is only latent in the isolated individual. R. Cudworth, R. Cumberland and S. Clarke are the chief representatives of intuitionism in English philosophy.

Of the followers of Kant, Fichte, Schleiermacher and, to some extent, Schopenhauer belong to the school of apriorism. Herbart's 'judgments of taste' (§ 9. 9) may also be denominated aprioristic, since the practical ideas which they express are regarded as eternal and immutable. Finally, Lotze must be ranked among the exponents of this phase of thought. He declares himself most explicitly for the apriority of conscience as law-giving function, and as explicitly denies the competency of empiricism to decide what ethical ideas shall be considered as obligatory.

5. Empiricism, particularly in the more special form of evolutionism, is the dominant form of philosophical ethics at the present day. Locke opened the campaign against intuitionism in ethics, as he did against apriorism in epistemology (§ 5. 3). His argument in disproof of innate practical rules or ideas sets out from the fact that there are no universally recognised judgments in matters of ethics: we do not find the same moral ideas in rude peoples, among criminals, etc., that we do in civilised nations and among individuals who submit to the regulations of the state and of society. In the second place, it is incompatible with the theory of an innate moral principle that in actual fact the dictates of morality should be so frequently disregarded, and that where our actions do conform to their (supposed) contents quite heterogeneous motives should be so frequently adducible for them. Lastly, there can be no doubt that the injunctions of morality stand in need of proof, if they are to make good their claim to validity; whereas innate truths neither require nor admit of demonstration. The only connate disposition to which Locke does not take exception is the capacity of feeling pleasure and pain; but religious, political and social sanctions have combined with it to determine the for-

mation of our moral ideas. This empiricism, and more especially its negative side, was hailed with great delight by the materialists. Helvetius and Holbach are more emphatic even than Locke in their denial of the originality of moral ideas. Nevertheless, it was impossible to formulate a satisfactory ethical theory along empirical lines so long as the burden of moral evolution had to be thrown upon the lifetime of the individual. For there is clear evidence of moral progress in society, in the community of individuals; and this cannot be explained while we conceive of each individual as starting afresh for himself, and refuse to posit any difference of connate disposition.

6. Schelling and Hegel are the first moralists to evince marked evolutionistic tendencies; but their view of the historical development of ethical norms is logical, not empirical. Hence they do not enquire into the special factors which have been at work in the alteration of moral standards, but content themselves with bringing the individual phenomena of the actual moral life under a general logical law. It is clear to us that this path can never lead to an understanding of the how and why of ethical ideas. The great advance which Darwin made upon previous theories of the development of organic life consisted in the specification of a whole number of empirical factors, which enable us to see how species originate and become transformed. Darwin carried over the same principles of explanation to the problem of the origin of conscience (*cf.* the *Descent of Man*). Three factors are concerned in its production: (1) the social instinct, which is connate in the animals as in man; (2) the power, gradually increasing with the rise of the animal in the scale of development, to compare the present with the past, to collect and utilise experiences; and (3) the general factor of habituation, which regulates all organic activities and inclinations. Added to these are natural selection, and the influence which the approval or disappoval of our fellow-men exercises upon our life and conduct. It is through the working of natural selection, *e.g.*, that races in which self-control has reached a high degree of development, or the social impulses have come to possess especial

significance, gain the advantage in the struggle for existence over others that have remained more backward in these respects.

7. More satisfactory from the philosophical point of view is the attempt made by Spencer to apply the doctrine of evolution to ethical problems. All action consists, on his view, in activities which are adapted to certain ends; and an action is the more perfect the more exact its adaptation. The natural ends of voluntary activity are either the preservation and furtherance of the individual life or the life of the race, or the promotion of a state of society which allows the individual to live and act in the greatest possible harmony with the aims and purposes of other individuals. The corresponding grades of conduct are termed by Spencer self-maintaining, race-maintaining and universal. It is the third stage that constitutes the principal subject-matter of ethics. Moral science has to deduce from the laws of life and the general conditions of existence why certain modes of conduct are harmful and certain others useful. That is 'good,' in the widest sense, which serves to accomplish some purpose; and the ultimate conscious purpose of all vital activity is the production or retention of pleasure, or the avoidance or removal of pain. There are, it is true, many ethical systems and moral judgments in which the reference to pleasure does not receive so great emphasis; but the reason is simply that they substitute for pleasure, the real and ultimate end of conduct, certain others which have acquired validity and significance as means to the attainment of pleasure. The most highly developed conduct is good conduct; and so the ideal end of action, regarded as a natural phase of human evolution, is identical with the ideal standard of conduct as judged from the ethical standpoint.

8. Wundt makes another and a different application of the doctrine of evolution in ethics. He finds the chief reason for the alteration of moral judgments or purposes in what he calls the 'law of heterogony of purpose'—the law, *i.e.*, that every voluntary action tends to go beyond its proposed end, so that unforeseen effects arise which may serve as the source of new ideas of purpose. This idea has proved extremely fruitful for

ethical enquiry. It enables us to understand how there can be so great a difference as there often is between the first and original purpose of a voluntary action and the end which it has come to subserve after a certain period of development. We see, *e.g.*, how an altruistic or universalistic action might gradually emerge from what was primarily egoistic or individualistic. Wundt further distinguishes three stages in the evolution of moral ideas: (1) a stage in which the moral aspect of life is as yet undifferentiated from its other aspects; (2) a stage in which ethical concepts become more sharply outlined, under the influence of religious ideas and social conditions, and (3) a stage in which moral conceptions become unified and systematised, as philosophy grows more powerful and religion loses its dogmatic character,—in which the notion of an ethics of humanity transcends the differences of race and custom. Lastly, conscience is manifested, Wundt says, by the dominance of imperative motives, to whose development many factors have contributed: external and internal constraint, enduring content, a moral ideal of life. The last factor is operative only in the introduction of the third stage, of fully conscious morality, where all the separate moral activities are controlled and determined by some single fundamental thought.

9. These examples of evolutionary ethics will suffice to indicate the general nature of its method. There can be no doubt that the requirements of a science of morality are very much better satisfied by evolutionism than by intuitionism. The question of the origin of moral judgments is not answered by the assumption of an innate conscience. In the first place, no account is taken of the actual differences of moral appreciation found in history, in the life of a nation, and in the conduct of individuals within the same epoch; in the second, no attempt is made to trace existent moral ideas to their conditions. And evolutionism is not open to the objections raised against the older form of empiricism. At the same time, we are bound to ask here, as we asked in the corresponding case of empiristic epistemology (*cf.* § 24. 6), whether ethics really has any necessary interest in an historical and psychological enquiry into the origin of ethical judgments. A

normative discipline, an art of volition and action, can gain nothing either for the validity or for the systematisation of its norms and precepts from the proof of their gradual development under a variety of conditions and influences. We can no more hope that ethics will be assisted in any direct way by an account of the course of moral ideas through the centuries than that logic would be helped to solve its problems by a psychological history of the development of its concepts and judgments and methods. Spencer's conception of an end of action, regarded as a natural phase of human evolution, is certainly not derived from a purely theoretical consideration of the course of history, but springs from a preformed ethical judgment which finds certain activities or purposes more valuable than others. Evolutionism is a theory, that is, but not a norm; it gives us an explanation of particular facts, but no precepts or laws by which we might regulate our actions. It follows that the antithesis of intuitionism and empiricism is not of essential significance for ethics. It applies to theories which have taken shape during the working out of psychological or sociological problems.

LITERATURE.

F. Brentano, *Vom Ursprung sittlicher Erkenntniss.* 1889.

C. M. Williams, *A Review of the Systems of Ethics founded on the Theory of Evolution.* 1893.

T. Elsenhans, *Wesen und Entstehung des Gewissens.* 1894.

§ 28. *The Ethics of Reflexion and the Ethics of Feeling.*

1. The question whether the motives of moral volition and action, as given in experience, take the form of feelings or of reflexion—some kind of rational consideration, concept, judgment, etc.—may mean either of two different things. The emphasis may lie upon the psychological nature of the motives to a voluntary action, and the answer to the question be sought by psychological methods within the psychological sphere; or interest may centre round the ethical character of the motives, which may

then be classified and valued without any regard to psychology at all. These two ways of looking at the question are not very clearly distinguished in the ethical literature, so that it is most difficult to name the supporters of the various possible theories. And there is still another difficulty. There is no general agreement as to what we are to understand by motive, and how motive is related to end. If motive is the same thing as cause, then, of course, the conscious ground of determination in choice or action is but a fraction of the total cause. But since a moral judgment has direct reference only to the conscious processes of volition and action, the idea of motive is restricted in ethics to this conscious ground of determination. Now, an end is the idea of a result of action, regarded in general as attainable; and it is clear that such an idea will determine and influence conduct. In this sense, an end is also a motive. Since, however, a single end may be regarded, if not as merely the *result* of choice, at least as the *most immediate* ground of determination in voluntary action, the term motive is still required to designate the occasion which led to the formation or selection of the particular idea of end. The distinction between end and motive would then be very simple. End is the ground of determination in voluntary action; motive the ground of determination in arriving at an end. Neither can be considered from the ethical point of view, however, except in the character of conscious processes. As we find the same lack of clearness in the ethical literature with regard to the meaning of these words—some books avoiding the difficulty altogether—it will again be very difficult to make our historical exposition anything but obscure.

2. The following account of the advocates of an ethics of reflexion, an ethics of feeling and a standpoint intermediate between the two, will (1) employ the idea of motive in the sense defined above. (2) It will further take its stand upon the modern definition of feeling as a state of pleasantness or unpleasantness, without, however, affirming the exclusive validity of any one of the various possible hypotheses of the quality of feeling. Some psychologists believe that the feelings are

homogeneous throughout, so that there are but two feeling qualities, those of pleasantness and unpleasantness; others distinguish a great variety of qualities within the general division: sensory, æsthetic, moral, religious, etc., feelings. We may quite well disregard this difference of psychological opinion as to the nature of feeling; and indeed we must do so, since we cannot always determine which position is held by a particular moralist. (3) Finally, we shall make no attempt at a separate treatment of sub-forms of the ethics of reflexion, of an ethics of understanding, *e.g.*, and an ethics of reason (*cf.* § 14. 7). The only alternatives that we have to consider, therefore, are contained in the question: Are the motives of moral volition intellectual or emotional in character? And we may accordingly substitute the phrase *ethical intellectualism* for 'ethics of reflexion,' and *emotional ethics* for 'ethics of feeling.'

3. The ethical systems of ancient philosophy are all alike intellectualistic. Socrates declares that reflexion alone can decide as to what will give keen and enduring satisfaction or happiness, *i.e.*, as to what can serve as moral end in the individual case. We find the same standpoint in Plato and Aristotle. Moral determination must proceed from the highest faculty of the mind, from reason. Hence the highest virtue of all is wisdom or prudence or foresight—a certain intellectual constitution. The same doctrine obtains also among the Stoics and Epicureans. The Stoics look upon passion as the root of all evil, so that the negative precondition for morality or goodness is a passionless frame of mind, apathy. Even in the Scholastic ethics we see traces of intellectualistic influence, in spite of its opposition to Christian theory. Thomas Aquinas says that rational foresight determines the will to choose the best among different possible purposes. And in modern philosophy the ethics of reflexion has found numerous adherents. Thus Hobbes' natural moral law (*cf.* § 9. 7) consists in an accurate weighing of the useful or harmful results of action; and immorality consequently rests upon an intellectual error, a wrong inference. Cudworth, too, makes correct foresight the source of all morality, and the same

idea recurs in Clarke, when he demands of a moral action that it be constantly and regularly controlled by reason.

4. The ethics of reflexion further includes the materialistic moralists in its ranks. They prefer the intellectualistic conception of ethical motives because it harmonises best with empiricism. For, evidently, our knowledge and judgment and reflexion may very well be made dependent upon experience; but the nature of feeling is determined by disposition and organisation. Intellectualism also dominates the metaphysical ethics of the seventeenth and eighteenth centuries. We cannot, it is true, assert that Descartes shows any very definite bias towards the position. Still, he defines morality as the intention of doing what one knows to be right, and holds that the emotions obscure clear knowledge and therewith debase the good will. Leibniz, on the other hand, makes moral and rational action identical. Moral action is the result of clear ideas, immoral action comes from confused ideas. And as the feelings of pleasantness and unpleasantness both belong to the class of confused ideas, they can be regarded only as obstacles to morality, not as positive grounds of moral determination. Through the writings of Wolff this became the accepted theory of ethics in the German philosophy of the first half of the eighteenth century. Kant, too, must be counted among the moralists of reflexion. The only motive to morality which he recognises is a law of the practical reason, an *a priori* rule; feelings are pathological grounds of determination in human volition. J. G. Fichte, during his first period, is Kant's truest disciple in ethical doctrine. None but those who act for duty's sake have reached the highest stage of the moral character. Hegel is also an intellectualist. Thought, of says, must decide what purpose shall be posited by the choosing will. And modern utilitarianism (*cf.* § 30. 9), as represented by Bentham and J. S. Mill, inclines towards the same standpoint. It is only by a quite complicated course of reasoning that we can decide whether a given action is or is not in accordance with the ethical end of general prosperity.

5. It is not until the advent of Christianity that the ethics he

feeling begins to assume definite form. Christianity sees the fundamental motive to moral action in the feeling of love. And it was then a long time before philosophical ethics assimilated the idea of an emotional ethics. In Shaftesbury it is very prominent. Emotions constitute the springs of all our actions, and moral conduct has its root in a harmonious relation of selfish and social feelings (*cf.* § 7. 9).

According to Hutcheson († 1747), purely disinterested love or unselfish preference is the sole source of moral action; while reason has but a secondary significance, as helping to determine the objects of action. For Smith, in the same way, sympathy is the only motive to morality. Rousseau also represents an ethics of feeling, but from a different point of view. His belief that nature is so far superior to civilisation necessarily led him to lay stress upon natural feelings, feelings undistorted by education. In the post-Kantian philosophy, Schopenhauer is an outspoken advocate of an emotional ethics. Sympathy is the one moral motive. L. Feuerbach also belongs to the school: he regards the impulse to happiness as the fundamental force in all action moral actions included. Comte, too, looks on love as the impelling motive in social activities. At the present day the ethics of feeling is undoubtedly in the ascendant. This is largely due to the tendency of modern psychology to identify feeling and motive.

6. Not all moralists are strict adherents either of the intellectualistic or of the emotional theory. Many have taken up an intermediate standpoint, recognising both intellectual and emotional factors as possible motives. Spinoza, *e.g.*, speaks of the enslavement of will by emotion as the source of all base and immoral conduct, and indicates clear or adequate knowledge as the only means of escape from it; but at the same time declares that emotions cannot be overcome except by emotions, and that truly moral conduct from inner freedom can therefore arise only by way of a special emotion which is stronger than the rest. This highest emotion is the *amor intellectualis Dei*. In English ethics Cumberland gives the feelings of benevolence and

trust a place beside rational foresight, as grounds of determination in volition; and Locke makes self-love an influential motive alongside of reasoned reflexion. Hume, too, thinks that conduct is affected in both ways, by sympathy and self-love upon the one side, and by understanding and reflexion on the other. Lastly, Herbart may be included in the present list, since his practical ideas, which give the standard of reference for all moral appreciation, acknowledge both an emotional and an intellectual motive. The emotional is clearly recognised in the idea of benevolence; the intellectual, perhaps, in the idea of perfection.

7. A psychological enquiry into the nature of the motives which determine choice or decision leads, on general grounds, and quite apart from the question whether feeling has two qualities or many, to the conclusion that neither emotional nor intellectualistic ethics is of itself adequate to the facts of the moral life. There are actions which must be referred to intellectual motives exclusively; but there are others which are instigated by an affectively-toned idea or judgment, and yet others whose selection is due simply to considerations of agreeableness or disagreeableness. Most moralists of the present day incline to think that feeling must be at least one, if it is not the sole factor in the taking of a resolution; and many assert outright that to will and to be pleased to will are one and the same thing. The actual judgment of the agent, however, returns a flat contradiction to this theory. Sometimes we think that we ought to do something, not from inclination, but because an external or internal force compels us; sometimes a simple reflexion, in which feeling plays no part at all, influences the will to decide. The assertion that feelings invariably help to determine volition—still more, the statement that they are the only possible motives to voluntary action—is a logical dogma of the most arbitrary kind. It is not an objective description taken from the facts, but a hypothetical construction of the course of events. And there is still another consideration. Working from the evolutionary standpoint, modern psychology has come to believe that pleasure and pain are connected with furtherance and obstruction of the

individual life. Hence those who regard self-preservation as the real or final purpose of all action find no difficulty in translating ethics into psychology, and defining their purpose as the pursuit of pleasure and the avoidance of pain. But to say nothing of the correctness or incorrectness of the evolutionary theory of feeling —and grave objections may be brought against it—the assumed connection proves nothing whatsoever as regards the particular action of the adult individual.

8. An unprejudiced psychological examination shows quite clearly (1) that voluntary actions often take place independently of feeling. (*a*) There are numerous cases in which a pleasure or the avoidance of a pain is experienced not directly, but only in idea. In all these, we *know* that if a certain event happens a pleasant feeling will arise or an unpleasant feeling be avoided. That is to say, we know theoretically what is the connection between the feelings and their conditions. Surely, no one will deny that choice can be made or resolution taken upon the ground of such knowledge. It is possible, of course, that the ideas may give rise to an emotion of expectation or fear, and so be accompanied by anticipatory feelings; but this is neither necessarily nor (so far as the author's experience extends) even usually the case. (*b*) Here belong further the 'habitual' or 'automatic' actions, whose sure and uniform course excludes them from the class of selective actions (actions involving choice) but not from that of voluntary action in general. They, too, require a certain impulse, which they receive from particular ideas. (*c*) And, finally, all dutiful actions seem to spring from other than emotional motives. They, however, are only one out of a large number of similar instances. Wherever principles, theoretical considerations, etc., determine a resolve, the equation of 'willing' with 'willingness' is quite without meaning. If the ethics of reflexion were content to state that intellectual motives are possible, or of actual occurrence, it would undoubtedly be entitled to general acceptance.

9. (2) But it happens hardly less frequently that affectively-toned ideas or trains of ideas are of determining importance for choice. When we act from benevolence or sympathy, from fear

or hope, from enthusiasm or despair, the influences at work are a more or less intensive feeling and an intellectual factor. Our choice is not decided by feeling alone, but by feeling in connection with particular ideas or judgments. The feeling of itself is oftentimes far too indefinite to give a concrete direction to volition and choice. And to abstract entirely from the theoretical factor would argue an inexcusable disregard of facts. (3) Lastly, it is a by no means uncommon experience that some idea assumes the dignity of a purpose because it carries with it an especially vivid feeling of pleasure, which prevents the realisation of other weakly-toned or indifferent possibilities. The relation of purpose and motive in such states of mind is the intimate relation of idea and feeling—indisputably the simplest, but not by any means the only case.

The result of our psychological discussion, then, is the rejection of any exclusive theory as to the nature of motives. We may note that the ethics of feeling, as it actually appears in the history of philosophy, has not as a rule drawn any hard and fast line in this respect. If the motive to morality is found in love or sympathy or benevolence, we may be sure that the writer has in mind actions which would fall under our second psychological rubric, actions where choice is determined by affectively-toned ideas.

10. We must now return to the ethical question, and ask which of the possible forms of motivisation in selective action is to receive the stamp of moral approval. According to intellectualism, none but the first; according to emotional morality, none but the third. The intellectualist would regard any admixture of feeling in the determination of choice as prejudicial to the moral quality of volition. But this theory, though it can point to Kant as its classical exponent, does not possess universal validity. Our moral judgment of voluntary action in cases where we have to assume benevolence or sympathy as motive is by no means a judgment of disapproval. On the contrary, such action appears especially to deserve the predicate of good or moral. And most moralists are here in accord with the judgment of every-day life. Under these

circumstances, an exclusive intellectualism must be rejected; the only tenable position, from the side of the ethics of reflexion, will be that which looks upon the intellectual and emotional factors as alike significant for our moral actions. But again, the moral consciousness regards with approbation actions which spring from the pure consideration of duty, and actions influenced simply by the *idea* of feeling. It is at all events not necessary, therefore, that pleasure or pain be involved in the origination of a moral act. And, finally, conscience does not condemn purely emotional actions, provided that it can approve their purpose. An act does not lose in moral value because it is prompted by a feeling of joy. At the same time, its moral character does not depend upon the feeling—unless, of course, we assume the existence of specific moral feelings. At this point the vexed psychological question of the homogeneity or heterogeneity of the qualities of pleasantness and unpleasantness (*cf.* 2, above) begins to have a bearing upon ethics. Since psychology has not as yet reached a final decision in the matter, we must simply suspend judgment as to the possibility of a specific ethics of feeling; though an exclusively emotional theory may, in any event, be rejected as untenable.

11. We may call the reader's notice, in the present connection, to an important fact which has not as yet received from ethical writers the attention that it deserves. There is a distinction between peripherally and centrally excited feelings, just as there is between ideas of perception and ideas of memory or imagination. But while the ideas produced by peripheral stimulation are very much more vivid and intensive than the centrally aroused ideas of memory and imagination, the pleasantness and unpleasantness set up by sense stimuli are not always, or even usually, stronger than those called forth by central excitation. Both facts are of great importance for the understanding of the more complicated processes which grow up round feeling or idea. A knowledge based predominantly upon perception would hardly be possible if the centrally excited sensations were as vivid as the peripherally excited; and, on the other hand, a standard of ethical or æsthetical appreciation, consistently applied over the whole

range of human activity, would hardly be possible if sense stimuli were the principal determinants of our emotional life. Moral education and moral progress are, therefore, closely bound up with this teleological difference between feelings and ideas.

§ 29. *Individualism and Universalism.*

1. Individualism and universalism return alternative answers to the question: Who must be affected by our conduct, if the conduct is to be termed moral? Individualism declares that it is always particular individuals, definite persons, that are the objects of moral volition; universalism declares as certainly that it is always a community, whether family or nation, social class or professional colleagues, etc., etc., to which moral conduct has to look. Individualism divides into *egoism* and *altruism*, according as the agent considers himself, his own person, as the end of his volition, or makes other persons the objects of his moral action. Universalism has as many forms as there are kinds of community; we can speak, *e.g.*, of a *social*, a *political*, a *national* and a *humanistic* universalism. As a general rule, however, it defines the supreme community, humanity, as the highest or final aim of moral conduct, and regards the other forms as merely preparatory stages, proximate ends or necessary means, to the fulfilment of the ultimate ethical purpose. There are various intermediate standpoints between the two extremes. Thus egoism and altruism may be united, and the different forms of universalism brought together into a single universal theory. Nay, even the extremes themselves, individualism and universalism, may subsist side by side within the limits of the same ethical system. We may acknowledge the justice or necessity of conduct which is directed towards particular individuals, as well as of conduct that takes the good of a community for its end.

2. We find both schools of thought represented in ancient ethics. Socrates, the Stoics and the Epicureans, are all individualists. Plato inclines to universalism; while Aristotle takes up an intermediate position. No moralist of antiquity stands for

pure altruism: the individualism is for the most part both egoistic and altruistic. We find an exclusive egoism, however, among the Cyrenaics (§ 9. 3), and, later, among the Epicureans. The founder of Christianity may be termed a humanistic universalist, since he felt himself called to bring salvation to all mankind. His ethical precepts are, it is true, characterised throughout by an individualistic tendency; but this does not include respect of persons, and the individualism is accordingly the fitting precursor of a humanistic universalism. Egoism and altruism are evenly balanced; it is only occasionally that the altruistic side becomes the more pronounced. The same point of view obtains in theological ethics. The duties of the agent to himself are placed side by side with his duties towards others. When the theologians further put forward the community of state or church as a special object of moral volition, they are not returning to the prevailing ideas of early Christian ethics, but rather extending and supplementing them to meet the needs of a different age.

3. In modern ethics we see all sorts and kinds of individualistic and universalistic theory. Spinoza and Hobbes are egoists who look upon the preservation, advantage and prosperity of the acting subject as the natural aim of all endeavour. Hobbes recommends an attitude of goodwill towards others, but only as a necessary means to the accomplishment of this end. Descartes and Leibniz, on the other hand, are individualists who unite egoism and altruism. Francis Bacon seems to be a pure universalist, of the social and humanistic type. Cumberland and Locke combine individualism with universalism; Hutcheson, Hume and Smith are very decidedly altruistic. Shaftesbury, Kant and Fichte are individualists in the general sense of the word; though Fichte in his later period leans towards a humanistic universalism. Schopenhauer, Comte and Lotze are altruists; Hegel and Wundt, humanistic universalists; Herbart, an individualist in both meanings of the term. Finally, Schleiermacher, Krause, Spencer and von Hartmann seek to harmonise individualism and universalism.

4. This variety of ethical standpoint is the reflexion (1) of an

actual difference in moral judgment, and (2) of a multiplicity of temporal and social influences. The cosmopolitan sentiment of the eighteenth century could not possibly have found expression in a national or political universalism, such as is proclaimed on all sides at the present day. In times when the individual feels himself and his needs to be at variance with the aims and regulations of the community to which he belongs by birth and right, ethics naturally takes the form either of individualism or of a revolutionary universalism: and so on. If we question the actual moral judgment of mankind, we receive an answer that tells as strongly for individualism as for universalism. An act of kindness done by one individual to another, without any idea of assistance to a community, is approved by our conscience as good,—provided, of course, that no egoism lies behind it. On the other hand, we approve equally of a mode of conduct whose purpose is nothing less than the advantage of humanity at large: *e.g.*, the production of works whose intellectual enjoyment is not confined to any particular persons or, perhaps, to any particular time. And again, we should not hesitate to call an action moral which aimed to further the interests of the narrower circle of the family, or the wider sphere of profession, social class, people or state. In other words, our moral judgment knows nothing of the exclusive antithesis of individualism and universalism. Nevertheless, there may be occasions when it has to distinguish and even to choose between them. A certain line of action towards individuals cannot always be harmonised with duty towards the community, and *vice versâ*.

5. It is a theory held by different moralists at different periods that there should be agreement between the individual and the social or universal emotions or tendencies. Kant's categorical imperative, *e.g.*, expresses this thought in the form of a law. But however much we may desire the reconciliation, we find ourselves, as a matter of fact, not seldom obliged to choose between the good of an individual and the good of the community. The difficulties which thus arise are not met by the simple statement that the community must of necessity

take precedence over the individual. The necessity exists only when the interests of the community coincide with those of the individual, or when their fulfilment at least promises the satisfaction of the just requirements of individual members. On the other hand, a case is quite conceivable in which the good of the community would not by any means appear more important or valuable than the good of the individual. Consequently we are always thrown back upon the question of the highest or ultimate end of moral conduct, the question of the *summum bonum*, and must let our answer to it decide whether particular persons or some form of community is to be the aim of our volition. It is only from the standpoint of a humanistic universalism that we can say *a priori*: universalism and individualism are never irreconcilable. And since Christianity has lent to this position all the weight of religious sanction, it is in the inalienable interest of ethics to give its full support to humanistic theory. The argument that individual persons must be the concrete point of attachment in moral volition finds direct refutation in the increasing development of social, political, national and humanistic forces.

Our discussion of these two schools of universalism and individualism must have brought home to the reader the fact of the *relativity* of moral judgments. This relativity will be impressed upon us still more forcibly, and in a still greater variety of degree, when we come to enquire into the ends of moral volition. It has found proverbial expression in the phrase: "the better is the enemy of the good." All judgments of value, including the æsthetic judgment and judgments based upon feelings of sense, have this mark of relativity upon them. Psychologically, it may be referred to the character of feeling in general. It has been the occasion of all the attempts of moralists in all times to set up some absolute standard of moral judgment, to discover some one supreme good or purpose to be achieved by moral volition. But no definition that has as yet been offered has been able to command universal and lasting assent.

§ 30. *Subjectivism and Objectivism.*

1. (1) *Subjectivism* defines the end of moral action as a subjective state, either of the agent himself or of other individuals. This 'state' must, evidently, be a feeling. The processes of pleasantness and unpleasantness are specifically subjective in character; they are the least capable of communication of all subjective processes; and they have no objective side at all (*cf.* § 26. 12). Moreover, they are admirably qualified to serve as final purposes, beyond which the question 'to what end' cannot go. At the same time, not all feelings are of equal value. They differ, at least, in intensity and duration: and psychology has drawn the further distinction of sensible or lower and intellectual or higher feelings, contrasting those that depend upon sensory stimulation with those produced by the activity of idea or thought (*cf.* § 28. 2). Subjectivistic ethics, following psychology, has taken two different forms, those of hedonism and eudæmonism.

Hedonism regards the pleasures of sense as the more intensive, and consequently the better worth pursuit; *eudæmonism* points to the greater permanence of the intellectual feelings, and makes an enduring contentment, 'happiness,' the end of moral endeavour. Both schools put a quite simple interpretation upon the antithetic predicates of the moral judgment. Conduct that tends to awaken pleasure is 'good'; conduct that tends to arouse pain is 'bad.'

2. (*a*) *Hedonism* appears only sporadically in the history of ethics. It was the position of the Cyrenaic school in the ancient world (*cf.* § 9. 3), and has been defended by certain of the materialistic moralists (especially Helvetius: §§ 9. 8; 27. 5). This slight historical importance is readily intelligible. (i.) It lies in the very nature of sense feeling on the one hand, and of the development of the higher civilisation on the other, that peripheral pleasures and pains, though constantly renewed, can exert but a transitory influence upon our inner life. (ii.) Moreover, the consequences of physical pleasure are often quite

the reverse of pleasant. (iii.) And lastly, our moral judgment, while it does not refuse to consider them altogether, tolerates them merely as means to other and higher ends, or in cases where they do not conflict with the more important interests of human life. For all these reasons, sense feeling cannot possibly rank as the sole and final end of volition; and any theory which attaches so great an importance to it must be rejected.

(*b*) *Eudæmonism*, which is still current in modern ethics, is far more adequate to the facts. The contentment that comes from a zealous fulfilment of duty or from a good conscience, from successful mental labour or artistic achievement, from stimulating companionship or the confidence of friendship,—this lasting contentment, it says, is an immeasurably more valuable and therefore more worthy aim than the brief and uncertain satisfaction of the senses. It is evident that eudæmonism is a theory to which the contents of most ethical systems can be subsumed. There is, probably, no moralist who would assert that the unhappiness of individuals is a necessary result of the conduct he prescribes, or who would declare himself indifferent as to its effect for feeling.

3. Socrates was the first to give a full and clear statement of the eudæmonistic position. Aristotle thinks it beyond all question that good fortune or happiness is the natural end of conduct. The Epicureans are also eudæmonists. Plato speaks of happiness in a transcendent sense; and Christian ethics accepts the doctrine, at the same time explicitly demanding the renunciation of earthly pleasures. It is doubtful, however, whether the ethics of Christianity is a pure eudæmonism. True, it insists upon the glories of the other world. But, although these glories follow from a moral and religious life upon earth, they are not necessarily to be regarded as an end prompting to action. In modern philosophy, Shaftesbury holds an eudæmonistic position; inner satisfaction is the end of morals. Utilitarianism (of which we shall treat more fully below: see 9) is also apt to appear in eudæmonistic dress, making the greatest happiness of all, or of the greatest number, the aim of moral volition. Lotze, too, may be termed an eudæmonist, since he looks on feeling as the only

real and final standard of value. Conduct that has no relation to pleasure or pain, he would say, can neither be approved nor disapproved; indeed, cannot be conduct at all. Lastly, we find eudæmonism in combination with other ethical theories, *e.g.*, with that of perfectionism. So in one form or another it pervades the whole literature of ethics down to the present day.

4. If eudæmonism affirms that the end which it formulates is the only end which can make moral endeavour and moral action worth while, we are bound to take issue with it. We can mention ends that are deemed worth while, altogether independently of the feelings connected with them. Suppose that we have chosen a community—the state, or perhaps mankind in general—as the object of our moral volition; it is absolutely impossible for us to consider the feelings of individual persons. You can make an individual happy, but not mankind or the state. Eudæmonism may, therefore, be combined with individualism, but is not to be harmonised with universalistic ideas. And since the ethical value of universalism is unquestionable, eudæmonism must be judged an incomplete theory.

Even in our conduct to individuals, however, the giving of happiness is by no means the only, or even the ordinary, end of moral purpose. The teacher who has in mind the efficiency of his pupil, the philanthropist who seeks to elevate the class of poverty-stricken indolents, the friend who lightens a criminal conscience by giving opportunity for full confession,—all these, we may be sure, do not aim at arousing agreeable feelings whether in others or in themselves. We may, therefore, think it desirable that the attainment of a moral end shall always bring with it an enduring satisfaction; but this will oftentimes be a mere secondary effect, welcome indeed, but not the one and only purpose of our volition. It is unnecessary to point out that the foregoing argument holds against egoistic, as well as against altruistic, eudæmonism.

5. (2) *Objectivism* regards the feelings as too vague and uncertain to serve as the objects of moral conduct, and accordingly sets up certain objective standards and ends whose validity

is independent of pleasure and pain. We have various forms of objectivism, corresponding to the different kinds of objective standard set up. (*a*) *Perfectionism* makes perfection or improvement the end of moral volition. It was introduced into ethics by Leibniz. On his metaphysical theory, the world is a graded series of monads (§ 17. 2). The highest and most perfect of them all is the divine monad; because it alone represents the universe with complete clearness. The more obscure ideas a monad has, the less perfect is it. The process of improvement, then, the advance towards perfection, means a growth in clear ideas. The theory was systematised and popularised by Chr. Wolff; so that we find a trace of it still lingering in Kant, in the statement that the duty of the agent towards himself is the duty of self-improvement. Indeed, the idea held its own after Kant's day as at least half-way entitled to a place in an ethical system; and in recent years Lipps has returned to it, though of course without accepting its original setting, the peculiar metaphysical assumptions of the Leibnizian monadology. Stripped of these, perfection means simply the unrestricted play and full development of all one's powers.

6. (*b*) Another closely related form of objectivism is *evolutionism*, which affirms that development or progress is the end of moral endeavour. Hegel was an evolutionist, but somewhat obscured his position by the logical phrasing that he gave to the idea of development. He also deprived morality of the independent and, in its own way, supreme value which we now ascribe to it, by making it only one, and that not the highest, stage in the dialectic process. Wundt has constructed a graduated series of ends, which culminates in an ideal conception, never to be attained in reality. He accepts self-contentment and self-improvement as individual ends, but still only as proximate goals of conduct, transition stages of moral activity. More important are the social ends, which find expression in public well-being and general progress. And highest of all stand the humanistic ends, which are chiefly effective to produce intellectual goods, and have as their immediate aim the constant and continuous improvement

of mankind. We must always look to religion, Wundt thinks, to furnish a concrete end of moral endeavour at definite epochs of human history. Ethics determines simply the tendency, the general direction of advance; so that development or progress itself is the only valid ethical end.

7. Neither of these two forms of objectivism is sufficiently clear and explicit to furnish a satisfactory ethical theory. It is meaningless to speak of perfection or progress or development, unless exact definitions are furnished. We must have criteria by which we can identify the process in a given case, or test alleged instances of it. We do not look with moral approbation upon any and every kind of development, but only upon that which follows from a quite determinate intention or serves quite determinate purposes. If we are told that it is moral perfection or moral progress that is meant, we reply that the definition is a logical circle: it contains the very term which needs defining. If we are told, again, that increase of knowledge or wisdom is a moral end, we have several objections to urge. (i.) Talent is irregularly distributed, and cannot on that account be regarded as a condition of moral achievement. (ii.) The proportionate exercise of all our powers, the development of a 'beautiful character,' cannot be brought into connection with the actual one-sidedness of talent and the restriction to definite sides or aspects of existence which a particular occupation requires. (iii.) We do not consider the absence or lack of cultivation of this or that capacity as necessarily constituting a moral defect. And if we are told, finally, that the trend of progress can be understood only from the observation of individual, social and humanistic purposes, as manifested in the conduct of particular persons, we reply that this conduct would then be caused or motived by regard to these purposes, and not by the indefinite ideal of infinite progress. For the question of the ends of moral volition expects for answer not a reference to some abstract effect, but the statement of an end which may be striven for by the individual mind in the individual case.

8. (*c*) A third form of objectivism is *naturalism*. For it, the

end of all moral conduct is a life according to nature. So far from regarding morality as a matter of commands, duties, in conflict with the 'natural man,' it affirms that the object of human endeavour should be to give full rein to natural inclinations, habits and impulses. The moral end may, therefore, differ very considerably in different cases, and naturalism offers no precise definition of it. If we feel the need of sensuous pleasure, we should adopt means to obtain it; and if we prefer work or a higher kind of satisfaction, we should take measures to secure that. It is noteworthy, however, that the historical descriptions of the life 'in accordance with nature' vary within wide limits from age to age. The Cynics introduced the idea into ethics. The Stoics, who were the first to turn it to ethical account, nevertheless identified the 'natural' with the 'rational' and 'dutiful' (*cf.* § 9. 3). Rousseau, on the other hand, looked upon 'natural' existence as an ideal, in contradistinction to the affectation and artificiality prevalent in his time. And in our own day Nietzsche (*Zur Genealogie der Moral*, 1887) has drawn a picture of a 'super-man,' who in exuberant fulness of strength may satisfy his desires and unfold his powers with total disregard of consequence. If naturalism really means what it says, it abolishes ethics altogether: for ethics can exist (as we showed above: § 9. 1) only where there is opposition between natural conduct and a conduct required or enjoined. In other words, the naturalistic position can be held in ethics only so long as the naturalistic ideal remains unrealised. Its doctrines grew, as we can easily see, out of a desire for primitiveness and vigour and simplicity of conduct: and it has a real significance as a criticism of the contrasting forms of life.

9. (*d*) In English ethics a fourth form of objectivism, *utilitarianism*, has become predominant. Francis Bacon struck the keynote of utilitarian ethics when he made the common weal the end of moral endeavour. Since his time it has followed a steady course, varying only as regards individualistic or universalistic tendency. Hobbes, Cumberland, and Locke were utilitarians. The theory was later revived by Bentham, and advocated

vigorously and in great detail by John Stuart Mill (*Utilitarianism*, 1863). In France it found a disciple in Comte, and quite recently certain German moralists, von Gizycki among them, have accepted it. At the same time there has lately been an energetic reaction against the whole point of view; and German ethics in particular—von Hartmann, Wundt, Paulsen—has taken up an attitude of strong opposition. The fundamental principle of the utilitarian school is that utility or prosperity is the end of moral conduct. But since the idea of utility is a relative idea, and so always leaves the question open as to what the useful is useful for, utilitarianism generally passes over into eudæmonism, attempting to define utility or prosperity by its necessary relations to pleasure and pain. The useful thus comes either to be regarded as that which secures pleasure and keeps off pain, or to be identified outright with happiness. The formula: "Work for the greatest good of the greatest number" becomes transformed into the eudæmonistic formula: "Work for the greatest possible happiness of the greatest number." This is the only escape from the excessive generality of moral concepts which follows inevitably from the adoption of the simple principle of utility. For there are assuredly very many useful things which do not make people happy: *e.g.*, a whole number of technical inventions, improvements of the means of communication, certain forms of division of labour, etc., etc.

10. On the points in which utilitarianism has identified itself with eudæmonism we can refer the reader to the criticism passed above (see 4) upon the eudæmonistic theory in its exclusive form. We would lay especial emphasis upon the fact that by the direct testimony of conscience there is no moral obligation to achieve happiness at any price. True, we normally feel an active sympathy with undeserved suffering; but we should be doing an ill service to one who had brought suffering upon himself by his own weakness and wickedness, if we put an end to his repentance simply in order that we might see him happy. Not pleasure absolutely, but only a pleasure which is possible under definite conditions, can be an end of moral conduct. And it is very

much the same with utility or prosperity. Some limitation is inevitable, if either is to serve as moral end.

Apart from this, however, utilitarianism does not seem broad enough to cover every instance of moral action. It has been pointed out that the soldier who remains at his post in the hour of defeat is doing useful service neither to others nor to his cause; and that the public man and head of a family who saves a drowning child at the risk of his own life is most probably endangering rather than furthering the general prosperity. Nevertheless, utilitarianism contains a core of truth, which becomes the more evident the more it breaks free from its connection with eudæmonism. The good at which it aims includes perfection and progress as well as satisfaction, so that rightly understood it furnishes an exceedingly comprehensive theory of moral conduct. Only it must not stop short at abstract generalities, but define as accurately as possible the various forms of prosperity, individualistic and universalistic.

11. We might put down as a fifth form of objectivism the theory that the good itself is an independent end of conduct. Differently expressed, the theory is that duty must be done for duty's sake. But plainly this is not any new form of objectivism. It simply affirms that in moral action the contents of motive and end must coincide. The reason for doing what is good is the good itself. The motive that prompts to the performance of duty is not some end which can thereby be accomplished, but an inclination towards duty. It is evident that a view of this sort—which has been supported with great energy by many moralists, Kant and Fichte among them—is compatible with the utmost diversity of ethical standpoint. For it says nothing whatever as to the contents of the good or of duty. If it could show proof that moral conduct and no other exhibits this coincidence of the contents of end and motive, it would be of value for the characterisation of action: but otherwise it has no independent validity.

We may now sum up our discussion of the various ethical schools. Only one of them, that of egoism, stands in direct contradiction with the moral consciousness. Altruism and universalism are both entitled to consideration. The ethical end, whether taken to regard other individuals or a community, may be very variously defined. Sense pleasure and enduring satisfaction, utility and perfection, may all be recognised as ends of moral conduct; and the principle of general prosperity is perhaps best adapted to bring them all under a single concept. We may demand, however, that any contradiction between the separate forms of this prosperity be avoided. As supreme rule of moral conduct we shall always have before us the increase and furtherance of moral activities and influences. Finally, we notice once more the relativity of moral judgments (*cf.* § 29. 5) and the necessity for their analytical and statistical investigation (*cf.* § 9. 11). The one-sidedness of the different schools of ethical thought that we have passed in review makes it desirable that the facts of the moral consciousness should be ascertained as accurately as possible, and then worked over into a system.

LITERATURE.

E. Pfleiderer, *Eudämonismus und Egoismus*. 1880. (Takes issue with Kant in particular.)

Chr. Sigwart, *Vorfragen der Ethik*. 1886.

J. Watson, *Hedonistic Theories from Aristippus to Spencer*. 1896.

For the ethical schools in general (§§ 27–30) *cf.* the literature cited under § 9, and especially the works of von Hartmann, Wundt and Sidgwick.

CHAPTER IV.

THE PROBLEM OF PHILOSOPHY AND THE PHILOSOPHICAL SYSTEM.

§ 31. *The Problem of Philosophy.*

1. In the first and second Chapters of this work we spoke of the necessity of finding a new definition of the problem of philosophy. All the attempts made so far to give an universally valid definition of philosophy break down when confronted with the facts of its historical development. The worst fault that a definition can have is to be too wide or too narrow; and the numerous definitions offered hitherto are guilty of both these errors. If we term philosophy a science of the inner experience, we cannot give either metaphysics or epistemology or logic or the philosophy of nature its proper place among the philosophical disciplines. Moreover, psychology, which is, of course, the real science of the inner experience, is just separating itself from philosophy and winning recognition as a special science: so that the definition is absolutely incompetent to bring out the peculiar features of philosophical work. If, on the other hand, we say that philosophy is the sum total of scientific knowledge, the systematisation of the sciences, we shall fail to understand its historical development and permanent significance: we have made the idea of philosophy too wide. In this way we might run through all the formulæ that appear in the literature as definitions of philosophy, and should always find the same mistake. The definition that we ourselves accepted provisionally and for reasons of expediency—that philosophy is the science of principles (§ 2. 8)—is no excep tion to the rule. A very little consideration on general grounds will show us that (and why) a simple definition after the ordinary logical pattern cannot apply to the subject-matter of philosophy.

2. The *genus proximum* that is usually given in definitions of philosophy is the idea of *science.* It then becomes necessary to distinguish philosophical science from other mental products of the same genus. But no *differentia specifica* can be proposed that does not strain the meaning of words, and none that even so is adequate to the facts. For (1) the objects with which philosophy is concerned are not of necessity specifically different from those dealt with in the special sciences; and the form or method of philosophic treatment is not of necessity different from the methods which they pursue. (2) Moreover, there is no settled rule as to what shall be included among the philosophical disciplines. The departments of philosophy that we discussed in Chapter II. represent approximately the body of knowledge that is called 'philosophy' at the present day; but the list is not by any means exhaustive historically. (3) Lastly, it is possible to distinguish within a scientific exposition (and the distinction is frequently drawn) a part that is philosophical and a part that belongs to the special object of enquiry.

Plainly, then, there can be no sharp line of division between philosophical science and the other species of the scientific genus. We must accordingly give up all hope of an unitary definition, and try to express what has been, is, and presumably will be essential to philosophy in another way,—by help of a divisive definition.

3. We believe that there are three quite different problems which have demanded philosophical treatment in all ages. (1) The first consists in *the development of a comprehensive and consistent theory of the universe.* Such a theory must, on the one side, take account of the whole scientific knowledge of its time, and on the other, keep a fast hold upon practical issues. It is, of course, for practice that it is chiefly needed. For the moment that our attempt to round off scientific knowledge takes us into the realm of the transcendent, the universal validity of ideas and

concepts and judgments ceases, not only in fact but in theory also. By theory, therefore, we can obtain no more than a survey, more or less adequate, of the different possibilities which open before the thinking mind at the limit of human knowledge. That every age has chosen some one of these, and expended upon it all the resources of subtlety and ingenuity, is due not so much to a constant curiosity to know, as to the inappeasable craving for a satisfactory background to human life, human volition and action,—for a comprehensive idea of what mankind and the universe are and mean that can be applied in every-day experience. That is why materialism has tried to recommend itself by asserting its power completely to satisfy all practicable requirements. *Metaphysics* is the old name for this first problem of philosophy.

4. (2) The second philosophical problem consists in *the investigation of the presuppositions of science.* Here belong, in the first place, certain general concepts, such as space, time, causality, etc., and, secondly, the methods and forms of scientific thought. In virtue of this problem, philosophy becomes a fundamental or central science, of a purely theoretical character, altogether remote from practical interests. On the other side, the problem demands from philosophy an independent analytical investigation of a definite group of facts, with which no other branch of knowledge is concerned. With the comprehensive outlook which it thus obtains, philosophy is in a position to offer a solid and sober criticism of work done in the special sciences. We all know how often the boundary line between fact and hypothesis or theory is overstepped, and how often the man of science presumes to judge of things which lie entirely beyond the range of special scientific knowledge. In all such cases the fundamental science, philosophy, is called upon to raise its voice in warning or correction. Knowledge of presuppositions thus becomes a criterion of the results that depend upon them. The general name which we attach to this problem of philosophy is *theory of science* (*Wissenschaftslehre*). It is evident that the contents and method of the theory of science must be essentially different from those

of metaphysics, and that we cannot argue legitimately from the one province to the other.

5. (3) The third problem of philosophy, and the problem whose subject-matter is especially liable to variation, is that of *paving the way for new special sciences and special scientific knowledge.* Remembering this third problem, we can understand the changes that have taken place in the number and contents of the philosophical disciplines, and show a real continuity of development in the aims and achievements of historical philosophy. There can be no doubt that metaphysics and the theory of science furnish material assistance toward the accomplishment of the desired end. Metaphysics calls our attention to the gaps that still exist in knowledge, but that may perhaps be filled up; and the theory of science uses its critical authority partly to insist upon a more solid foundation for scientific hypothesis, partly to indicate the general direction in which scientific work may be pushed on with greatest prospect of success. Nevertheless, the task requires for its fulfilment something which is possessed neither by the theory of science nor by metaphysics. It is so closely related to purely scientific enquiry that the reader may question whether it should be relegated to philosophy at all. And as a matter of fact we cannot point to any intrinsic or necessary criterion, whereby we may decide exactly when a special science, the way for which has been paved by philosophy, shows its right to an independent place in the sum of knowledge. The matter depends upon extraneous circumstances: when material or range of application has reached a certain limit it becomes inconvenient to regard the science any longer as a department of philosophy. Nevertheless, it is not a simple accident that philosophy has discharged this third function with such signal success. The man of science who exercises his powers exclusively on minor problems, on particular sections of experience, has naturally no comprehensive grasp of what is possible to science as a whole.—We cannot give the problem a special title. It is most fittingly designated by the names of the special disciplines which owe their origin to philosophical initiative.

6. It is not necessary that the three philosophical problems should be approached separately. There are, on the contrary, a number of philosophical disciplines, in the strict sense, where the two first, if not all three, receive treatment at the same time. Suppose, *e.g.*, that we are setting out to write a natural philosophy. We shall (1) first of all go to the theory of science, and try to turn its criticisms to account in the special field of natural science. We shall, that is, pick out and examine the particular presuppositions upon which natural science depends. (2) We shall endeavour, secondly, to bring together in our natural philosophy all the contributions that natural science makes to metaphysics, and so clear the ground for a theory of the universe, so far as it can be built up upon scientific foundations. (3) Lastly, we may be able to work upon the third problem by raising new questions or erecting new hypotheses upon the basis of facts already known. —The same thing holds of philosophical psychology, and would hold of a philosophical ethics, if there had been opportunity for its development alongside of a special moral science.

These facts show that we were right to give up an unitary definition of philosophy, and recognise a number of heterogeneous philosophical problems. In no other way could we explain how a bundle of entirely different ends or purposes, held together by the unity of the subject-matter in which they are realised, comes to constitute a distinct discipline. And we are now further in a position to decide how far philosophical questions or philosophical points of view may justly be introduced into scientific exposition. Philosophy must not assume an attitude of calm aloofness towards the special sciences, and must not shield itself behind the high sounding—and empty—generality of the systematisation of scientific knowledge. It must stand in close and constant relation to the sciences, acting and reacting, taking from them what they have to give, and giving to them liberally of what they need.

§ 32. *The Philosophical System.*

1. From a scientific system we demand on the one side a complete classification of the ideas employed, and on the other a complete deduction of the positions held. That is the ideal of a scientific system; but there is hardly a single discipline that even approximates to it. Logic and mathematics are the only sciences which meet the requirements in any degree at all. It is, further, an essential precondition of an unitary system that the science admits of accurate definition; the definition is the only guarantee of an internal and necessary connection among the principles or ideas distinguished by classification. It follows, therefore, that philosophy as a whole—the philosophy of § 31—cannot be reduced to a system. (1) In the first place, the heterogeneity of the separate philosophical problems renders deduction from a single highest definition impossible; (2) and secondly, the variation in the subject-matter of the third problem makes philosophy dependent upon time and accident to a degree that is incompatible with the logical and universal validity of a systematic structure. But if we can have no hope of framing a system of philosophy in general, we need not despair of systematising certain departments of philosophical activity. We will therefore attempt, in what follows, to set forth the main heads of a systematic arrangement within the three great divisions of philosophy. At the same time we shall append brief remarks upon the method of exposition best suited to the different problems.

2. *Metaphysics*, as a theory of the universe based both upon science and upon the experience of practical life, falls into a general and a special part. *General* metaphysics developes the highest or ultimate principle of a world theory, and tries to make it adequate to all the various requirements of scientific hypothesis and daily practice. *Special* metaphysics paves the way for this general treatment, by shaping the results of science to meet metaphysical needs. Adopting the current classification of science as mental and natural, we may subdivide special

metaphysics into a *metaphysics of nature* and a *metaphysics of mind*: the expressions have found acceptance in philosophy, though neither of them is free from objection (*cf.* § 8. 11). From the metaphysics of nature we expect an orderly exposition of the material which the natural sciences contribute to a theory of the universe. It will get this material, for the most part, from astronomy, physics and geology on the one hand, and the biological sciences on the other. The metaphysics of mind we expect, similarly, to gather metaphysical material from the mental sciences. It will receive most assistance from psychology, ethics, the philosophy of religion and the philosophy of history. Since a metaphysics without transcendence seems to be impossible, and speculation can be exercised so much more freely and boldly in general than in special metaphysics, it would seem that the *synthetic* method is that best suited to the first great department of philosophical enquiry. Special metaphysics is an indispensable precondition of general. Hence we do not approve of the ordinary plan of placing ontology (*i.e.*, general metaphysics) before cosmology and psychology (*i.e.*, practically, the metaphysics of nature and of mind). Such an arrangement completely inverts the logical relation of the disciplines.

3. The *theory of science* has to investigate the presuppositions of all the sciences. It falls at once into two parts, corresponding to the distinction of *material* and *formal* presuppositions. Any thought can be considered separately under the two aspects of form and contents; and any science, or system of thoughts, can be looked at from the same points of view. The great divisions of the theory of science thus obtained are *epistemology* and *logic*. Epistemology deals with the contents of the most general or highest concepts of all the sciences; logic with the uniformities of scientific thought. Within this first division we may make another, and distinguish between *pure* or *general* and *applied* or *special* epistemology and logic. The former are restricted to so much of form or contents as is common to all the sciences; the latter analyse and verify the formal and material presuppositions of particular sciences or groups of sciences. There are accord-

ingly an epistemology and logic of the natural sciences, of mathematics, of the mental sciences, etc. The method which, in the nature of things, can best be followed by the theory of science is the method of *analysis*. Philosophy is not here concerned to supplement scientific results by new ideas, but only to analyse and classify, as accurately as may be, the material that the sciences themselves provide. Here too, therefore, the special or applied enquiry is the logical presupposition of the pure or general. Epistemology and logic most nearly approach the ideal of complete classification and deduction; and so have yet another claim to rank as the fundamental philosophical sciences (*cf.* §§ 5. 5, 6; 6. 4).

4. It is, of course, impossible to give *a priori* a list of sciences for which philosophy shall pave the way, or in which its methods shall stimulate to new activity. We cannot, therefore, hope to obtain any systematic classification of the lines of work included in the third philosophical problem. We can only indicate the status of affairs at the present day, *i.e.*, name the special sciences which, as things are, stand indebted to philosophy. It follows from what we said in our second Chapter with regard to the special philosophical disciplines, that psychology, ethics, æsthetics, sociology and, in part, the philosophy of religion, would fall under this category. We must note, however, that when a department of philosophical knowledge becomes capable of standing alone, as a special science, it does not break free of philosophy altogether, but simply divides up into a philosophical and a scientific part. This is what will, undoubtedly, occur in the case of the five disciplines just mentioned. The division has gone farthest in psychology, and next farthest, perhaps, in sociology. In both instances it would be easy to show the need and scope of philosophical treatment, alongside of independent scientific work. The path which philosophy follows under such circumstances is best seen by reference to the philosophy of nature, where the separation is already complete. All departments of philosophy—metaphysics, epistemology and logic, and perhaps the unnamed discipline that points out new scientific problems or criticises the

theories of the special sciences from which it takes a name—all departments of philosophy have here combined to devote their energies to one definite object (*cf.* § 31. 6). For this reason we took pains in Chapter II., when we were formulating the special problems of a philosophy of nature, a philosophy of law and a philosophy of religion, in the philosophical meaning of the terms, to emphasise the great variety of their contents.

5. The country of science was at first a monarchy; but in the course of ages monarchy has given place to democracy. In the old time Queen Philosophy held undivided sway over the special disciplines,—settled their differences, gave them wise counsel, and offered freely of her treasure of ideas and methods to satisfy their needs. And they came in brilliant companies, zealous to follow the hest of their sovereign, to model their carriage upon hers, to use her wealth for the increase of their own portion. Then on a sudden they awoke, as if from an evil dream. The way that had been shown them had led them astray; the treasures they received were but worthless tinsel; and the fair proud form of the queen herself, the form they had all aped and envied, a lying perfection. So they hurled her from the throne.

There followed years of self-reliance, that were years of prosperity and success. But prosperity quickly led to arrogance and impatience of restraint. Soon there was no trace left of the order and system of the old kingdom: anarchy reigned, and the sciences were an unruly mob, none regarding its neighbour. In the meantime the outcast and despised queen had pondered much: she had thrown aside the hollow fruits of dialectic, and learned to be careful and accurate in small things, and to bow to the constraining power of facts. And when the busy-bodies of her old court would have laid violent hands upon the abandoned sceptre, and in their blindness chosen the soulless puppet of materialism to rule over them, then she stepped forth in the strong armour of epistemology to turn the storm, and with plain, wise words send back the rebels to their borders. Since that day her authority has steadily increased, not least because men see that the lust of power is gone out of her. She lives to-day in peaceful intercourse with her former subjects. By science, with science, and for science she works in all her forms: as metaphysics, as theory of science, and as pioneer of scientific enquiry. And science, on its side, is ready to accept the aid of philosophy, with her to serve the cause of knowledge, and for her to gather facts. It has been the aim of this Introduction to show that in the democracy of science philosophy has lost nothing of her true and proper usefulness, but labours and struggles with the ideal of her past glories ever present to her.

INDEX OF NAMES

INDEX OF SUBJECTS

References to the more important passages are printed in italics

OTHER BOOKS BY BERTRAND RUSSELL

ROADS TO FREEDOM:

SOCIALISM, ANARCHISM and SYNDICALISM.

Cr 8vo. New and Cheaper Edition. Cloth, 5s. net; post free 5s. 4d.
Limp Cloth, 3s. 6d. net; post free 3s. 10d.

"A remarkable book by a remarkable man. Mr. Russell is a far-going Revolutionist, he is avowedly an Anarchist, but his anarchism is of a kind with which, as regards one of its tenets, a good many people who are not Anarchists will sympathise. He explains with great clearness and accuracy the form of State Socialism in which he believes."—*Times.*

"Mr. Bertrand Russell could not write a dull book if he tried, and 'Roads to Freedom' is an extraordinarily interesting one. What he has done, and that with brilliant success, is to raise the whole social controversy out of the fog of words in which it has lain so long enwrapped."—*Common Sense.*

"Mr. Russell is a philosopher, and the distinction of his admirable survey of the three most radical schemes for the regeneration of Society is his 'sweet reasonableness.' Avowing himself convinced that Guild Socialism provides the safest and best programme for Reconstruction, he examines the history and doctrines of the other systems, and argues that Guild Socialism avoids the hazards of Anarchist Communism and the bureaucratic tendencies of State Socialism, yet comprehends practically all the benefits they offer."—*Athenæum.*

PRINCIPLES OF SOCIAL RECONSTRUCTION

Cr. 8vo. New and Cheaper Edition. Cloth, 5s. net; post free 5s. 4d.
Limp cloth, 3s. 6d. net; post free 3s. 10d.

"Mr. Russell has written a big and living book. We question whether a more brilliant statement of the Liberal Philosophy has been written since the last world war created Liberalism."—*Nation.*

"Essentially a discussion rather of principles than of any definite programme, being an examination and comparison of the possessive and the creative impulses."—*Times.*

THE PRACTICE AND THEORY OF BOLSHEVISM

Cr. 8vo. Second Impression. 6s. net; post free 6s. 4d.

"There have been few more incisive and penetrating criticisms of all forms of Communism than Mr. Russell's candid admissions."—*Times.*

"A powerful and conclusive book . . . as trenchant and original as anything he has written."—*Daily News.*

Library of Philosophy

General Editor: Professor J. H. MUIRHEAD, LL.D.

ANALYTIC PSYCHOLOGY By G. F. Stout. Two Vols. *4th Edition.* 25s. *net.*

APPEARANCE AND REALITY By F. H. Bradley. *6th Edition.* 16s. *net.*

ATTENTION By Prof. W. B. Pillsbury. *2nd Impression.* 12s. 6*d. net.*

CONTEMPORARY PSYCHOLOGY By Prof. G. Villa. 16s. *net.*

HISTORY OF ÆSTHETIC By Dr. B. Bosanquet. *4th Edition.* 16s. *net.*

HISTORY OF ENGLISH UTILITARIANISM By Prof. E. Albee. 12s. 6*d. net.*

HISTORY OF PHILOSOPHY By Dr. J. E. Erdmann.

Vol. I. Ancient and Mediæval. *4th Impression.* 16s. *net.*

Vol. II. Modern. *6th Impression.* 16s. *net.*

Vol. III. Since Hegel. *6th Impression.* 16s. *net.*

HISTORY OF PSYCHOLOGY By G. S. Brett, M.A.

Vol. I. Ancient and Patristic. 16s. *net.*

Vol. II. Mediæval and Early Modern Period. 16s. *net.*

Vol. III. Modern Psychology. 16s. *net.*

MATTER AND MEMORY By Henri Bergson. Translated by N. M. Paul and W. S. Palmer. *3rd Edition.* 12s. 6*d. net.*

NATURAL RIGHTS By Prof. D. G. Ritchie. *3rd Edition.* 12s. 6*d. net.*

PHILOSOPHY AND POLITICAL ECONOMY By Dr. J. Bonar. 16s. *net.*

RATIONAL THEOLOGY SINCE KANT By Prof. O. Pfleiderer. 16s. *net.*

THE PHENOMENOLOGY OF MIND By G. W. F. Hegel. Translated by J. B. Baillie. Two Vols. 25s. *net.*

THOUGHT AND THINGS; or, Genetic Logic By Prof. M. Baldwin.

Vol. I. Functional Logic. 12s. 6*d. net.*

Vol. II. Experimental Logic. 12s. 6*d. net.*

Vol. III. Real Logic (I., Genetic Epistemology). 12s. 6*d. net.*

TIME AND FREE WILL By Henri Bergson. Translated by F. L. Pogson. *3rd Edition.* 12s. 6*d. net.*

VALUATION: THE THEORY OF VALUE By Prof. W. M. Urban. 16s. *net.*

THE PSYCHOLOGY OF THE RELIGIOUS LIFE By Prof. G. M. Stratton. 16s. *net.*

THE GREAT PROBLEMS By Prof. Bernardino Varisco. Translated by Prof. R. C. Lodge. 16s. *net.*

KNOW THYSELF By Prof. Bernardino Varisco. Translated by Dr. Guglielmo Salvadori. 16s. *net.*

ELEMENTS OF FOLK PSYCHOLOGY By W. Wundt. Translated by Dr. Edward L. Schaub. *2nd Edition Revised.* 16s. *net.*

GIAMBATTISTA VICO By Benedetto Croce. Translated by R. G. Collingwood. 16s. *net.*

ELEMENTS OF CONSTRUCTIVE PHILOSOPHY By Prof. J. S. Mackenzie. *2nd Impression.* 16s. *net.*

SOCIAL PURPOSE By Prof. H. J. W. Hetherington and Prof. J. H. Muirhead. 12s. 6*d. net.*

INTRODUCTION TO MATHEMATICAL PHILOSOPHY By Bertrand Russell, F.R.S. *2nd Edition.* 12s. 6*d. net.*

GOD AND PERSONALITY (Gifford Lectures) By Clement C. J. Webb. (Part I.) 12s. 6*d. net.*

DIVINE PERSONALITY AND HUMAN LIFE (Gifford Lectures) By Clement C. J. Webb. (Part II.) 12s. 6*d. net.*

MODERN PHILOSOPHY By Guido de Ruggiero. Translated by A. Howard Hannay, B.A., and R. G. Collingwood, M.A., F.S.A. 16s. *net.*

THE ANALYSIS OF MIND By Bertrand Russell, F.R.S. 12s. 6*d. net.*

LONDON: GEORGE ALLEN & UNWIN LIMITED
RUSKIN HOUSE, 40 MUSEUM STREET, W.C. 1